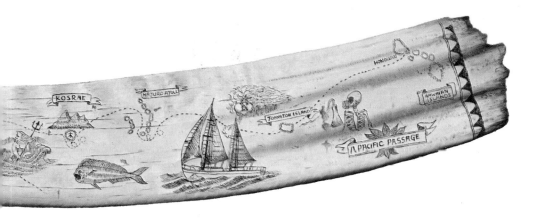

BOOKS BY WILLIAM F. BUCKLEY, JR.,
ON EXPERIENCES AT SEA

AIRBORNE: A Sentimental Journey
ATLANTIC HIGH: A Celebration
RACING THROUGH PARADISE: A Pacific Passage

Racing Through Paradise

RANDOM HOUSE   NEW YORK

RACING
THROUGH
PARADISE

A Pacific Passage

WILLIAM F. BUCKLEY, JR.

Photographs by Christopher Little

Grateful acknowledgment is made to the following for
permission to reprint previously published material:

People Weekly: Excerpt from issue of September 6, 1982,
Josh Hammer/*People Weekly* © 1982, Time Inc.

St. John Telegraph-Journal/Evening Times-Globe:
Excerpts from the *Telegraph-Journal* and
Evening Times-Globe, July 16–17, 1982.

Portions of this book previously appeared in
The New York Times and *The New Yorker*.

Library of Congress Cataloging-in-Publication Data

Buckley, William F. (William Frank), 1925–
Racing through paradise.

1. Buckley, William F. (William Frank), 1925–
2. Sealestial (Yacht)   3. Pacific Ocean.   I. Little,
Christopher.   II. Title.
G530.B   1987   910'.09164   86–26209
ISBN 0–394–55781–6

Manufactured in the United States of America
24689753
First Edition

For
FRANCES BRONSON
With gratitude

Contents

ACKNOWLEDGMENTS   xi

PROLOGUE   xiii

1. SETTING OUT: PACIFIC PASSAGE   1

Book One: AT SEA, *1981–1985*   13

2. PATITO   15

3. THE ANGEL OF CRAIG'S POINT   36

4. IN & AROUND LONG ISLAND SOUND   46

5. CHARTERING, AND A CHRISTMAS CRUISE   54

6. THE AZORES   64

7. GALAPAGOS, A SHORT STOPOVER   75

8. TAHITI   80

Book Two: RACING THROUGH PARADISE   89

9. THE DECISION: SAIL THE PACIFIC   91

10. PREPARATIONS   101

11. TO JOHNSTON ATOLL   118

12. THE MAGIC OF GPS   135

13. AT SEA   155

14. AT JOHNSTON   179

15. TO MAJURO   197

16. MAJURO   223

17. TO KOSRAE   236

18. KOSRAE   258

19. REMEMBERING PHIL WELD   270
20. TO KAPINGAMARANGI   276
21. KAPINGA   298
22. TO KAVIENG   312
23. ARRIVING—THE FINAL EVENING   329
EPILOGUE   338
INDEX   341

Acknowledgments

I am primarily indebted to my son Christopher, for reasons that will become evident to the reader.

Christopher Little did the fine photographs. Those on the first page of the second color signature are by Claudio Veliz, Jr.

To my other companions: I am grateful for their company, for their journals, and for their friendship.

Several friends read and commented on the manuscript, including Charles Wallen, Jr., Professor Thomas Wendel, Richard Clurman, Reginald Stoops, Priscilla Buckley, Reid Buckley, Lois Wallace, and Jeff Cohen. I owe special thanks to the distinguished editor and translator Sophie Wilkins, for yet another set of shrewd and original recommendations. But above all, I am obliged to Samuel S. Vaughan. This is the tenth volume by me that he has edited, and I would not know what to do without his sage, generous, and acute counsel.

I thank Dorothy McCartney for her invaluable help in research, Tony Savage for his patience and skill in typing three drafts, and Frances Bronson, to whom I dedicate this volume with great affection, for what I have come to call (*mot juste!*) her "editorial coordination."

My thanks to Joseph Isola for his fine copyreading—twenty-three times he has seen me through from galleys to book. I rejoice that Chaucy Bennetts consented to copy edit, as she has done on many of my earlier books.

My congratulations to George Thompson for the oil paintings of both sides of the scrimshaw presented me by my companions at a reunion in New York City in November 1985. They are reproduced as the endpapers at the beginning and end of the book. And my special congratulations to the superb scrimshander David Lazarus for his ingenious and artful creations after sketches by my son Christopher. David Lindroth did the fine artwork and sketches, and Lillian Langotsky did the book's design. My thanks to them both.

I take pleasure in acknowledging the *Galapagos Guide*, written and photographed by former U.S. Peace Corpsmen Alan White, Bruce Epler, and Charles Gilbert under the sponsorship of the Charles Darwin Research Station in the Galapagos Islands. A fine and readable guide. In the text I refer with admiration to *Landfalls of Paradise: The Guide to Pacific Islands*, by Earl R. Hinz (Western Marine Enterprises, Ventura, California).

I want to acknowledge, even though I run a risk in doing so, those who, during the month of June 1985 paced the widows' walks, if indeed they did. On that assumption: My affectionate thanks to my wife Pat Buckley, my daughter-in-law Lucy Buckley, to Shirley Clurman, Betsy Little, Bootsie Galbraith, and Gloria Merritt. Their patience, understanding, and fortitude were exemplary, though here and there a little practice is indicated.

Prologue

"Here's a package for you, Pup." From the sunny dock, my son Christo handed me down to the deck what looked like a shoebox. From below, the voice of Liz: "There is literally not room to stow one more hot dog." I have been a little queasy about Liz; there's a professional irritation in her voice. Whatever was in that shoebox wasn't going to sink our 71-foot, 70 ton ketch, granted that we are stuffed to overflowing. Reaching for the package, I said simply, "Don't worry, Liz."

It was a bottle of champagne, to which a note was appended. "This champagne is yours," the donor had written, "because you were responsible for naming our boat. You're welcome to come aboard if you want." She had designated the pier. The letterhead carried the printed name Querencia, and she hailed from Vancouver.

I looked up. The donor was at the corner of the dock, talking to Dick Clurman. I climbed up and approached her. She was in her late thirties, animated, pretty, tanned, competent in manner, and warm. She told me, a little shyly, that she had run into the word for the first time in one of my books and on reflection had thought it just right for the boat she and her husband had been planning for years. She had needed to check it out—she smiled—just to make *absolutely sure, but I had been right, the word doesn't translate. It is used in Spanish to designate that mysterious little area in the bull ring that catches the fancy of the fighting bull when he charges in. He imagines it his sanctuary: When parked there, he supposes he cannot be hurt. It is the first responsibility of the matador carefully to interpret the bull's initial roaring about the ring, as he is teased this way and that by the peones with their capes. The matador must discern exactly where in the ring is the little twenty or thirty square feet this particular bull has designated in his mind's eye as the area of imagined immunity, because when the time comes for the final, dangerous, exhibitionistic passes preceding the kill, the matador must not initiate them so close to the querencia as to risk the bull's deviation from his normal, rectilinear charge. If the bull doesn't charge directly at the cape, deviating instead toward his querencia, he might run his horns into the matador.*

So it is, borrowing the term, that one can speak of one's "querencia" to mean that little, unspecified area in life's arena where one feels safe, serene. In the company of one's wife or husband, say. Within the shadow of the Statue of Liberty, perhaps. In due course, for all men, such an area will be underground, the graveyard's bower. But meanwhile—the lady smiled—she thought it just right for her boat, and so did her husband; a boat that had brought them peace of mind. I told her how very sorry I was I could not visit her Querencia, as the hectic final minutes before our setting out preempted distractions, however pleasant. We would drink to their querencia that very night, I promised, hoping that, in Sealestial, we would find our own.

Racing Through Paradise

1

SETTING OUT:
PACIFIC PASSAGE

It had been a busy morning, each of us occupied with his own concerns, though Dick Clurman located on behalf of us all the clinic that would inject us with gamma globulin, to fortify against hepatitis, and several of us assembled for that protection, fanning out afterward to attend to our special commissions.

I went back to my hotel and attended Mass in one of its little ballrooms, where I prayed also for the safety of the journey. Back in my room I wrote out my final newspaper column and phoned it in to the automatic recorder in my office. It was easy to write, and caught my mood. Oddly lacking in excitement, I think back, perhaps adumbrating the relative detachment Danny and Christo would detect early on . . .

Five years ago, setting out from Bermuda to the Azores on a sailboat, I advised friends and critics of this space that for the first time I would take two weeks' holiday at one time, instead of the customary one week at Christmas, the second in midsummer. The experience apparently entered my bloodstream because, however unremarked, building within me were seeds great and strong in effrontery, blossoming one day in outright contumacy. What happened one month ago ranks with the day Oliver Twist held out his porridge bowl to the beadle and asked for "More."

I asked my editor for one month's leave.

It isn't exactly sloth. It is that, one month ago, I addressed the question of how to transmit my punditry from wherever I would be all the way to Kansas City, home of Universal Press Syndicate. I will be on a sailboat wending my way through Micronesia, propelled by the trade winds. I shall be pausing only four times in a four-thousand-mile journey, in exotic atolls where telephones function irregularly. One of these atolls is unfriendly to visiting yachtsmen, allowing them to disembark only if wearing gas masks . . . The prospect of telephoning in my injunctions through a gas mask proved the conclusive argument, my spies tell me, in this unusual act of indulgence by my friendly editors, one of whom is said to have remarked, "He's hard enough to understand speaking through plain ether. I wouldn't want to listen to him through a gas mask."

And so it is that this is the final column. Final, that is, for four weeks, after which, if the Pacific is pacific, the column will resume. As for the Pacific Ocean: from North Latitude 21 degrees in Honolulu to South Latitude 5 degrees in New Guinea the wind tends to dawdle pretty gently during the summer months, and if we have any indication of a typhoon, we shall show it great respect. I do not believe in confrontational engagements with nature.

To get out of the way of a storm whose location you have established requires of course that you know where you are. Well, I will have on board two secret instruments, one conceived by me, a second by a conglomerate of geniuses. This last permits measurements of one billionth of a second, and translates, or will by the year 1989, into a little box that will tell you where you are so exactly that you can double-park your car by following its instructions. The other is computer software. If the navigator feeds the computer: 1) where I think I am, within thirty miles; 2) in which direction that star I just shot lies, within thirty degrees; 3) what second, minute, hour, and day it is in Greenwich, England; 4) exactly how high up from the horizon it was—then lo! the star's identity is vouchsafed. The computer will say, "By Jove, that was Arcturus!" And I will know where I am.

Our preoccupations during this period will be with the nitty-gritty. Heat, for instance. We shall be hovering over the equator, propelled by winds that come astern, as we travel at seven or eight knots. If the wind behind you is sixteen miles per hour and you are

moving forward eight miles per hour, the net force of the wind on
your back is a mere eight miles per hour. I have never measured the
velocity of the wind from a house fan perched at the corner of a
desk, where they used to perch before God gave us air conditioning,
but I would guess the wind comes out at twenty or thirty miles per
hour, which is why the skin stays tolerably cool. It will be otherwise
when the sun is more or less directly above you, and the temperature, hour after hour, is in the high eighties, and your ocean fan
dribbles out only one quarter of the air you get from an electric fan,
as though the motor had a gear marked "Extra Special Slow." In
such moments sailors dream less of wine, women, and song than of
Frigidaire.

Do such concerns get wished away, under the category of Problems of the Idle Rich? Well, the case can be made: Nobody forced
me to undertake to sail from the United States to the East Indies.
But it is the human way to exert oneself, every now and again, in
eccentric enterprises. Yesterday in New Haven I listened to a classmate describe his ascent of Everest and wondered how it is that
anyone should willingly engage in such madcappery: Dick Bass had
taken risks I do not contemplate in my irenic passage with my son
and my friends, my books and my music, across the great Pacific
Ocean.

We had made no arrangements to forgather at noon, permitting
me to lunch lightly with two old friends, residents of Honolulu,
while Danny spent a poignant couple of hours with his wife,
Gloria—the young husband going off to sea—and his sister-in-law,
Marian, there to console and to enjoy a few serene days in Hawaii;
and we had convened aboard the *Sealestial* an hour or two before
the gift of champagne.

The sun overhead was hot, as one might have expected on the
second day of June in Honolulu. It didn't occur to me at the time,
but I now note, looking in the almanac, that on June 2 the sun
circles the earth (that's the way navigators are trained to reason:
the earth never moves; the moon, the sun, the planets, and the
stars rotate above us) almost exactly at the latitude of Honolulu,
which would make that day theoretically the hottest day of the
year.

A farewell: Gloria and Danny Merritt.

But there was wind to cool us off, and excitement to distract us from the heat. *Sealestial* had been scrubbed by its standing crew for six weeks, two of whom—the mate Noddy and the stewardess Maureen—would join my crew—the captain Allan, and the cook Liz—for the passage. Four of my cruising companions (Reggie, Christopher Little, Danny, Dick Clurman) had been aboard for two or three days. Van Galbraith arrived only last night, from a commencement address in Utah; and Christopher, my son, and I also arrived only last night. I had been busy the day before in New Haven, where I did an hour's television on the reunion class of 1950 (my own and Van's), and a second hour on the graduating class of 1985. *Vive la différence* was the sour aftertaste following the second hour (a not terribly bright dean at Yale, acting on the request of my program's producer to nominate five graduating students, had selected five with pronounced and rather disheveled political biases over in left field, reasoning that my own presence required ideological counterweight. She overdid it).

On Saturday morning, before Christo and I left on the afternoon flight for Hawaii, my lawyer had driven over to my house in Stamford to have me sign my Last Will and Testament. He had assured me that his fitful initiative had nothing to do with my projected Pacific passage. We had the farewell and slightly strained lunch with wife/mother (Pat worries when we go off sailing). On top of which Mrs. Reagan called from Camp David to advise me that this ocean trip of mine was to be *"the last time"* I would do such a thing, that she had exacted a similar promise from her husband a few years before to give up steeplechasing on horseback. I was both reassuring and evasive. Ten hours later, Danny and Reg met us at the airport in Honolulu.

I tactfully stowed the *Querencia*'s champagne myself, in a remote and neglected little hollow I unearthed in the back of the hanging locker, and looked now at my watch.

It was just after 3:30. Seven months earlier I had sent a memo to all hands saying that we would set out from Honolulu at 1600 (4 P.M.) on June 2. I went back up to the cockpit. Quite suddenly there was, well, no bustle. I looked about. Dick, shirtless as usual, was seated, smoking of course, fussing with one of his radios; opposite, Dan was wedged between wife and sister-in-law, drinking a beer, of course; Van and Reg bent over the cockpit instruments—Reg was quietly explaining something. Christo was testing the new 24-volt fan in the saloon below. Christopher Little, twenty yards abeam, waved to me from his rented power boat—they call it a chase boat (its function is to pursue a departing vessel for the convenience of a photographer who wishes to record the scene). After a few miles, the chase boat would pull alongside, Christopher Little, with his photographic gear, would leap onto the *Sealestial,* and we would wave goodbye to the power boat. *Sealestial* would sail on toward the little island, 716 miles away, which I plotted to stop at on our southwesterly course to the East Indies. About the same distance, I was reminded, as Newport–Bermuda.

"What do you say we shove off?" I announced.

We proceeded to do so, twenty minutes earlier than scheduled, on that bright afternoon—suddenly experiencing that blend of elation, excitement, and apprehension one feels when heading out into the ocean on a long passage. Such moments live on in the memory. We hoisted the spinnaker on a broad reach and the heavy-laden ketch sprang to life, the meter rising quickly to eight and one-half knots. The seas were lively without being boisterous. The sun was at about two o'clock on our course, still high but a little less white-pallid than at noon. To our left, at nine o'clock, was imperious Diamond Head. Aft of the windward beam, at five o'clock, we could make out Pearl Harbor. From the wheel I could

Departing Honolulu. Next stop, Honolulu.

see, a couple of hundred yards to windward, Christopher Little with his camera, hanging on tightly to what looked like a huge cleat on the chase boat: Houston Control had never had a better launch. Christopher's journal (my son is hereinafter designated as Christopher, or Christo, his nickname; Christopher Little, our crewmate and photographer, is always "Christopher Little") logged what then happened.

Christopher.   Knew something dreadfully wrong yesterday when we left the dock twenty minutes early, ahead of schedule. We were up forward putting up the Multi Purpose Sail (MPS), me, Noddy, and Van, when the gods exacted their propitiation for our effortless departure. (Well, effortless qualified by WFB's spending three years getting us ready.) We had one wrap of the MPS halyard around the winch, getting it raised okay. It hourglassed, but then filled out. Then when Noddy tried to get another wrap around the winch, he got his fingers caught between the halyard and the winch. I thought he was awfully calm under the circumstances.

Under way: Diamond Head in the background.

"My fingers are caught," he said.

This is the all-time, proverbial, BAD SITUATION, and it gets worse as his fingers are vised onto the winch. Soon his voice has an edge to it.

"Get the winch handle on!"

I lock it on, but it's no good: The wind, at 20 knots, is putting a thousand plus pounds of pull on the halyard.

Yelling, rushing forward, Van lets the halyard go. Noddy's three fingers play through the winch, counterclockwise. He falls back, not making a sound, but his face shows pain. I look at his hand, expecting a bad sight. He's clutching it close to his chest. His index finger has a hole in it and his thumb looks crushed. He plunges his hand into the ice chest.

The MPS, meanwhile, is now being dragged on our starboard side like some hyper-sea anchor. Much shouting. We lift it in. Chris Little, on the chase boat, is catching the whole sorry spectacle on film. The chase boat skipper, who apparently doesn't like sailboat types—a neat inversion of the usual formula—is now bent out of shape laughing, on account of this photo session turned into something of a training film on how *not* to set off on a trans-Pacific sail. My heart, meanwhile, is pumping too hard (I dunno, jet lag?). We manage to transfer Noddy to the chase boat without crushing his legs, and make our sorry way back into the Elewai boat harbor.

I suggest to Van we pretend we've just sailed across the Pacific the *other* way and that this is our final landfall.

Van: "Declare victory and go home, eh?"

There was no one at the dock to cheer us on when we limped in. Gloria and Marian had left, the friendly couple were back in their querencia, and the dock, at a little after five on Sunday afternoon, looked sleepy. A taxi was called and Reggie, always calm, took Noddy to the same clinic where, that morning, we had gone to get our gamma globulin.

Aboard *Sealestial*, we waited. We didn't know whether the bones in his hand were broken. It was dismaying to see him go off, his hand in a bucket of ice. Already we had got used to his steady smile—oxymoronic, given his Rastafarian hairdo, all those tiny little braids, twenty or thirty of them circling his face: One asso-

Noddy—first-rate mate, first victim.

ciates such hairstyles with surliness, at worst, hostility. Noddy is from Barbados, where his father is a high-ranking officer in the army. Ambling along the streets of Fiji a few months earlier, having been let go as supernumerary by the sailing vessel that, needing extra crew for the long passage, had brought him from the Caribbean, Noddy fell in with the captain of *Sealestial* who soon learned —as we would—that even as all men with wooden legs don't behave like Long John Silver, so all men with Rastafarian hairdress don't behave like Idi Amin. We engaged ourselves, as one tends to do when feeling strain, in make-work, pending Noddy's return from the hospital.

Next stop, the clinic.

It was very good news. The X ray had shown no broken bones; he wore a bandage, and the doctor cleared him to proceed on our Pacific passage, provided he was cautious in using his hand.

We needed two hundred feet of three-quarter-inch line to replace the shredded spinnaker halyard. A Good Samaritan manqué, a few boats down from where we were tied up, stepped forward and grandly offered us the line—for five hundred dollars. Twenty percent above the catalogue price, he acknowledged, but that would only just do to take care of the surcharge getting it over from the mainland—"Everything is more expensive in Hawaii," he consoled our captain, Allan Jouning, ever silent, a little skeptical but resigned, when Allan came to ask my okay. The alternative was to wait until the ship vendors opened up the following morning. Wait thirteen hours? Why, if we were thirteen hours late landing in New Guinea that would wreck a half-dozen careers. The check was made out, and the halyard run up to the masthead by Danny, on the bosun's chair.

An hour later we were well under way, tacking downwind. Even with the spinnaker up, I was 35 degrees south of course, but I couldn't do any better: *Sealestial* will not sail downwind under spinnaker. The wind steadily strengthened—"good, reliable offshore breeze," Allan commented. Maureen asked for drink orders, and most of us asked for a nip. We were relaxed, and moving briskly as the sun edged down. Dinner was called, and Allan relieved me at the wheel.

> **Christopher.**   The seas are six feet and following. The conversation at the dinner table turns to seasickness, and soon Liz's lovely pilaf is lost on me. Allan calls out from the wheel, "Big one!" to warn us to hold down the pilaf, glasses, forks, salt, salad, and wineglasses. We manage, mostly, but still a piece of mango lands on my lap. WFB turns to Chris Little and says, "Christopher, you look pale." Indeed, when the seven of us sat down, we were all talking. Then six of us were talking. Then five of us were talking. Then four of us were talking. I excused myself, cat-walked over three pairs of legs and made my way to the scopolamine stash [a seasick prophylactic]. After I'd got the patch behind my ear, Reg reminded me to wash my hands, scopolamine not being good to rub into your eyes in the middle of your sleep.

Christopher got no sleep. His grand idea, that he and Danny would share the vast expanse of the after cockpit for thirty days and thirty nights, was one more chimera, of which there are always a lot when you plan anything at all unconventional at sea. We had over four thousand miles of downwind work to do, and the rear end of a stately ketch wriggles like a stripper's. Add the waves that occasionally break over the transom or slurp in over the sides, and you have a no-win situation. A few nights' experimentation would prove enough.

Christopher wrote with vague misgivings that he "watched Hawaii" from his turbulent bunk, watched it "recede into the wake, its lights resembling lava flow. This was different from setting out from Miami in 1975 [when the winds were abeam and steady as we moved sedately with the Gulf Stream]. Seasickness has a way of casting a pall, shipwide. My musings were interrupted by the sound of retching from the starboard midships. Turned out to be Reggie. Danny was trying to console him." Dick, age sixty-one; Van, age fifty-seven; and I, age fifty-nine, were spared. (The last time I was seasick was when I was thirteen. But that is no guarantee that I shan't be seasick tomorrow.)

Dick wrote in his journal, "I stand the first midnight watch. It is glorious. The moon is bright, its luminous glow spreads over three-, four-foot sparkling waves, the wind behind us, a near-musical accompaniment to the undulating motion of boat and sea. It is truly a reverie."

It was that, as the lights from Honolulu finally disappeared and we were charging our way now across the Pacific. Not going quite in the right direction—we'd have to jibe the spinnaker before too long, and harness our headsail so as to give us something better than thirty-five degrees off course. Tomorrow. Tonight a rig change would be cruel and unusual punishment for the sick and the weary. There was only the sound of the sea. We were making eight and a half knots. Eight people were asleep. Time edges its way out of the picture, time narcotized. Yesterday you thought in minutes, even half minutes, an hour at the most, and it was the year before yesterday, and the year before that—reaching back to the last time you crossed an ocean. Time loses its meaning. You just sail, and sail, and watch the moon descend ever so slowly, the stars in steady rotation, the waves rushing alongside, creating that comfortable, cozy companionship, you and the waves, traveling in the same direction. We were off.

Book One

AT SEA,
1981–1985

2

PATITO

Sailing is a continuous experience as, I suppose, other avocational sports are—a skier more or less keeps on skiing, and though one episode (a week in Alta? a summer ski in Chile?) may stand out, you tend to think of it as in some way seamless. If the moment comes when you lose your eyesight, or suffer a stroke, then you stop sailing. I tend to think, perhaps naturally, in serial episodes bounded by books, of which this is the third, so that my mind turns, as a skier's might in comparable circumstances, to experiences I have had since I crossed the Atlantic in 1980 on *Sealestial*, with my friends.

It was soon after doing so that I felt the unmistakable longing to acquire my own boat again. It had been sad, parting with my *Cyrano* after twelve years, but the financial strain of maintaining a sixty-foot wooden boat was great. I can't think of any expedient I failed to explore in order to devise the means of keeping her. My brightest idea, I thought—I still do—was to locate a couple of grandparents, he/retired, she/hospitable, who live in the Midwest, summering there and wintering in Florida somewhere between, oh, Miami and Palm Beach. The two cities are connected by the southern leg of the Intracoastal Waterway and there has got to be, on both sides of that waterway, a concentration of affluent older

folks surely unrivaled in number anywhere on earth over an equal
stretch of land. Many live in condominiums, but thousands have
houses, large and small, along the waterway, and a good many of
these maintain powerboats they use serenely to parade up and down
the waterway, occasionally venturing outside into the ocean to fish
or to cruise.

Cyrano, with its silent engine, its air conditioning, its roomy
interior saloon, its unexcelled sheltered cockpit-saloon, would have
been perfect for cocktail cruises in the late afternoons, perfect for
a modest sail in the ocean—say, Fort Lauderdale to Miami—then
perhaps back inside the waterway, 125 sheltered but glamorous miles
right down to Key West. Moreover, when the children—or grandchildren—visit, and want a real cruise, they could take the doughty
Cyrano across the Florida Straits to the Bahamas, to Bimini, to Cat
Cay, on over to Nassau and beyond, along the exotic, the gorgeous
Exumas. Then (my imagination was in high gear) I would recapture the boat toward the end of April, about the time my Florida
partners began to itch for their annual summer visit to their home
in the Midwest. I would sail the boat from time to time during the
summer, enjoying the two coastal passages, up to New England,
and back to Fort Lauderdale, say in October . . . How appealing,
the thought of cutting the bills in half and keeping the boat active
for more than the three or four weeks, plus the commercial chartering, *Cyrano* was being used. Chartering out the boat hadn't
really worked out: to charter what the trade calls a "character"
boat is always difficult. *Cyrano*'s profile is distinctive, even provoca-
tively so, with its twelve-foot bowsprit; and I never did get more
than a dozen charters per year. I needed a steady partner.

Here and there I advertised my plan, but got not a single nibble.
I continue to be surprised by this. I calculate it would have cost
the co-owners something on the order of thirty thousand dollars a
year each (in 1975 dollars) to maintain the boat (that would include a captain and a mate). I have no doubt my idea will one day
flower, but probably it will need to be sold to the brokerage fraternity, who broker not only boats but ideas to clients who vest
confidence in them. Big boats are really too expensive to be hus-

Off to a flying start . . .

My Cyrano, *1958–1976.*

banded by a single owner. And the seasons—Florida, New England —accommodate the idea of co-ownership.

During the same period I had *Cyrano* I continued to own, and to charter, *Suzy Wong*, which I bought in 1962 from four young men who, upon being discharged from the Air Force in Tokyo, commissioned the Sparkman & Stephens yawl and sailed her from Hong Kong, traveling west to Miami, an eighteen-month journey. I raced her heavily for three years, and chartered her extensively during the summers with a succession of young captain-mates of which my neighbor Danny Merritt was the latest. But as his own responsibilities grew—away at college and, after his graduation, busily indentured to an insurance company—he had less and less time to look after the affairs of Caribbean Enterprises, Inc., the unit that chartered out both *Cyrano* and *Suzy Wong*.

A twenty-year-old wooden boat requires semi-constant maintenance, and if it happens that you are made happy spending your
weekends sanding and varnishing and lubricating and doing minor
carpentry, as distinguished from, oh, gardening, playing golf and
tennis, doing crossword puzzles, or reading books, then a wooden
boat is made for you. I have never developed an interest in boat
maintenance. I have done it, but then I have done everything,
including latrine cleaning in the army. To have done everything is
not necessarily to cultivate a taste for doing everything, and by the
time I was thirty or so I resolved I would contrive alternatives to
varnishing my own boat.

The transaction I faced, then, having sold *Cyrano*, involved sell-
ing *Suzy Wong* after twenty years and buying a smaller boat, this
one made of fiberglass, whose maintenance would therefore be reduced by, say, 75 percent.

An attractive and enthusiastic young couple bought *Suzy Wong*
in 1982, and on the Fourth of July, 1984, I called Danny and told
him quick to go out and buy that day's *New York Times* (sigh,
Danny and Gloria do not regularly subscribe) and look at the front
page. Because there, sitting on top of a caption illustrating the
languorous summer holiday season, was a picture of—*Suzy Wong*.
It did not surprise me that the owner, and his wife, and a little boy
whose profile was startlingly like Danny's, were pictured industri-
ously at work, varnishing dear old *Suzy*. That little boy's grandchildren will be busy varnishing dear old *Suzy*. Meanwhile, I set to
work looking for *Patito*.

At first I took an active interest in the boat I would next acquire,
looking at this model and that, but I found myself attracted to the
more expensive, intricate models, and this was not the idea at all.
The idea was to economize, while getting a boat a single person
could easily sail. I turned the commission over to Christopher and
Danny, who have enjoyed joint ventures since first they became
fast friends at age twelve, and one day I had a phone call. They had
located *the* boat. *Exactly* what "you" have been looking for. Moreover, the boatyard was willing to sell it at a 10 percent discount if
I came up with the cash, and I *had* to see it—36 feet long, a sloop

of course (yawls are out of fashion), a nice little owner's cabin, a quarter berth, and a wonderfully comfortable saloon which in a trice made up into two berths, the unhinged table serving as leeboards.

Before one buys a boat one has it "surveyed." This brings into the picture an expert who goes over the boat from stem to stern, advising the prospective purchaser of the boat's condition and what the surveyor thinks should be done in order to put it in first-class shape. We reckoned all the changes he recommended as costing not more than a few thousand dollars, and so the check—the mortal remains of my interest in *Cyrano*—went out.

Christopher wanted to name it after the protagonist of my spy novels, but I recoiled (as, a couple of years older, he'd have done); he then suggested calling it "Ducky," that being, for reasons unknown, unknowable, and uninteresting, the cognomen both my

Christo, mischief-making in his journal.

wife and I go by when addressing each other, assuming the domestic temperature is not below zero. I thought the idea appealing but a little cute by far for someone of my august, conservative habits, and so I compromised, translating the term into Spanish, whence *Patito*, little duck.

I fell quickly in love with the little boat. She sails with a light-heartedness I hadn't experienced since lake-sailing my 17-foot *Sweet Isolation* before the war. Yet *Patito* isn't skittish, and water seldom comes in over the rail. One quickly gets over the missing forward section that comes in forty-foot boats, but presently I discovered this about my 36-foot Lancer, which was that four people aboard is perfect. Five people and you have the distinct impression there are three people too many aboard. Odd, but true. I have never known a situation in which the addition of one body has such adverse social and mechanical leverage on comfort aboard.

We prepared, in June 1982, for our first cruise aboard *Patito*, and I resolved to sail it to my paramount love, which is the St. John River in New Brunswick. I have elsewhere described this seventy miles of paradise, with the pastel pastures and the huge oak trees and the warm, clean water (notwithstanding that it is brownish in color, from the tannin from upstream pulp factories). It is the Land of Oz you are catapulted into after groping your way across the treacherous Reversing Falls that take you through the grimy manufacturing city of St. John. It is the perfect ending to a blue-water cruise: the protected, sunny, stretch from St. John to Fredericton with fields and woods and intimate riverbanks and a dozen river byways, large and small, in between.

Normally, we'd have asked Reggie to join us as the fourth man, but that year he was determined to race again to Bermuda, and so we asked Tom Wendel to come over from California. He found this less strenuous than my summons in the summer of 1980, that he hop over from San Jose, where he teaches colonial history at the university, to Horta in the Azores, to take the place of Van Galbraith, who jumped ship to keep a professional engagement in London. I learned after our six-day sail from the Azores to Spain

Patito, *en route to Treasure Island.*

that Tom would more likely master the hieroglyphics on the Rosetta stone than learn the difference between starboard and port. But never mind; Danny and Christo and I could always point to a ship's line and say, "Tom, please pull that rope," and he would willingly, not to say unthinkingly, oblige. Meanwhile he would keep us wonderful company, and during the evenings—and sometimes during the day—we would plug in my four-octave Casio and play together, on the cockpit table or in the saloon, an hour or more of Bach (he is truly expert, but indulges me, and so I play one hand, he the other).

The big navigational adventure ahead of us was the discovery of a Loran-C computer that—I cannot overemphasize the meaning of this for a navigator or a pilot—*really* worked. I had had Loran (Long Range Aids to Navigation) on board my boats off and on for several years, and I even remember one occasion, searching out the light on Isla Mujeres in Mexico en route to Cozumel, when Reggie actually got it to work. That was my single successful experience with a Loran, until now.

When I experienced that new Trimble Loran-C, my memory went back to a movie.

I don't remember what it was called, and in any case it doesn't matter.

Quiet!

. . . You see, seven thieves are engaged in robbing the house where the big jewels are kept. They manage, with great acrobatic skill, to get through the attic window and to descend, ever so silently, into the room adjacent to the inner sanctum where, they know, the jewels are housed. Not a word is spoken (*mustn't alarm the neighbors!*). The problem now is to penetrate the wall to the room where the jewels are.

But Leopardo, the leader, has thought of everything. He has brought along a portable wall-breaking machine! The idea is simple: You set up what amounts to a wooden beam stretching from the sturdy wall opposite to the target wall. You manage this by

end-to-ending lengths of wood sufficient to create a continuous composite beam of the right length. The robbers prop up its constituent
segments with anything convenient they can find—books, um-
brellas, chairs, boxes. Finally they insert into the little space left
between the end of the beam and the target wall the operative
link—a jack! A *regular automobile jack*, used to lift the car when
time comes to change a tire.

The completed beam now stretches twenty feet, from the firm
wall to the target wall, the idea being to cause the target wall to
collapse under pressure, permitting entry into the treasure room.
So . . . Leopardo grabs the jack handle, looks about smugly at his
associates, and begins to . . . shhh!—not a word, not even a whisper
—t-u-r-n the jackhandle.

The pressure mounts. The makeshift beam begins . . . slowly . . .
inexorably . . . to compress.

But   whew! It's insufferably hot. A Roman evening in mid-July.
Leopardo is sweating heavily as he adds one turn after another on

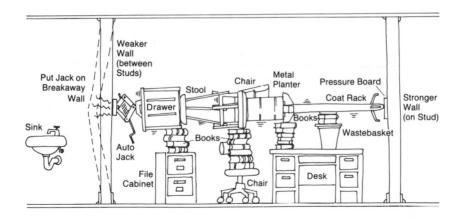

the squeaking jack, in that tense, expectant silence. Any moment now the weaker wall will collapse, and Leopardo and his gang can rush through the gaping hole into the treasure room—and live happily ever after on the spoils.

But Leopardo can't, finally, stand the heat. So he signals to little Squatto. "Get me a glass of water," he whispers. Squatto disappears in search of water. Leopardo goes back to the jack, the room ever-so-silent, his colleagues sweating. He gives the handle one more—the terminal!—turn.

Crunch!

That does it! The wall to the jewel room shatters like broken glass. And there, on the other side, is Squatto, filling a glass of water from a tap.

The movie audience is hysterical with laughter. All of Leopardo's architectural ingenuity—all those beams and tripods and jacks—was utterly unnecessary. The whole time, you see, there was a side door into the jewel room. Unlocked. Squatto, in search of a glass of water, opened it, and walked blithely in.

That is how I felt when I discovered my Trimble Loran-C.

It had been thirty years since I presented myself, along with Reggie, at a nearby house in Stamford to learn celestial navigation from an accomplished amateur. We went there once every week for a month. And then, bored by the slow pace of instruction, I studied some books and procured my first sextant. In due course, I was practicing at sea and corresponding with the fraternity on the subject. I have never fancied myself expert, but I was satisfied to make do with operational mastery of a technique that would permit me, when at sea, to know where I was, always supposing there was a sun or a moon or a planet or a star to look at, that weather conditions made it possible to spot them, that my watch was accurate, and the horizon visible.

And then came Trimble Loran-C.

It was as if you had spent an entire lifetime learning languages so that you might communicate with other people and then suddenly, in an expansive mood, the Holy Spirit had acted again, and this time, instead of granting the gift of tongues only to a chosen few disciples, He had vouchsafed it to absolutely everyone: so that, using glossolalia, we had awakened with powers of instant inter-communication. All those laborious hours spent learning Aramaic and Greek and Latin and Hebrew were, quite simply, redundant.

That is how I felt. If I wanted to get into the treasure room all I needed to do was to consult my Trimble Loran-C. Forget all that other, cumbersome stuff.

I must now behave responsibly and go through the ritual, cautionary motions. This is the point where the medicine bottle says, "If side effects occur, consult your doctor." Okay:

If your Loran-C doesn't work, make sure you know how to find out where you are by other means. Bring out your sextant, if the sun is shining. Bring out your rusty direction finder, if you are in range of a beacon. Turn on your radar, if you have one and land is in range. Call the Coast Guard and ask them to give you a bearing, if none of the above. Throw out a sea anchor, or heave to, and wait for a passing boat and ask where you are, if a passing boat comes by before you run out of K rations.

By all means be prepared to do any of these. But meanwhile, permit me to notify those who do not know it, and care, that as far as I have been able to discover, the problems of coastal navigation are over—kaput, like smallpox. And Loran-C has done it. Not only done it, but done it with perquisites absolutely undreamed of by anyone who learned navigation during this century and went to sea not knowing that, just over the rainbow, a miracle was waiting to happen. But realize this immediately, that Loran-C is not a worldwide system. For instance, it will not, as I'd soon discover, take you across the Pacific . . . And I would learn about something coming soon, more miraculous even than Loran-C. But I write now of the epiphany of 1982.

It was about then that Loran-C, whose range is longer than the Loran-A's it superseded, came in with a bang. The tale quickly got around that Loran-C was remarkable. Its disadvantages were that it used a distinctive set of intermediates (lines running through the charts) to define position, rather than the familiar latitude and longitude. That and the irksome chart problem. Most of the charts we carried made no provision for Loran-C. The Loran lines were depicted only in the very small-scale models, and with those it is difficult to fine-tune your navigation. To locate, using one of the old 1200 series charts, the entrance to Burnt Coat Harbor in Maine using Loran-C was simply impractical. What a lot of us did was attempt to trace in the lines on our larger, detailed charts, taking geographic positions from the larger chart and plotting them in. This, however, was misleading because Loran lines are not straight; but it was better than nothing, as we sat around waiting for progress. What kind of progress?

I am on record, during the Great Hiatus, as having remarked to several technologically sophisticated friends that the time had clearly come to devise a computer program that would convert a Loran fix into a latitude/longitude fix. "Look," I said to Reggie, who is a scientific genius and went to M.I.T., "surely it's got to be simple? Why couldn't I say to the computer, 'We are on a point somewhere southeast of Nantucket, with Loran TD [Time Distance] readings of 44444, 55555, and 66666.' There, insert those figures in one of your calibrated chips, and give me a fix expressed in longitude and latitude." Reggie said it would be too complicated.

Too complicated!

Well, there arrived a period, 1981–82, when you could buy new Lorans that did indeed convert TD readings into Lat-Long (geographical) readings, permitting the use of conventional charts. But the manufacturers made heavy weather over that perquisite, charging you one thousand dollars or even fifteen hundred dollars extra for the facility. Some people went the distance, but most of us held back.

Meanwhile an idea was brewing, and Charles Trimble (and I suppose others simultaneously—we are always being told that someone other than Columbus really discovered America, or almost did, or already had done) came out with it.

What was waiting to be done was the wedding of the Loran and

the computer, which were born for each other and were living together in a few experimental models. The Loran knew where you
were. This it knew by measuring, in millionths of a second, the
time between the dispatch of a signal and its receipt by a vessel at
sea. That intelligence, coming in from more than one transmitter,
provided you with a fix.

So the computer was given the relatively modest commission of
taking Loran-C information and finding the corresponding language
in the vocabulary of latitude and longitude. Now that was a fine
achievement, but what was then done by Trimble stirs the imagination. Granted that the first question at sea is the most important
(where am I?). But having got the answer to that question, you
will want more. And the infinite exploitability of the union between
Loran-C and the computer has made it possible to ask more.

When Christo, Danny, Tom, and I set out, we projected a
course. Stamford, Connecticut (leaving at 6 P.M.), to Port Jefferson (on the North Shore of Long Island); to Block Island (second
night); to Nantucket (third night); to Monhegan Island (night
five, allowing for a day's layover at Nantucket); to St. John (night
six).

Accordingly, a week before setting out, Danny and I spent about
an hour on the living-room floor with charts, dividers and parallel
rules, and a clipboard and a notebook into which, one after another, we wrote down the latitude and longitude of convenient
waypoints.

You ask, what is a "waypoint"?

So did I wonder what it was, on getting Trimble's Operating
Manual.

I pause to note that I have railed for years about instruction
manuals that succeed only in mystifying. I doff my hat to the
Trimble people. Their Operating Manual for Model 200 is a triumph of lucidity. It is a pleasure simply to read it, engaging as it
does in John-hit-the-baseball prose—direct, active: just the sort of
thing one needs when explicating scientific mysteries to technically
untrained people.

"Waypoints [the manual tells us] are locations (latitude/longitude coordinates) on the surface of the earth, and may represent destinations such as harbor entrance buoys, a string of lobster pots, turning points on a cruise, etc." It isn't easy to devise a more straightforward way of defining a waypoint. But of what use are they?

Trimble's machine has a memory of ninety-nine waypoints. Suppose that you were to assign one waypoint each to the principal corners of the continents of the globe. You'd have about seventy-five left after you completed a circumnavigation.

On the other hand, suppose that you planned such a trip as we undertook, through New England waters from Stamford, Connecticut, to St. John, New Brunswick. The distance, depending on which passages you select, is on the order of six hundred miles. So that, without repeating a waypoint, you could have a fresh one every five miles.

But suppose that you were an agoraphobic who couldn't stand the thought that your next destination was an infinite five miles away. Why, you could give yourself waypoints one mile away, and when you had consumed the first one hundred, you would simply reassign them to ensuing latitudes and longitudes. I mean to make clear that one hundred waypoints is as many as you could conceivably use for any purpose whatsoever, going from anywhere to anywhere else, along a course as straight, as or crooked, as you chose.

And, of course, when voyaging between one point and another at sea, most of the time there are no buoys, which is why the waypoints are programmable as positions—geographical abstractions. What would be the point, you ask, in having waypoints between Pollock Rip, where land ends, and St. Peters Cut, where you first see Prince Edward Island? The answer is that two purposes are served. The first is that successive waypoints, using the Trimble program, signal the Great Circle course, so heading for a waypoint means that you are guiding your vessel along the Great Circle navigational route, which is the shortest route.

From which you have stayed?

Yes.

By how much?

Ask Trimble. You merely depress one of his buttons and it tells you. Graphically, and in letters: You are, at this moment, 800 feet to the right of where you would be if you had stuck to the Great Circle route.

And you are just beginning to exploit Trimble.

The first day of our cruise was encumbered by bad weather and other problems. So, taking stock at Branford Harbor, an unscheduled stop, we revised our itinerary. In fifteen minutes our waypoints were adjusted. We pulled out of Branford at 6:30 A.M. in a deep fog that was still with us fifteen hours later when we arrived at Menemsha's narrow little cut at Martha's Vineyard. At what time did we arrive at Menemsha?

I've already said that we took fifteen hours which, added to 0630, gets us there at 2130; but when did we know that was the likely hour of arrival?

Early in the afternoon. It happened that the weather conditions did not change. The wind was steady from the east at about 10 knots, so that we were always under power. After passing Race Rock, whose gong we could hear but not see, so dense was that fog, we depressed another of those little Trimble keys. The TIME key. You ask it for an Estimated Time of Arrival. It tells you, in about two seconds, "ETA 2142." What it has done is taken the speed you have made good over the preceding five minutes in the direction of your waypoint. It has then divided this speed into the distance between where you are now and where the waypoint is toward which you are headed, and added this to the time of day. The answer is 9:42 P.M. I confess that the first time I had this experience I simply sat and stared at the computer, in dumb admiration.

How does it know the time? I mean, does it have an internal clock? Yes.

Alarms? There is no end of them. You can, if you wish, set the alarm to advise you when you are one-tenth of a mile from the next waypoint. (Minor complaint: The alarm should have a volume control. You would not hear mine over, say, a music cassette.) Or you can set it to go off one-half mile before; or never.

Can the alarm alert you to other situations? Short of impending seductions, the answer is: Yes, practically anything.

You are at a harbor and throw out the anchor, letting out 100 feet of line. You set the alarm, instructing it to go off if your vessel drifts more than 125 feet away from where you dropped the anchor. If something wakes you at midnight, it won't be the sound of your vessel hitting rocks. It is the alarm, advising you that vessel-on-rocks will be the next sound you hear unless you do something about your dragging anchor.

The Trimble of course tells you in what direction to head for your next waypoint, and how far away it is. *Does it track that distance continuously?* Yes. Every six seconds your position is updated.

Well, that way, I could figure out exactly how fast I am going, couldn't I?

Yes, you could, but Trimble will do it for you. Just push one of the other keys.

I must be careful—must I not?—to make allowance for magnetic variation, as I slide from one magnetic zone to another?

Yes, you must—unless you decide to let the Trimble do it for you. In which event you reprogram the computer, a maneuver that takes about six seconds. It will then automatically give you the proper magnetic heading for your destination. Its memory, you see, tells the computer where you are. And depending on where you are, the computer knows what is the appropriate magnetic variation. So it simply changes the course heading by the relevant sum. Needless to say, it advises you that, as of that point, you are now getting Magnetic, rather than True, courses.

And so it goes. The Trimble Loran-C, I should have mentioned earlier, is designed for maximum accuracy and range (it suggests modestly it will take you to within 300 feet of your buoy, but my experience is that, most of the time, it is more like 50 feet), and has other features.

Dropped your wife's wedding ring into the water? Dropped your wife into the water? Quickly push the button that has HOLD written on it, and it will freeze the exact location of where it all happened, so that you can mosey the boat back to go to exactly where you were, in order to undo the damage. And on and on.

What we had, when we set out for St. John that day in June,

thanks to the wedding of Loran-C and computer technology, was a simple, relatively inexpensive instrument that, in a word, did away with common navigational problems. Yes, there are moments (and the Loran clearly tells you when these moments come) when there is something going on in the skies that gets in the way of clear readings. Yes, the Trimble, like every other machine, may blow a transistor, if transistors blow. Your batteries may short and suddenly you have no juice (the draw, on 12 volts, is a mere .4 amps, about as much as a small bulb). A stroke of lightning may do away with your antenna, or, for that matter, you.

I do not suggest that any or all of these things cannot happen. It is unhappily true that there is much less than worldwide coverage by Loran-C, though I'd guess that if you added up the areas Loran-C now does cover, you'd end up with coverage for those areas of the world where 75 percent of yachting goes on. (The one conspicuous void is the Caribbean. There they are waiting for the Global Positioning System, about which an explanation down the line.)

My sermon is less than a recommendation that sailors rely exclusively on their Trimble Loran-C; it is only that in the history of

Trimble's Loran 200.

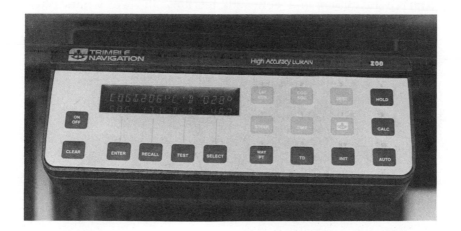

modern navigational progress nothing could compare with it—up to that time. Loran-C was the anchor achievement. But the combining of it with the computer quite simply takes the work out of navigation.

We knew, setting out from Stamford, where we were, where and at what speed we were headed, what if any was our drift, when we were likely to arrive at Port Jefferson, how far we had left to go.

Sure, I would continue to bring along all the other paraphernalia. But better resolve, I thought that night, when after traveling for fifteen hours without sight of any land, any buoys, any other boat, sometimes straining to see our own bow, we came at dead of night upon the little cut leading into Menemsha—not easy to spot even at high noon—resolve to give yourself refresher courses every year or so in the other stuff, because you will have got used to relying on this system. It was the hottest navigational aid since the sun sight, and, unlike the sun, it does not sleep half the time, just when you need it most, or tease you, at other times, behind cloud banks. Loran-C, like the Constitution, or IRS, is full-time.

We rejoiced over our liberation from the conventional rigors of navigating and piloting, and rejoiced in a great deal else. Just north of the tip of Cape Cod, we ran into the most prolific school of whales I have seen anywhere in the world. They were disporting about a mile to starboard, the sun, setting opposite, playing on their frolics. Christopher and Tom took pictures, and we sat down happily to our steak dinner. The wind had picked up nicely and we were on autopilot, the southeasterly wind blowing the seakindly boat on its comfortable course toward Monhegan, which we thought to hit at about noon the following day. The boys (as I am likely to continue to call them, inasmuch as the same clock that graduates them into middle age graduates me toward senescence) knocked off at ten. Tom and I listened to music and to the wind until two in the morning. To spare the batteries, we took the wheel, which is my diplomatic way of saying that I took the wheel, since Tom has a problem distinguishing between a course of 330 degrees and a course of 033 degrees—what one might call (see below) a Clurman-problem. The following day we bathed and explored in Monhegan and dined wonderfully on fresh lobster, setting out after dinner for St. John, and running into sheer hell the next day.

It was midmorning. We were in total fog, somewhere between Grand Manan Island and the easternmost stretch of American soil, fifty miles or so from the bend into St. John. Danny, checking out the Loran, called out to me from below that a current was clearly taking us swiftly to the north, as the bearing on our next waypoint now read not 0100, but 0300: we were slipping. I made the necessary adjustment in my course and a few minutes later Danny reported that we were dangerously close to land, so I turned sharply to starboard, gave the wheel to Christopher, and went below. I checked several waypoints on my beloved Trimble. I found: chaos. No two bearings were consistent. Either the whole unit had gone berserk, or else—we were out of range.

We had with us only the first draft of the Trimble Manual, in mimeograph form. The succeeding draft would have solved our problem: It would have given the code numbers to turn to in order to receive Loran-C from Canadian stations. I didn't know these even existed, having assumed that U.S. Loran would easily carry us as far as St. John. We were reduced to what seemed the antiquarian resources of a sailboat caught in a fog, not knowing, given the confusion of the apparatus on which we had relied, within ten miles where we actually were.

I charted a course parallel to the northeasterly direction of the mainland and proceeded watchfully, hoping the fog would lift.

It did so for about an hour in the late afternoon, and it was after that that our situation got worse.

Two hours later we spotted a buoy and one of the boys, with binoculars, sang out its identifying number. It was by now dark and cold, and the fog was back with us. I calculated, based on the buoy, that we were seven miles from Point Lepreau, a promontory on the lee side of which we could throw out the anchor and get some relief from the northeasterly that was now roaring at about 20 knots.

As often as not, any singular stretch of time at sea teaches lessons one would think, in retrospect, were rudimentary. In this case, the first thing I should have done was turn the wheel over to Christopher or Danny, go below, and come up dressed for arctic circumstances. Instead I put on, offhandedly, an extra sweater, and calculated that a mere hour's exposure, never mind the dropping temperature, would hardly hurt. Two hours later, on the stipulated course, having traveled not seven but eleven miles, we still didn't see the flashing 5-second, 16-mile beacon on which we depended, even though the fog had lessened sufficiently to make us confident that we would be able to descry it. I was now almost paralyzed by the cold and rain, as were my mates, and infinitely depressed by the incomprehensible failure of the vessel to traverse the seven mythical miles. When finally we spotted the beacon we all but collapsed with relief—I had considered heading out to sea and heaving to, which is to say making a sailboat as immobile as a sailboat can be, accomplished by running a small jib aback to the windward side, reefing the mainsail, and adjusting the tiller until minimum sway is effected. We found conditions at the proposed anchorage far less auspicious than anticipated, but I ordered the anchor thrown out —it is a heavy Danforth with twenty feet of chain, followed by two hundred feet of one-inch nylon. It held; but the boat rocked, and sleep was fitful. The buoy had been misidentified, and we were four miles further away than we had thought.

The following day the wind abruptly ceased, but the fog gave limited visibility. Under power, we followed the rocky Canadian coastline, secure only in the knowledge that eventually the land's profile would lead us into St. John. Visibility was about a quarter of a mile. We spotted a buoy, and I made out the letters "GR," and concluded happily that we were at Negro Head, a mere three miles from the entrance to St. John. In fact we had twelve miles to go. Once again, misidentification. (There was nothing on the chart that corresponded with my GR. To be sure, we were relying on a five-year-old chart.)

That night we truly rested. At St. John we did some provisioning while waiting for the Reversing Falls to let us by. I never forget the prescription: *two hours twenty-five minutes after high tide, three hours fifty minutes after low tide.* These magic moments usher in the ten minutes' stability during which boats can come and go. On the eleventh minute after low tide, the great force of the Bay of Fundy with its forty-foot tidefall rushes into the St. John River. Eleven minutes after the tide is high, four hundred miles of river, whose tidefall is a bare inch, thunder down into the depleted Bay of Fundy. We had had an eventful four hours, but now we nestled in the bower of the loveliest river in the world.

Unhappily, the next day's wind was a brisk northerly, right on our nose, so that we did not reach Fredericton, seventy miles up-river. After two bracing, exquisite sunny days we were back in St. John, at the Royal Kennebecasis Yacht Club by the Reversing Falls, and there we would leave *Patito* to be ferried back to Connecticut by two young professional pilots.

3

THE ANGEL OF CRAIG'S POINT

That last day on the river, after sailing briskly downwind with only the headsail for two or three hours during which we lunched, we thought to take a little exercise—a good walk—and while at it, to get rid of two sackfuls of garbage, neatly tied up in plastic bags and riding in the dinghy we were towing.

I spotted a little private wharf on Craig's Point and glided in toward it, intending to ask the owner's permission to use his garbage container and perhaps even to tie up the boat on his dock for an hour while we walked. As we approached the dock, Christo leaned forward, a docking line in his hand ready to toss to the man in his early sixties who approached us in the usual manner in which boats are approached when coming in for a landing—i.e., prepared to receive the bowline and to cleat it to the dock. I signaled Tom to make the request from amidship. He said, "Is it okay if we tie up here for a few minutes? We'd also like to get rid of the garbage, if that's all right." To our astonishment, he answered: "It is *not* all right. Go away. This is private property." I intervened. "How far from your house is the public road?" He pointed in the general direction of his own house.

"It's back there."

"Well," I said, "could we just walk across your property to find a public place to leave the garbage?"

"You may not. Go away."

To put it calmly, sailors are not used to being treated that way. To begin with, our anxiety to put the garbage on an assembly line to the city dump was a presumption of our concern for the cleanliness of the water that ran by Craig's Point, where the gentleman lived, not Wallacks Point, where I live. But of course there was no alternative than to retreat from his dock area. We consulted hastily, calculated the probable distance of his shoreline property, went safely beyond it, threw out a hook, and three of us went ashore. At least we could get our walk. The garbage could continue to accumulate until we reached the yacht club next morning.

After our walk we sailed another hour, spotted a seductive minicove nestled among tall cypress trees, and let down the anchor for our last meal aboard *Patito* on that trip. Christopher and Danny set about preparing a gourmet dinner while Tom played an entire Bach toccata on the Casio. I sensed an ungovernable urge, and reached for my portable typewriter. Before we sat down to dinner, I announced that I wished to read to my crew a letter I had written to the editor of the afternoon paper at St. John. I intended a catharsis for the unpleasant experience at Craig's Point, and achieved it.

Four days later, back in New York, my secretary, Frances Bronson, told me that the editor of the *Telegraph-Journal* of St. John, New Brunswick, was on the line and wanted to speak to me.

I was stuck. Journalists should always take calls from other journalists (my rule). But I knew that there was no way I could take *this* phone call and speak the truth without undermining my own enterprise. So I instructed Frances to tell the editor, "Mr. Buckley has nothing to add to the letter he addressed to your paper a few days ago at St. John, and sends his best wishes."

A few days later, someone sent me in the mail a copy of the *Telegraph-Journal* for July 16, 1982.

Bill Buckley Loves Hospitality In N.B.

(Editor's note: William F. Buckley, editor of National Review, a conservative magazine published in New York and host of the popular 'Firing Line' program on the educational television network, was in New Brunswick recently with his family. They had a few problems but were delighted with the help they received. And he wrote to us to say so.)

* * *

Dear Sir:

Indulge, if you will, a vacationing American journalist with Canadian connections (my wife, even after 30 years' marriage, is obstinately Canadian), a word or two about our recent voyage in my small sloop with three companions, from Stamford, Connecticut to Saint John, via Nantucket.

1) Near Lepreau Point, west of Saint John some twenty-five miles, we ran out of fuel — and there was no air. My son and his companion took the dinghy, approached the nearest house, and explained our predicament. The gentleman convoyed them to the nearest gas station, where they filled two five gallon containers, returned them to the beach, wished them godspeed, and rejected mostly amiably a proffered bottle of champagne.

2) At Saint John, while waiting for the current's equilibrium in order to make the passage across the Falls, a resident volunteered to drive us in his work-truck to the restaurant where we lunched. En route he spotted our five-gallon container, ascertained that we intended to buy some diesel,

volunteered to do so for us while we lunched, and to place the container in our dinghy; where, an hour later, we found it, together with the receipt from the gasoline station.

3) The following day, heading up the River, I radioed to my office to ascertain whether the details had been completed involving the ferry pilots retained to bring my sloop back to Connecticut. After the telephonic exchange had been completed, the operator said to me: "Excuse me, sir, but I heard your secretary give the telephone number of the hotel where she booked your pilots. She gave you an area code of 709. That is the area code for St. John's, Newfoundland, not Saint John, New Brunswick." I quickly called back to New York, explained the confusion, and thanked the marine operator whose merciful intervention spared us a geographical solecism that would have qualified for the annals of, well, something.

4) But I must close by mentioning what my shipmates have come to refer to as "the Angel of Craig's Point." That may really be overstating it, but the gentleman who owns the house on Craig's Point, at Latitude 45 degrees 23.5, Longitude 66 degrees 12.3, is certainly very special. We had accumulated some garbage, and went by dinghy to the gentlemen's little wharf, where he met us with open arms, guiding us to a disposal point, complimenting us effusively on the thought we took to preserve the ecological purity of your beautiful river. Such ardent attention he gave us that we soon

WILLIAM F. BUCKLEY

gathered that he devotes himself substantially to welcoming any yachtsman or passers-by who have garbage or any form of detritus to dispose of. Such heartening concern for nature, and such hospitality evidenced to strangers, prompts me to send a copy of this letter to the editor of the famous Cruising Guide to the New England (and Canadian) Coast, so that future editions will assure that no yachtsman will pass by Craig's Point without paying respect to its Angel, and leaving him his garbage.

We are all very much in debt to the citizens of Saint John for your hospitality.

WILLIAM F. BUCKLEY, JR.

New York, N.Y.

On the right, there was a large picture of me, smiling. The headline read,

BILL BUCKLEY LOVES
HOSPITALITY IN N.B.

An editor's note began the story . . .

(Editor's note: William F. Buckley, editor of *National Review*, a conservative magazine published in New York and host of the popular "Firing Line" program on the Educational Television Network, was in New Brunswick recently with his family. They had a few problems but were delighted with the help they received. And he wrote to us to say so.)

Dear Sir:

Indulge, if you will, a vacationing American journalist with Canadian connections (my wife, even after thirty years' marriage, is obstinately Canadian), a word or two about our recent voyage in my small sloop with three companions, from Stamford, Connecticut, to St. John, via Nantucket.

1) Near Lepreau Point, west of St. John some twenty-five miles, we ran out of fuel—and there was no wind. My son and his companion took the dinghy, approached the nearest house, and explained our predicament. The gentleman convoyed them to the nearest gas station, where they filled two five-gallon containers, returned them to the beach, wished them godspeed, and rejected most amiably a proffered bottle of champagne.

2) At St. John, while waiting for the current's equilibrium in order to make the passage across the falls, a resident volunteered to drive us in his work truck to the restaurant where we lunched. En route he spotted our five-gallon container, ascertained that we intended to buy some diesel, volunteered to do so for us while we lunched, and to place the container in our dinghy; where, an hour later, we found it, together with the receipt from the gasoline station.

3) The following day, heading up the river, I radioed to my office to ascertain whether the details had been completed involving the ferry crew retained to bring my sloop back to Connecticut. After the telephonic exchange had been completed, the operator said to me: "Excuse me, sir, but I heard your secretary give the telephone number of the hotel where she booked your crew. She gave you an area code of 709. That is the area code for St. John's, Newfoundland, not St. John, New Brunswick." I quickly called back to New York, explained the confusion, and thanked the marine operator whose merciful intervention spared us a geographical solecism that would have qualified for the annals of, well, something.

4) But I must close by mentioning what my shipmates have come to refer to as "The Angel of Craig's Point." That may really be overstating it, but the gentleman who owns the house on Craig's Point, at latitude 45° 23.5, longitude 66° 12.3, is certainly very special. We had accumulated some garbage, and went by dinghy to the

gentleman's little wharf, where he met us with open arms, guiding us to a disposal point, complimenting us effusively on the thought we took to preserve the ecological purity of your beautiful river. Such ardent attention he gave us that we soon gathered that he devotes himself substantially to welcoming any yachtsmen or passers-by who have garbage or any form of detritus to dispose of. Such heartening concern for nature, and such hospitality evidenced to strangers, prompt me to send a copy of this letter to the editor of the famous A *Cruising Guide to the New England* (and Canadian) *Coast,* so that future editions will assure that no yachtsmen will pass by Craig's Point without paying respect to its Angel, and leaving him their garbage.

We are very much in debt to the citizens of St. John for your hospitality.

Wm. F. Buckley, Jr.
New York, N.Y.

The following day I received a copy of the *Telegraph-Journal* of St. John for July 17, 1982. The headline was too good to be true . .

THE ANGEL OF CRAIG'S POINT STRIKES BACK

On the left of the boxed story, another headline:

MORE ABOUT
BILL BUCKLEY'S
GARBAGE BAGS
BY JIM WHITE
ASSOCIATE EDITOR

Where is William F. Buckley's garbage?

That's the big question facing residents of the Craig's Point area on the St. John River north of Westfield.

Mr. Buckley, the well-known American writer and editor of the *National Review,* wrote a letter to the editor of the *Telegraph-Journal* which was published yesterday, complimenting New Brunswickers on their hospitality during a recent visit.

But the vituperative Mr. Buckley struck out at one resident of Craig's Point in a seemingly innocent passage and that resident wants to set the record straight once and for all.

4   THE TELEGRAPH-JOURNAL, SAINT JOHN, N.B., SATURDAY, JULY 17, 1982

The Angel Of Craig's Point Strikes Back

By JIM WHITE
Associate Editor

More About
Bill Buckley's
Garbage Bags

Where is William F. Buckley's garbage?

That's the big question facing residents of the Craig's Point area on the St. John River north of Westfield.

Mr. Buckley, the well-known American writer and editor of the National Review, wrote a letter to the editor of The Telegraph-Journal which was published yesterday, complimenting New Brunswickers on their hospitality during a recent visit.

But the vituperative Mr. Buckley struck out at one resident of Craig's Point in a seemingly innocent passage and that resident wants to set the record straight once and for all.

Mr. Buckley in his letter referred to the "angel of Craig's Point" who assisted him in disposing his accumulated "detritus" from his "small sloop."

Mr. Buckley went on further to suggest passing yachters should not miss the opportunity to deposit their garbage at Craig's Point.

But the so-called "angel" has an entirely different recollection of the encounter.

Aubrey Pope, a retired Saint John businessman, remembers the July 1st encounter with Mr. Buckley's party very well.

The Buckley sloop had spent the night in the shelter of a cove off Craig's Point, Mr. Pope said.

The next morning, Mr. Pope's wife noticed "three chaps in a rubber dinghy heading toward the shore."

Mr. Pope, who is well known up and down the river, went out to greet the landing party.

By the time Mr Pope arrived at the shore one of the men was standing on the wharf and the others were handing out two boxes and a couple of bags of garbage.

"If they had only asked permission, I would have been happy to give them a hand," Mr. Pope said.

But the party arrogantly went about their work and told Mr. Pope they

were going to dump the garbage beside the road.

When Mr. Pope told the group there was no roadside pickup they insisted they wanted to get rid of their unseemly cargo.

At this point Mr. Pope informed them they were trespassing on his private property and were no longer welcome. They could pack up their garbage and return to their boat.

"They got in their boat and rowed into the river," Mr. Pope said. "Then they put into shore a little way's down river. They walked ashore with the boxes. I don't know where they dumped it, but they didn't have their garbage when they came back to the boat."

Attempts to get through to Mr. Buckley at his New York office failed. But Mr. Buckley's assistant, Francis Bronson, said Mr. Buckley had submitted the letter for publication and had no further comment.

Kempton Pope, son of the owner of Craig's Point, said the rudeness of the Buckley party was what really riled his father.

WILLIAM F. BUCKLEY

"If they had introduced themselves we probably would have been proud to have Mr. Buckley's garbage," he said with a chuckle.

Because of his actions in writing the letter Mr. Pope suggests Mr. Buckley confine his cruising to the Love Canal.

Meanwhile the search continues at Craig's Point for Mr. Buckley's garbage.

Mr. Buckley in his letter referred to the "angel of Craig's Point" who assisted him in disposing his accumulated "detritus" from his "small sloop."

Mr. Buckley went on further to suggest passing yachters should not miss the opportunity to deposit their garbage at Craig's Point.

But the so-called "angel" has an entirely different recollection of the encounter.

Aubrey Pope, a retired St. John businessman, remembers the July 1st encounter with Mr. Buckley's party very well.

The Buckley sloop had spent the night in the shelter of a cove off Craig's Point, Mr. Pope said.

The next morning, Mr. Pope's wife noticed "three chaps in a rubber dinghy heading toward the shore."

Mr. Pope, who is well known up and down the river, went out to greet the landing party.

By the time Mr. Pope arrived at the shore, one of the men was standing on the wharf and the others were handing out two boxes and a couple of bags of garbage.

"If they had only asked permission, I would have been happy to give them a hand," Mr. Pope said.

But the party arrogantly went about their work and told Mr. Pope they were going to dump the garbage beside the road.

When Mr. Pope told the group there was no roadside pickup they insisted they wanted to get rid of their unseemly cargo.

At this point Mr. Pope informed them they were trespassing on his private property and were no longer welcome. They could pick up their garbage and return to their boat.

"They got in their boat and rowed into the river," Mr. Pope said. "Then they put into shore a little way's down river. They walked ashore with the boxes. I don't know where they dumped it, but they didn't have their garbage when they came back to the boat."

Attempts to get through to Mr. Buckley at his New York office failed. But Mr. Buckley's assistant, Frances Bronson, said Mr. Buckley had submitted the letter for publication and had no further comment.

Kempton Pope, son of the owner of Craig's Point, said the rudeness of the Buckley party was what really riled his father.

"If they had introduced themselves we probably would have been proud to have Mr. Buckley's garbage," he said with a chuckle.

It had been ages, historian Tom Wendel wrote me from California, since he had seen such a farrago of misinformation as that given to editor White by Aubrey Pope. But we had had our laugh, and I resigned myself to living with the consolation that misrepresentations of *Patito*'s behavior were limited to a modest circulation centered on Craig's Point, New Brunswick.

Not so.

On September 6, *People* magazine (circ. 2,850,000) ran an item in its Chatter column, written by Josh Hammer.

Dumping on the Locals After a recent cruise down New Brunswick's picturesque St. John River, writer-skipper William F. Buckley, Jr., sent a letter to the *St. John Telegraph-Journal* praising a fellow whom he dubbed "the angel of Craig's Point." According to Buckley, the man had helped his crew dispose of its shipboard garbage. Aubrey Pope, 67, a local businessman, recognized his description but surfaced with a somewhat different version of Buckley's tale. As he told it to an editor at the *Telegraph-Journal*, three of Buckley's crew members had indeed sought to unload their trash—by dumping it all on Pope's private dock. Pope happened to intercept them and ordered them off. "I'm not very big, but I can get ugly," he said, adding that he "would have been glad to help"—if it hadn't been for their "arrogant attitude." Buckley's response was to dump his trash without permission at a scenic spot farther down river and then fire off his sarcastic missive, in which he "thanked" Pope for his help, gave the exact location of his dock and advised mariners passing through not to cruise by Craig's Point "without paying respects to its angel" by dropping off their garbage there.

Oh dear, I thought. It was all really getting out of hand. Mr. Pope's story had now elevated into rarer atmospheres. Not only had we obstreperously arrived at his dock, landed on it without his permission, and (in effect) threatened him, we had actually thrown our garbage into a scenic spot next door. So, of course, I needed now to write to *People*. I did so, patiently straightening out the story. *People* did not publish the last half of the sentence that began, "It would not occur to us to dump garbage on private property without permission"—which sentence went on to say, "or to publish a story to the effect that Mr. Hammer [the author of *People*'s Chatter column] had done so, without first calling him up and asking him whether so bizarre an allegation was correct."

And then, on top of all that, I had a pleasant letter from Roger Duncan, the editor of *A Cruising Guide to the New England Coast*, the Bible of New England sailors. I hadn't actually sent him a copy of my letter to the St. John paper—but somebody else had done so. And now he was writing to *thank* me for thinking to send him such random information about cruising experiences as I was collecting. He advised me that his own experience with Canadians, like my own, reaffirmed that they were the most hospitable breed of people on earth. He finished:

I appreciate your thinking of the *Guide*. It is only with the help of cruising men who write in their experiences of various harbors that we can possibly keep the book current. I visit a great many harbors and so does [my associate] John Ware, but we could never accomplish the project without help. Any other information of interest to cruising yachtsmen will be welcome, either now or later.

I needed to straighten Mr. Duncan out in a hurry.

And then, on reading the correction published in *People*, the editor of the St. John paper wrote to remind me that he had tried to reach me over the telephone but I had not taken his call. He added that Mr. Pope was now asserting that his own story of what had happened was confirmed by someone who had used binoculars from the other side of the river. I replied:

Dear Mr. White:

Thank you for your amiable letter. You will perhaps have reflected on the reasons why I did not take the telephone call from you that day in July. Obviously my letter, while composed three parts of genuine praise of Canadian hospitality, was composed one part of sarcasm at the expense of Mr. Anti-Pope. I could hardly have talked with you over the telephone without giving away the show, and obviously I wouldn't have wanted to do that.

On the astonishing point that there was a live witness via binoculars: That would suggest, given that the verbal exchanges with Mr. Pope were exactly as described by me, that the binoculars disposed of facilities for picking up the sound of human voices several hundred yards away. Since to my knowledge such stuff as this is limited to the CIA and KGB, then you have more to worry about than my inaccessibility. If your reporter advised you that we proceeded to dump the garbage ashore, why he is just plain wrong, and if it were necessary to prove the point, you could have four sworn affidavits. My own guess has been that Mr. Anti-Pope is industrious in elaborating circumstances that vitiate his rudeness. I note that *People* magazine edited my letter, leaving out the last sentence, which was the only trenchant remark on their own misbehavior. Ah well. Could it be that journalists are also human?

I took occasion to express my gratitude to the part of the world he lived in. And closed,

I take the liberty of sending you a copy of my book *Airborne*, published five years ago. There is a section in it in which I pay tribute to St. John. I stop smiling when I tell my friends it is the most beautiful river in the world, because I fear that they might think I am exaggerating. By the way, the use of the word "vituperative" in the newspaper story on me is incorrect. I am other things.

Thank you again for your hospitable note. The next time I am in the area I shall give myself the pleasure of calling on you. We might discuss the nature of a Garbage Memorial to the memory of the Angel of Craig's Point.

Exactly a year later, Tom Wendel, Danny, Christo, and I found ourselves once again on the St. John River. We had planned to cruise to the Bras d'Or Lakes in the northern part of Nova Scotia, but a tight schedule plus headwinds rerouted us, and now we were at anchor within sight of the Angel's spread, a few hundred yards upstream. We had consumed, with dinner, a magnum of fine Bordeaux, a cruising gift from a friend, which greatly animated us. Accordingly, we typed out a note, stuck it in the bottle, corked it tightly, and let it float downstream. The note read:

Important . . . Reward . . . The finder of this bottle can claim a fifty-dollar reward by presenting the bottle to Aubrey Pope, Esquire, at Craig's Point, Morrisdale, NB. The reward will be payable on saying to Mr. Pope, "This bottle represents the gratitude of the Canada Beautiful Society, Ltd, Garbage Collection Division, W. F. Buckley, Corresponding Secretary, Care Editor, *St. John Telegraph-Journal*."

Somewhere in the oceans of the world that bottle is floating about. That, or else it has been presented to the Angel for the promised reward.

4

IN & AROUND
LONG ISLAND SOUND

Patito is a great pleasure to me, but the one trip planned with my wife Pat also aboard proved, as she would put it, "a disaster" (a *Women's Wear Daily* word for uncomfortable). I am being harsh, because setting out from Block Island I decided to go to my destination, Edgartown, by heading northeast, by Chappaquiddick, in order to avoid an adverse current on the westerly route up Martha's Vineyard Sound, which would not turn for five hours in our favor. This decision meant close windward sailing, of the kind that causes a sailboat to lean dramatically to one side, the going bumpy, wet, disagreeable. And the going this day was very choppy, indeed so much so that the mate I had retained to ferry the boat back to Stamford from Nantucket, and who was with us for this leg of our little cruise, was himself a little chagrined at the punishment I permitted *Patito* to take.

Matt Craven was about twenty-seven. We had crossed paths when I cruised on one of the Delta Line's cargo/cruise ships in 1980, from Rio de Janeiro to Valparaiso, an ocean trip I had greatly looked forward to in part because it gave me the time I needed to complete a book, in part because I longed to go through the Strait of Magellan. It was November, midsummer in that part of the world, but Punta Arenas, at 53° 10' latitude, is cold, and the two pilots who board at Rio, one of them Chilean, the second Argentine, are properly tense as they guide the vessel through the narrow strait, a day and a half's anfractuous journey to the open ocean.

To amuse myself I had brought along a sextant and a Plath calculator, my then-current enthusiasm, and every night I took star sights, along with another American passenger also hooked on celestial navigation. The two of us were given the courtesy of the bridge and became familiar with the officers. Matt had had four years' training at Kings Point and I noted with some awe the meticulousness of operations on a modern bridge manned by professional seamen. I had been in the Gulf of Tonkin, aboard the aircraft carrier *Forrestal*, and it was on the order of being inside the clockwork of an atomic timepiece. I have been in the cockpit of a Boeing 747 when it made a mind-dazzling all-blind landing, and I have seen high-tech precision at work. Something of the same sort happens in the belly of an icebreaker charged with keeping a shipping lane open to McMurdo Station in the Antarctic. There a young man who cannot have been more than eighteen, guided by radar and other instruments that register the least palpability, ordered the icebreaker's hull to rampage forward, shattering the ice; then reverse-engine back, then full-throttle forward; then back, repeating the sequence for about five months, surely the most grueling peacetime assignment in military life. I have been inside an atomic submarine, satisfied that the team of navigators knows the submarine's position within a matter of inches.

All of this engages rapt admiration, but taking the same sights with virtually the same equipment used two hundred years ago is quite another world. Standing fifty feet above the water, with a (gyroscopic) compass and fixed binoculars, predicting with the aid of the tables within a half minute or so the ideal moment to catch the premeditated navigational star—these are laboratory navigational conditions, I thought; but even so, I admired the profitable routinization of the navigational enterprise, making any error almost instantly transparent. Matt, a tall, blond American of Scandinavian background, told me on that cruise that his profession was subject to long layoffs and if ever I needed crew to ferry my little sailboat from anyplace to anyplace, he would probably be very much available.

So here he was, as I pounded close-hauled against the heavy seas off Block Island. He turned to me, finally, and said that, really, he thought I was asking too much of the vessel. This observation delighted my wife, who thinks I ask too much of a vessel if I hoist a handkerchief up the mainmast. But, to be agreeable, I took a second reef on the mainsail, and reflected that at Kings Point they probably do not expose the cadets to very much ocean racing. I abandoned racing after a number of years in part because I did not have a suitable boat for competitive work; in part because the administrative burden of collecting a crew, weekend after weekend, gets terribly burdensome; in part because the activity is progressively antisocial if your family does not participate. And, also in part, because ocean racing can be protractedly uncomfortable. Necessary discomfort at sea is one thing. Unnecessary discomfort is quite another thing, and I have devoted a substantial measure of my sailing career, if that is the word for it, to distinguishing between the two.

But the major problem, where *Patito* is concerned, is that my wife suffers from arthritis. She has had two hip operations, and that night at Nantucket (from which she flew home) she told me, resolutely, that she would not again sail on *Patito*, and she has not. This is saddening, because one aspires to share all one's pleasures; but it is better that way than the other way—the other way being to take along one's wife on the clear understanding that the passage in prospect will be no more adventurous than sailing across the window of Abercrombie and Fitch. Often it isn't more than that; but one can never tell. And the preeminent anxiety one feels for the biological and temperamental well-being of one's wife quite upsets the experience you seek from sailing.

So then, for four years Pat and I have not sailed together aboard *Patito*. We have sailed a great deal together, but on vessels 70 feet or longer; and, with the single exception of our annual overnight run from Anguilla to Virgin Gorda, no overnights, thank you.

It was then that I developed what has become a practice I most heartily recommend. My friend Peter Flanigan, in the summer of 1985, thought to buy a 45-foot sailboat and to keep it in Essex, Connecticut, even though he lives in Greenwich, Connecticut. This would mean, I pleaded with him, that every time he used the boat it would need to be for a proper cruise. It is hardly worth driving two hours to Essex for a day's sail, followed by two hours' drive back, never mind the hour it requires to reach the Sound from Essex by boat. Why not do as I do?—I asked seductively.

What is that?

Well, I said, I have now a routine, and I do it about fifteen times every year. For one thing (I slip quickly into the didactic mode) you must not think of putting your boat away, as most people do, right after Labor Day. This is a habit associated with children going back to school, children being at once the most convenient menials in a sailing family, as also very often (though by no means always), the greatest enthusiasts. So that when they go off to school the boat tends to sit, forlornly; and is soon put away in the boatyard.

No more! I said. If you have a boat that requires little maintenance, a boat two people can easily operate, why, keep it in the water and use it. But develop your own routine.

I have one, and it suits and pleases me hugely and, I gladly report, gives pleasure to others. It always includes four people, and almost always all male—36-foot boats are inconveniently small for privacy. We meet at my house in Stamford between six-thirty and seven. Danny, who lives a few hundred yards away and who exercises supervision over *Patito*, is always invited; but half the time, and even more these days (he is preoccupied with his wife and three children), he is not free. I then gladly invite Tony Leggett, who sailed across the Atlantic with me in 1980, an Olympic-class sailor also aged about twenty-seven, a splendid companion, bon vivant, and conversationalist who rusticates in a bank vault somewhere in Brooklyn during the week and aches for the mere sight of salt water.

He and I are absolutely all that is needed to sail the boat, leaving room for two jolly good fellows, and it matters not in the least whether they know the difference between the mast and the boom. We serve up a drink and watch the first fifteen minutes of the evening news with Pat and, more often than not, her houseguest, all in my enchanted, littered music room. Before the news is concluded, we go to the station wagon in the rear of which is everything we will need to dine royally. We are at the boat basin in five minutes, the food is stowed in ten minutes. If the wind is severe, I will take a reef. With the roller-furling genoa, we can get exactly as much pull from the headsail as we desire. I rejoice in activating every electric and electronic device I have aboard *Patito*, and these would sink the average boat show. I put on the radar, and show my guests how we can track our way out of the harbor. I pause to note that the new digital radar (I have Raytheon's 200) gives a wonderfully clear reading, avoiding the revolving wand that left one, over the years, forgetting what lay out there at one o'clock, by the time the wand had reached eleven o'clock. For fun and instruction, one summer night after a picnic dinner, I made Christopher pledge not to look out from the cockpit. He must stare only at the face of the radar and from there issue me instructions on how to pilot *Patito* back to my slip. He guided me past two beacons, then into the mouth of Stamford Harbor, up the main channel, past the rocky beacon at the north end, into the 50-foot-wide channel leading to the yacht basin. We'd have run aground just at the point where the channel was the narrowest. The radar, in short, guided us almost to our berth.

I turn on my beloved Trimble, which now has an extension on the cockpit bulkhead so that by pushing this button or that you can learn everything you'd have needed, earlier, to go below to learn: your course, the distance to your destination, your drift, your speed made good—all these are sitting in front of you. When you reach the mouth of the harbor, you set your course, first to the little reef one mile south, then—unless the wind is from the southeast, which usually it is not—I sail to my favorite little harbor at Eatons Neck, a nine-mile sail.

Sometimes the passage is completely calm. Sometimes the wind is raging ferociously and with a double reef—once or twice under reduced headsail alone—we travel at hull speed, over 8 knots. We do our best simultaneously to nibble at our foie gras and to drink our spring vinho verde. In an hour and a half we have wended our way through the serpentine channel, always a little bit of a breath-catcher as the sands run erratically, requiring, at low tide, concentration on how you managed the channel a fortnight ago. Occasionally we go aground, and use one of the standard devices to claw our way into navigable water. But then the final northerly undulation and we are in the little harbor, more like a lagoon. The low-profile beach does nothing to protect you from the wind, if it is heavy from the north. But it shields the water, which is wonderfully still, and you throw out the anchor, and feel wonderfully refreshed.

Danny or Tony lights the fire on the grill that hangs out over the rear pulpit, and you go below and attend to a) music (your kind of music), b) lights (your kind of lights—candlelight), c) heat (when it is cold outside, you light the kerosene 13,000 BTU heater), d) picture lights (two, forward, carefully designed to light up two charming oil paintings by Richard Grosvenor), and e) wines (you open the wines you will have for dinner, and pass about a preview). One of the guests usually volunteers to mix the salad, already prepared, or preheat the corn before it gets its roasting on the grill, or light the oven (careful: lighting an alcohol oven is not the kind of thing one lightly turns over to the amateur to perform), or to heat the dessert.

In a half hour you are eating and drinking and listening to music and conversing. The question eventually arises whether to dip into the ocean. Danny and I once did this on December 13, and have no wish to break that record. But last year I did it on Thanksgiving weekend, and the survival rate is remarkably high. The pain is intense, but only for about five seconds—to be sure, four seconds more than, they tell you, someone being electrocuted experiences pain. But you feel splendid when this is over. You help to make the beds. One guest occupies the quarter berth (a coffin open at one end, stretching aft along the ship's hull; Tom Wendel has the quite extraordinary habit of going into the berth head first,

Patito. *Home under power.*

which most vertebrates would find impossibly claustrophobic). Two guests are comfortably ensconced in sleeping bags on either side of the collapsed saloon table, their reading lights on; and I am in my little private cabin, having dutifully checked the strength of the battery bank we are not using, to make certain that when we need the engine the following day we will have it. And if the kerosene heat is left on, however reduced, we must have an opening through the cockpit doors to let in air (otherwise we all die at night).

The most unattractive half hour of boat life is immediately after you wake up. There is so much to do, and the old yo-ho-ho has yet to kindle. You need to get dressed, in cramped quarters. You need to perform your toilette. Probably you will swim. The alcohol stove must be lighted.

I therefore tend to favor the quick getaway. Tony will weigh anchor, while I run the boat forward with the engine, and our two guests below are making toast, coffee, and asking who wants what cold cereal. By the time we are out of the little harbor, as a rule, we have had our breakfast, leaving us only the second cup of coffee to drink, and attention to pay to the sails. Generally in the morning the wind is not brisk, but usually it is enough to take us home at about six knots. At 10:30 you are in the car, the big garbage bag dumped in the boatyard's huge receptacle designed for that, the second plastic bag, containing all the saucers, plates, and utensils used during dinner and breakfast (they will be stuck into the automatic dishwasher), in the car trunk.

We go to the cellar of my house, into the swimming pool, first using the hot shower from the Jacuzzi, then the pool. In twenty minutes we are fresh as the newborn, sitting upstairs reading the Saturday *Times* with fresh coffee. The diaspora, almost by pre-understanding, begins. Your guests take the train to New York, or else drive off if they came by car; you go to your study in the garage and get to work, and you feel . . . They used to remark, in Gstaad when she lived part of the winter there, that Elizabeth Taylor, stretching her arms out in the morning on her porch, looking over the beautiful valley, would sigh and say, "I feel like a new man!"

I don't know how many guests I have taken on these little miniature cruising experiences, but I think they are almost all quite taken with them. There is so little fuss and bother. And yet you have had a genuine experience at sea. Call it a sailing haiku.

I should add that Peter Flanigan's boat rests now in Stamford, fifteen minutes from his house, not in Essex.

5

CHARTERING, AND A CHRISTMAS CRUISE

References to blue-water sailing tend to frighten people away because of the expense associated with the sport, and that is understandable. What is not right is that it should frighten away as many people as it does.

What is truly expensive is the large boat (defined arbitrarily as over 40 feet) maintained for ocean racing. The cost is heavy in gear, sail inventory, refinements of one sort or another, electronic aids, feeding and transporting your crew . . . It is a heavy drain, though what is remarkable about it is that so many Americans appear to be able to afford it. But the cost of maintaining a 45-foot cruising sailboat is, I'd estimate, about one half the cost of maintaining a 45-foot racing sailboat. Those who wish to get from the competitive sport only the sensation of the sail itself can satisfy themselves by buying a very small one-man boat, and perhaps racing it with a yacht club. The pleasures to be got in doing this are enormous. They do not, however, include the pleasures of life on board, which are reserved for those who like to cruise.

The trick, of course, is to charter a boat. If one consults the charter pages of the sailing magazines, one has the impression that chartering is a major business. It isn't, in fact, and this is so, I think, for two reasons. For one, the fear of the cost; for another, the reluctance to expose oneself to an experience with which one isn't familiar. The fear of not knowing how to act.

Someone recently sent me a clipping from a magazine called *Latitude 38*, published in California. I cannot imagine that it is read much in Latitude 39, or even in Latitude 38, if the prose I went through is characteristic. To be sure, the opening sentence was not exactly an icebreaker. It read, "There are two words that explain why the general public thinks of boat owners as the idle, indolent, insolent rich. One word is William. The other is Buckley." The author was reacting to a piece published in *Life* magazine in November 1985, in which I gave a brief account of the Pacific voyage I am celebrating in this volume. The author does not like my style of life on board, nor, do I suppose, would he like my style of life ashore. The final sentence of his essay reads, "Between William Buckley and $12 million America's Cup campaigns, it's no wonder the non-boating public has the wrong impression."

I was twice affronted here, having publicly defended the campaign to recapture the America's Cup, even while acknowledging that it is an expensive business. There is no way in which sponsors of an event as publicized as the America's Cup can disguise its terrible cost. For one thing, the entrepreneurs need to go out and raise the money, and they need to approach dozens, even hundreds of contributors. It is not as in days of yore, when one afternoon cocktail with Cornelius Vanderbilt and *zap*! the money is pledged. I know from my brush with the committee that they are as diligent as the professionals who raise money for Harvard or for the Red Cross.

But I think that the dyspeptic editor of *Latitude 38* does not pause to reflect on how much one can accomplish, in the way of sailing experiences, with moderate expenditure, here sadly but dutifully acknowledged as obviously out of the reach of most people (there are 440,000 power-and-sail cruising boats in the U.S.). But angry editors do not write editorials denouncing families who go off to spend a week or ten days in a Caribbean hotel, and it is here, slyly, that I begin my analysis.

When, for the first time, our son Christopher would not be with us for Christmas, we lost interest in spending it at home and accepted an invitation to go to La Romana, a budding resort on the southeastern point of the Dominican Republic. Ever since then we have gone to the Caribbean at Christmastime, seventeen years straight, excepting only the Christmas I spent at Tahiti on *Sealestial*, more or less monitoring its way to Honolulu where, six months later, we would set out on our Pacific passage.

Accordingly, although I have cruised the Caribbean more thoroughly than Christopher Columbus, I don't feel qualified to communicate the "magic" of the Caribbean, as they regularly refer to it when lesser words seem tongue-tied. *"If you begin to meet the people, you'll find striking differences from island to island— from Trinidad to Barbados, or Martinique to Guadeloupe. The better you know them, the more different they become."* That is from one of those coffee-table books about the Caribbean. And, later on in the same essay, *"The contemporary Caribbean has much in common with ancient Hellas—its sense of community in sports and art and religion."* These are asseverations I wouldn't deny. But I'll probably leave this planet before discovering whether they are true, because I never intend to explore the question. I don't want to live in the Caribbean, and I have too many friends I neglect in Connecticut to aspire to neglect yet more in the Caribbean. But I am here to say that it is hard to have a happier time than cruising in the Caribbean.

On your own boat.

That is, chartered, not necessarily owned. One pauses to examine, briefly, the commercial cruising pleasure liner spending the conventional one or two weeks in the Caribbean with 300–700 passengers aboard. Probably there is much to be said for this way of seeing the islands, in preference to hotel life. But your very own boat is really the way to go, and right away one needs to confront the question, "Isn't this out of the question for the average pocketbook?"

The answer is: Yes. But so is a week aboard the Royal Viking *Sky*, or a week at Paradise Beach, or Little Dix, or Caneel Bay. In round figures—if you include meals, drinks, tips, taxis—you are talking about four hundred dollars per couple per day, times seven comes to about three thousand dollars a week. In 1984 we chartered a boat that cost one thousand dollars per day, including food but not drinks, tips, or taxis. Throw these in, even profusely, and you are still short of nine thousand dollars per week. But there are three couples sharing the boat, so that the cost per couple—at three thousand dollars—is comparable to that of the hotels.

Until 1978 we vacationed on our own *Cyrano*, which when last I chartered her out went for three thousand dollars per week. In the years after losing her, we experimented with several boats, discovering in due course the 71-foot ketch (it is a class called Ocean 71) *Sealestial*, my enthusiasm for which led me, one spring, to charter her from St. Thomas to the Mediterranean, whither she was in any case bound for summer charters. I have found *Sealestial* the (almost—she is not air-conditioned) perfect cruising boat. And here is what you get when you charter a boat like *Sealestial*:

First, the tangibles. There is a crew of four. A skipper, a first mate, a stewardess, and a cook. There are three cabins. In descending order of luxury, the owner's cabin, which includes a dressing table, a huge stuffed chair for reading and working, a private bath including shower; a smaller but commodious cabin with hanging lockers and two bunks, sharing a shower and separate toilet with the third cabin, slightly smaller but entirely comfortable, provided it is not used by three persons sailing day and night across the Pacific Ocean.

The main saloon, as boat people call what at home would be called the living room, is square and would hold, comfortably seated, sixteen people. Eight can be seated around the coffee table that lifts up and becomes the dinner table, opposite the bar, music quarry, and screen for night movies. You may choose to eat in the main cockpit, to take advantage of the air and the view; or, usually when under way, at noon, in the after cockpit, which fits snugly six people, the awning giving protection from the sun. On deck there is more room than can be consumed by twelve people who wish to lie and read, or to sun, whether or not the vessel is under sail. The rubber dinghy holds eight people, and there is diving equipment aboard for four, with tanks that recharge in about a half hour. There is a radio that (usually) works, giving you contact as required with whomever you need to reach.

And the intangibles? You can rise in the morning, take stock of the wind, and decide which island to visit next. You can decide when to set sail, after breakfast or after a tour of the island. You can, sailing along offshore say a quarter of a mile (after you leave the Bahamas, the islands are nicely sheer and the water deep), spot a beach and decide impulsively you would like to swim off it. It happens to appeal—so that day you go no farther. There is no fixed itinerary, no deadlines, save the day and place of your disembarkation. When there is such a thing as a deadline—a couple of friends are flying down for a few days—you make contingent arrangements. It is easy to book a little airplane to meet your boat at a convenient island, the cost approximating a long taxi ride through Los Angeles.

It is most important, in the winter months (and, for that matter, also in the summer months, a point I have made before), to turn your watches to Buckley Watch Time. There are those who call this Daylight Time. But the two do not always correspond, because in some circumstances Buckley Watch Time advances the conventional time by two hours. The practical meaning of it all is that you can start the cocktail hour as the sun is setting, and eat dinner one hour later, at eight o'clock. Otherwise you can find yourself drinking at six o'clock and eating dinner at seven. "The former offends the Calvinist streak in a Yankee; the latter, the Mediterranean streak in a yacht owner," I once wrote. Dinner is protracted and leisurely, and after dinner, according to the inclinations of one's companions, we gamble (poker), or we watch a movie, or we read; and before retiring we swim, and stare a little at the stars, and the moon, and listen to the little waves, from whose busty sisters we are, on the leeward side of the island, protected.

I reflect on the last Christmas cruise we had in the Caribbean, before our Pacific passage. There are always variations, but the principal features are unchanging.

On this occasion, a week or two before we were to fly down, I had a phone call from Judy Papo, the broker and wife of the owner. A most unhappy development! Poor *Sealestial*! What outrageous people one finds in the world! And a brand-new motor at that!

The tale unraveled, and it transpired that, coming down from a berth in England after a summer in the Mediterranean, the yacht's brand-new engine gave trouble—somewhere off Casablanca, I think it was. The captain accepted a friendly offer of a few miles' tow, upon the completion of which the Good Samaritan asserted salvage rights, putting in a bill for the entire value of the boat, something on the order of three-quarters of a million dollars. They settled for less than that, but the negotiations would keep the boat from arriving in time for Christmas.

The resourceful broker, however, was armed against such a contingency. She proposed that we accept one of *Sealestial*'s sister ships for one week, and that for the balance of our ten-day trip we ride, without extra charge, on the brand-new vessel built by Dr. Papo, the owner of the *Sealestial*, a monstrous big sloop yclept the *Concorde*, 88 feet long, with room for twelve passengers and a crew of six.

Boats that size move, for me, on just the other side of manageability; but we were talking about only three days, and in any event there were no practical alternatives. The nuisance lay in packing and repacking, freedom from which is one of the splendid perquisites you inherit if you elect not to visit the Caribbean island-hopping from hotel to hotel.

And so we flew to St. Martin (a practical hint: Endeavor to begin your cruise from an island to which you can fly without changing planes).

The very first night out on a boat in warm air redolent of salt and sand and perhaps the scent of the island, if you have left a city in bitter cold, is a pleasurable experience difficult to surpass, unless you elect to reminisce about the day the gates opened and you left prison a free man. I suspect that subconsciously people cultivate, during the days and even weeks before such a vacation, specially strenuous schedules, to heighten the complementary relaxation of stepping into a boat with nothing pressing to do, and setting out immediately for the privacy of a cloistered lagoon. The sensation has got to be on the order of what the dope-afflicted call a rush.

St. Martin has two harbors, neither of them memorable, both pleasant. We set sail for St. Barts, which is east, its harbor so very picturesque and always full of conventionally sleek but also idiosyncratic boats—the loners who, after transatlantic passages, usually make land at Antigua, and almost always sail on to see St. Barts, 75 miles northwest.

But we had a secret destination. A few years ago we discovered a little cove on the west side of Anguilla which, apart from Quemoy and Matsu, is I think the only piece of property that has ever inclined me to imperialism. You will remember that before the Falklands affair, the last major sally of the British fleet was in 1969, an attack on Anguilla which, backed by a constabulary of, I think, eight people, had declared its independence. The Wilson government sent a formidable flotilla to put an end to this contumacy in the Antilles. I would like to become an imperialist, conquer Anguilla, and reward myself with that little cove.

I don't really know what-all goes on in Anguilla, and it is this ignorance of Caribbean life I do not wish to conceal. All I know is that the word *anguila* in Spanish means eel, and that the island, about eighteen miles long, slithers its way southwest to northeast rather like an eel, that a little bit south of our anchorage and a couple of miles offshore is the quintessential little island, the kind you see drawn by cartoonists for the convenience of the caption-makers. You know—a sandy beach not much bigger than a giant turtle, one palm tree jutting up from the middle of it, and such captions as, "Well, the population problem went away." It is visible from our little anchorage, a most awful tcasc, as though the man who does Macy's windows had sneaked in the night before to make fun of our idea of perfection by lily-gilding. Never mind, I say; never mind, Pat says; never mind, Dick and Shirley say, and Schuyler and Betty, and we raise our drinks to our perfect little anchorage, and pity the rest of the whole wide world.

I intended an overnight sail to the Virgins. I like one such, even

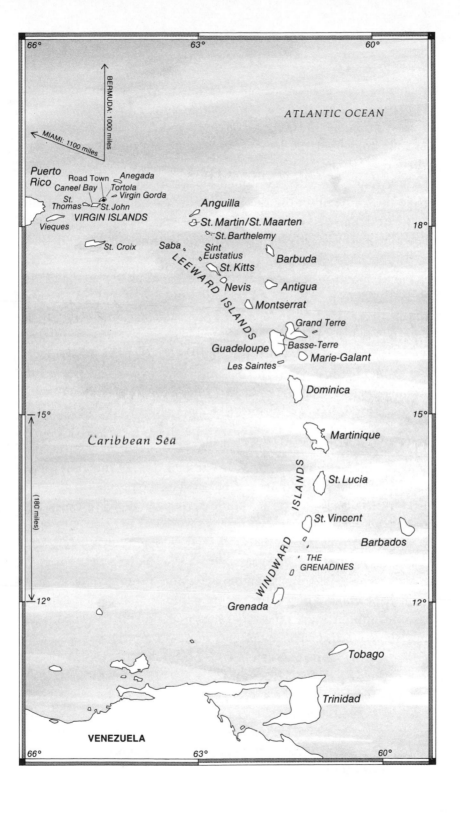

when one cruises hedonistically. It has a way of reminding you
that somebody has to grow the peaches, and whip the cream. It is
really quite uncomfortable to wake at midnight and stand watch
for four hours, but the idea was not more than a velleity, so that
when the captain of the substitute boat, unaccustomed to the
docility that goes with my imperious ways, said he would rather
make the long sail during the day, I suffered him to go ahead and
do so, and we left at dawn and arrived just before dark at Road
Town in Tortola, with its orderly, rounded quay, the yachts lined
up European style, stern first, the museum reminding us of the
bloody history of the Caribbean, where for so many centuries the
idea was that everyone should kill everyone else, and all the flag-
makers were kept busy changing prevailing standards, Dutch,
French, Spanish, English, Danish.

But we had come to Tortola primarily to pick up two passengers,
one of them Christo, and the next morning we set out with gusto,
running over to Virgin Gorda for a dive, and then a long downwind sail to St. John and Caneel Bay, where we would yield up our
vessel and board the *Concorde*.

We spent Christmas night at a bay just north of Caneel, and
that was wonderfully happy, with Pat's glittering Christmas lights
and trees and a great volume of gifts exchanged, some of them in
the form of I.O.U.'s bearing pictures of gifts that lay in waiting
for us back home, too bulky to transport. I was not about to bring
to my son, for example, the Collected Works of the Beatles on
C.D.'s to a vessel that does not have a disc player. The music on
board was splendid. Boats enjoy the same advantage cars enjoy:
their shape makes for a natural sound baffle, so that even indifferent
cassette amplifiers give off a very full sound, and we had aboard not
only the conventional Handel, but some arrangements, absolutely
perfect, of the Christmas carols (the Bach Choir, David Willcocks
conducting, PI Records) done with a special originality, designed
to please even those whose cup is already very full.

Oh yes, the *Concorde*. It began to blow quite hard from the
north, so the question was where to go with it, and we ended by
taking it on two or three twenty-mile triangular courses, as if racing.
It is a most exquisitely designed boat, and the cuisine below cannot

be surpassed in the best hotel in the Caribbean. But it is a little disheartening to see two young women on deck huffing with coffee-grinder winches to hoist the vast mainsail. To sail the *Concorde* for an hour or two, returning to your point of origin, is on the order of what Virgil Thomson once wrote about an overbearing composition by—was it Vaughan Williams?—that it was like boarding the *Queen Mary* in Manhattan in order to travel to Brooklyn.

But there is pleasure to be got, if that is the kind of thing that appeals to you, in studying this boat at sea, driven by the hugest single sail I have ever seen. The silky smooth, light, suntan-oil Caribbean we all think of, and indeed often experience, can work its way up into quite a lather. When these things happen at sea, and you are bound for remote places, they can bring protracted discomfort. But when you cruise, the pain is going to go away sometime before sundown; and you are suddenly floating again, quite still, save for the little motion that reminds you you are on a vessel, quite alone if that is your mood, or socializing with good friends, if that is your mood; and that nothing is pressing, and tomorrow we will see what the wind is like, and acknowledge that the Caribbean's weather, like its people, can be pleasant, hospitable, and also all those other things.

I despair of ever persuading great lots of vacationers who spend the same money at hotels to try cruising. I experimented with every conventional inducement when I had my *Cyrano*. As I've suggested, I don't really know the reason for the general resistance, though of course in many cases seasickness or the fear of it figures. In others I suspect it is a slight fear. Of what? I don't really know, but again I suspect it is a fear that, on a boat, it is feared that it is too easy to—somehow—act maladroitly.

Well, true, it's easy to goof if you're crewing for the America's Cup. But on the Caribbean, in a good boat, with a competent crew, there isn't really anything you can do to disgrace yourself—I mean, that you couldn't as well do at the Paradise Beach Hotel. You should give it a try. But not on the *Sealestial* at Christmas time, because that's reserved until they lower me down.

Or was—until, unexpectedly, Dr. Papo decided to charter it to me when the idea came to sail across the Pacific.

THE AZORES

I haven't ever made a systematic study of the offbeat availability of charter boats, and probably never will. There is now a useful monthly, *Charterers* (P.O. Box 1933, Jensen Beach, Florida 33457). But I was astonished, on deciding in 1983 to sail again in the Azores, to discover that the only boat I could rent was a ferry boat with room for 150 guests. What you depend on is the great treks, one eastward in the late spring, one westward in the fall: the silvered fleet that winds away from the Caribbean in mid-May, bound for the Mediterranean in search of commerce; and, in October (with due regard to the hurricane season), goes back to the Caribbean.

It isn't hard, when there is that density of traffic, to lure a west-bound boat to travel the 750 extra miles to secure a charter in the Azores for a couple of weeks. Something I learned quite by the way was that the owner of a boat similar to the boat I finally chartered was actually disposed to dispatch his ketch all the way from Antigua, where it rested awaiting the December charter season, to the Azores just to capture our two-week charter. This offer meant that I could safely decline to pay the owner of the boat we did engage the requested surcharge for the 750-mile detour. Chatting with the captain one evening about this extraordinary disposition of one of his competitors to submit his boat to a two-thousand-mile sail (Antigua–Azores) for the sake of a single charter, I was reminded that the difference in the cost of maintaining a sailboat in port and the cost of maintaining a sailboat under way is negligible—put it, he said, at $150 per week. "The owner doesn't care that the captain and the mate, the cook and the steward, are at sea. Their wages and food are the same. And, as a matter of fact, we're just as happy at sea as in port." I have never, while at sea, managed to slide quite into that overdrive, the condition in which you don't seem to care if the voyage is endless; but I know now that for some people (see Chapter 12), landfall can, the excitement of it to one side, be something of a disappointment. I assume this has to stop somewhere short of Flying Dutchmanitis.

Why doesn't everybody in the whole world know about the Azores?—I kept saying, to my wife Pat, to my sister Priscilla, and to Betsy, Christopher Little's wife. Christopher Little knew the Azores because he was with me on my second Atlantic crossing and had been as struck as I by the beauty of the islands. After the first week in October, I would learn, you run into something of a letdown, because although the flowers are still abundant, they have begun to wither, so that the prodigal fullness of spring and summer isn't there to knock you off your feet, but there is plenty there to do all but that.

If you collect great sensual experiences, you have got to add to your list off-loading into a comfortable cruising boat after a hectic jet trip (we were held over—fog—in Lisbon twenty-four hours). It is a generic experience, applying not alone to sailboats but also to ocean liners and, I would suppose, to trains that rescue you from where you don't any longer want to be. My high point of emotional excitement as a boy came, I think, when, a month after I was thirteen, I traveled with two sisters and a governess aboard a tender at Southampton to the *Normandie*, which would carry us away, from boarding school in England to holidays in America. The excitement as we approached the dormant giant and its sanctuary was, for me, unique.

I remember also a hot and tormenting two days in Kenya in

1974 during which the Foreign Minister had badly misbehaved. He refused, moments before our scheduled taping, to go on the "Firing Line" television program unless I would agree not to mention critically *any* leader of *any* African country, with the exception of South Africa. To agree would have left me powerless, in what was advertised as a general discussion of Africa, to mention the peccadilloes of the Emperor Bokassa, or Colonel Idi Amin. There was an audience of five hundred waiting in the auditorium, and a crew of four that had flown from New York, and a sweating producer, while Dr. Mungai smilingly repeated his last-minute ultimatum. It finally ended when I said wearily, "Well, Dr. Mungai, it's your country, but it's my program," and called the show off.

After that came the brief flight to Mombasa—hot, dispirited. Followed by the hot taxi ride to the harbor. And then the tender to—the *France!*

There is something distinctive about the sense of security of a vessel that massively assures you it will take you away from it all; something also, I suppose, about the vessel's sitting there, waiting for you. In the case of a chartered vessel there are folks aboard waiting to help you to relax, eager to give you food and drink; the opportunity, in Terceira, to wipe away the cobwebs of thirty-six hours of New York-Faro-Lisbon-Terceira. We felt just that creaky, on reaching the Swan 65 ketch on which we would spend ten days. David Cadogan, the bright young captain, and Penny, his friend and cook, and Ronnie, the mate, made us feel as though their just-completed one-week sail from Gibraltar, an agitated beat against hard westerlies in order to make our charter date, had been the happiest overture in their lives to the happiest cruise they ever expected to undertake . . . We ate a meal of Portuguese fish and fruit, and drank local wine, and ate fresh bread, and made plans for our cruise the next day to Horta.

I was reminded how very little people know about the Azores. I had read, before visiting them for the first time, the entire stock of literature available from the Portuguese Tourist Agency, a library that fits easily into the jacket of a 33 rpm record. The liveliest account had appeared in a three-part series published years earlier in *The New Yorker*, and I learned that I was borrowing the agency's only copy, which I promised to return and did, neglecting to write down the date of the issue or the name of the author.*

Such ignorance doesn't surprise the Azoreans. Gazpar, who guided us about Faial, one of the seven principal islands, told us quite resignedly about his own experiences. "When I was drafted into the Portuguese army, I arrived in Lisbon. And do you know what? Zay ask me, why you are not a Negro? And then when I tell them zat I am a Portuguese from the Azores, zay do not know even zat the Azores are Portuguese!" That's hard to imagine, I said, but then I told him that a recent survey published in Boston had revealed that an American college freshman thought Shirley Temple was the author of *Uncle Tom's Cabin*, and Gazpar said, What was *Uncle Tom's Cabin*? so I decided to stop the cultural cross-pollination, and instead just to listen. But even if Gazpar happened to have hit a singularly ignorant group of Portuguese fellow recruits, his complaint is distressingly plausible. I know, because I have tried explaining the islands—and, after a while, I usually just give up.

My life as an evangelist for the Azores began when I sailed through them, when crossing the Atlantic on *Cyrano* in 1975. I came back vibrating with the experience. *"Let me tell you about the Azores!"* I would begin. I wanted to tell about more flowers than in the whole rest of the whole world put together, about volcanoes some of which continue to erupt with astonishing frequency, about jeweled lakes surrounded by a hundred different varieties of trees and shrubs, about hydrangeas so thick they serve as fences to keep the Swiss white-brown cows confined within their undulating, irregular pastures, about great cliffs overlooking volcanic beaches, about a gentlefolk so proud and gracious . . . But always I found I needed to start at the very beginning. It was as if Pavarotti, embarked on "Celeste Aida," was always being stopped after the first few bars—"Wait a minute, Maestro, just who *is* Aida?"

---

* Subsequent records reveal that I had read Emily Hahn's "A Reporter at Large in the Azores," *The New Yorker*, November 14, 21 & 28, 1959.

Granted, in 1975 we had slept on board my boat, and had had a chance to explore several coastlines. But we had also rented cars and roamed about three of the islands. And I was breathless on the subject of the Azores, because I deem them the most beautiful islands in the world. Or, necessarily to modify that claim, the most beautiful islands I have ever seen.

And so I would begin again, patiently . . .

The Azores (I explained) are islands that sit approximately two thirds of the way between us and Portugal, which is the country that owns them. (I grant that here I flirted with Dick-Jane-Gyp pedagogy, but in dealing with the Azores you sometimes really have to. Even David Cadogan, our skipper and a man of cosmopolitan experience, knew practically nothing of them, save as a port of call, convenient, e.g., when voyaging from Bermuda to the Mediterranean.)

But to resume: There are nine of them, islands that stretch out across 400 miles of the Atlantic and about 150 miles north to south. They comprise, all told, about 900 square miles. Distances between them vary from five miles to 150 miles. One of the islands—Terceira, where we had just landed—has a huge American-Portuguese air base responsible for reconnaissance over the entire central Atlantic. The islands were discovered nobody exactly knows when (they first appeared, if somewhat astray, on Catalonian maps in the 1350s), but the Portuguese got there some seventy years before Columbus discovered America, and get this: Do you know why we are missing the name of the captain who formally—i.e., in the name of the Portuguese king—claimed them in 1427? Because in 1836 George Sand, the French author (who was, of course, a she), spilled ink over the one chart that bore the fellow's name (typical of she-authors who call themselves "George"), forever obliterating, in those pre-Xerox days, the identity of that dauntless historic figure.

On and on I would rattle, but after a while, *pari passu* with my listeners' wandering attention, I would run down. The whole subject was somehow fanciful, too remote; my enthusiasm somehow surrealistic. So that, in October 1983, our trip was on the order

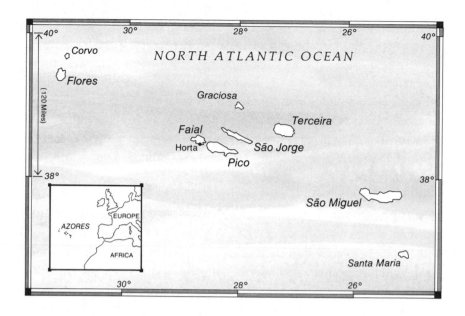

The Azores.

of enlisting an expedition to verify that I had indeed laid eyes on a hanging garden of Babylon.

The following day we set out in a northeast wind (the *Scarlett O'Hara* having arrived at its westward destination, the wind, naturally, turned from west to east). It was a bracing day under spinnaker leaving Priscilla and Betsy, alas, feeling sick. We sailed at hull speed, close to nine knots. We covered the distance of eighty or ninety miles, going around the eastern tip of São Jorge, arriving in Horta in the late afternoon. Cadogan is a fine seaman, and likes to forswear the engine when weighing anchor, and when dropping anchor, something we all got used to as children sailing little engineless boats; a little lingering of macho, the attraction of which continues. David believes that absolutely everything aboard should be absolutely ready before you set sail, which includes all the lines, all the sails, all the winch handles: but he does these things other than in the spirit of the master sergeant, and I learned a great deal from him, as I learn always from other skippers: most particularly, in the case of David, about the uses of the rudder when the current is running against you, or when you are in reverse gear and everything goes upside down. Thus, in such circumstances, if you wish the bow to head left, you turn the rudder to the right. Funny that it should take me about fifty years fully to grasp that one.

This was the third time I had approached Horta by sail, though the first time from the east. I closed my eyes and recalled the two previous approaches, both in the early hours of the morning.

After a day and a half at Horta, we sailed across the little strait to the anchorage at Pico, under the imposing snow-capped volcano. My designs were to tour Pico, to dine on board the boat, and then to leave Priscilla, Pat, and Betsy to spend the night at the little motel there, after which they would fly the next morning, leaving it to the crew and Christopher and me to take the boat the 110 miles to Ponta Delgada. My point was that the trip would be exceedingly uncomfortable, as the wind was blowing right into our teeth and would be doing so until we emerged from the strait caused by the islands of Pico and São Jorge, lying parallel, fifteen miles apart, for thirty miles.

We were visited by the governor of Pico and his translator, and the good governor not only gave us each a half-dozen tiny inch-square silk facsimiles of the official flag of Pico, plus the little wooden matchlike rods on which they would, with careful prompting, slide, plus the little wooden mount into which, with some care, you could wiggle in the wooden rods—but insisted on piecing together all eighteen of them, which required about five minutes per flag, the governor's energy sustained by one glass of scotch per four or five flags.

Dear Pat got progressively skeptical about my plans as, waiting for the governor to finish his petit point, we gazed at the full moon and felt the gentle breeze wafting in at us. She concluded feistily that she and my sister and Betsy were being "dumped" while we menfolk would have a glorious moonlight sleigh ride to São Miguel. By the time the governor left, volunteering to drop the ladies at their motel, my wife was not speaking to me, so certain was she that she was being robbed of a motionless night in her comfortable stateroom.

That was just after ten at night. Five hours later, just after three in the morning, I shouted to David through the howling wind to come back to the wheel to confer. "*I say*," I shouted, "*it's a no go. Let's head back to Horta.*"

"I hate to give up," David said.

"I do too," I said. "But I figure we have eight more hours of tacking to do at this rate."

The islands had acted as a funnel, and though we had a double reef and a tight Yankee headsail, and sailed as close into the wind as forty degrees, the wind and current kept edging us back, so that after five hours of tacking we had made only ten or twelve miles on our course.

So . . . I eased the helm around; we let out the main boom and the headsail and glided back toward Horta, reaching it soon after dawn. We threw out our anchor and went to sleep. It was with mad pleasure that, at about noon, I telephoned Pat at her hotel in São Miguel to tell her that our lovely moonlight ride to São Miguel had been aborted at 0300, and we would fly in on the afternoon plane for our visit in São Miguel. We would fly back to the *Scarlett O'Hara* in two days, and then cruise back to Terceira to catch the plane for New York, stopping by for the night at São Jorge.

How to describe São Miguel? One tourist, deft at recording detail, saw in a single day "geranium, fuchsia, rose, carnation, orange, lemon, lime, guava, grape, magnolia, palm, sugar cane, banana, tobacco, India rubber, camellia, apricot, oleander"—and then, one assumes, stopped listing.

Why aren't there more tourists? A very interesting question. The promotion of the Azores is lackadaisical. The Azoreans are ambivalent on the subject of tourists. Yes, they would like more people to feast their eyes on their beautiful islands. No, they do not want to transform the Azores into another Bermuda. (*We have nothing*

against Bermuda! they will add hastily, with habitual courtesy.)
There are no white sand beaches—though one quickly gets used
to the darkness of basalt beaches. (Who knows, if we were accustomed to dark sand, São Miguel's might be advertised as guaranteed
not to turn white in the sun.) The salt water is cool, not languid-
warm. No nightclubs (they could easily be started), no roulette
wheels (again, easy). There are superb little eateries, run not for
tourists but for natives. The Cabalho Blanco on São Miguel would
rate three stars in New York if they gussied up the serving plates
and decor. You wouldn't need to do a thing to the food.

What else is there, beside splendid cruising grounds?

Well, that depends on whether quite awesome beauty pleases
you sufficiently to frustrate boredom. Look, on São Miguel, for instance, there is the phenomenon of Lagoa das Sete Cidades. You
drive up to 6,000 feet and suddenly you are staring down at a
crater two miles in diameter. Within it are two mini-craters, lakes
now, eye-to-eye. Where the nose would be is a gleaming white
village with its characteristic, indigenous architecture—the austere
Portuguese colonial white, dark brown trim—way down there, 3,000
feet below you. The nearer lake, you suddenly notice, is emerald
green. The adjacent lake, a cerulean blue. Why? Well you see, the
horrible King Sete discovered that his young princess had fallen in
love with the humble shepherd, and so he tore them asunder.
Their separation—by a 10-foot-wide land bridge—caused great
sadness, such that they continued to weep copiously, his green
tears filling the one lake, her blue tears the adjacent lake; lakes that
touch each other, even as the boughs of Baucis and Philemon nestle
together in the legend.

What kind of people inhabit the Azores? Such people as you
would expect if you came upon islands inhabited primarily by
people concerned with survival. The first preoccupation of any
people is food, and it is only after food is available that other appe-
tites awaken, concerned with cultural amenities. On the islands of
Terceira and São Miguel there is a bit of light industry, but not
much. Even so, as is true in almost any poor country, there are the
niches in which people express themselves, the inevitable individua-
tion of the species.

If you are lost in Horta, you will find Pete's Bar. It is a room in which twenty-four people, at most, can be uncomfortably seated, but it is also the center of sailing life. It is at Pete's that you leave messages, for instance. For other sailors? For anybody. And it is Pete who will change your money, or tell you where to go to find a gasket for your engine. A hundred yards from Pete's Bar, up on wooden horses, there is all that remains of a 36-foot steel-hulled yacht, discovered, without identifying documents, a few weeks earlier by a fishing boat. Its eighty-year-old owner-captain, a Dutch-man, was ever-so-dead—the bones were actually protruding. He had died from starvation, and the reconstruction of his last days, done by examining the boat and its accoutrements, advises us that he had attempted to flag one or two passing vessels in order to adver-tise his having run out of food, failed; and just passed away, at the wheel.

It was to Pete, of course, that the information was given, since it was more or less assumed that he would get the word to some-body in Holland, and perhaps someday someone will come and claim the hull. It is still seaworthy.

There is a great will to assist people. The Azores is the kind of

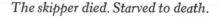

The skipper died. Starved to death.

place where if you ask someone where the post office is, he is most likely to lead you there. Pete and Otto, the scrimshander about whom I have written (*Atlantic High*, page 222), are in their own way unique but they do not misrepresent the Azorean temper, which seems to desire to be as agreeable to visitors as nature is agreeable to them.

Our final sail, back to Praia da Vitoria in Terceira, was, for the first time, in weather a little nippy, even at midday. There are, the natives like to say, as many as four seasons in a given day in the Azores, so changeable is the weather. But it is never very cold or very hot (the temperature is never lower than 43 degrees Fahrenheit, or higher than 78). And there is every kind of topography save dry desert—though the most recent of the titanic eruptions, in Faial, would look like desert if the ash were yellow instead of brown. But there is everything else. Moors and pastures, cliffs and ponds, mountains and valleys, spas and geysers.

The impact of these islands makes poets of people, for instance, a great-granddaughter of John Bass, sometime U.S. consul in Horta. Of Faial she wrote that the "name is freighted with magic charm; it recalls an ideal home life; it suggests hedges of camellia trees, or fragrant pittosporum, tangles of roses and fields of sky-blue flax; it brings to mind all manner of picturesque island scenes; and truly there are times when we feel God's presence, as, with the mind's eye, we behold the mountain of Pico standing like a heavenly beacon, only a few miles away from our own beloved Island." You can't say that kind of thing about just any old place, now can you?

You should promise yourself to visit the Azores, ideally by boat, before you die, or before a definitive eruption causes that haunting archipelago to sink into the vasty deep, rejoining the continent of Atlantis to which legend has it belonging, adding to the luster of underwater life.

7

GALAPAGOS, A SHORT STOPOVER

The *Sealestial* left Fort Lauderdale in early November 1984. It was headed for Honolulu, for our rendezvous on June 2. The vessel needed to travel to the Panama Canal (distance: 1,030 miles), then to the Galapagos (872 miles), then to Tahiti (3,600 miles), then to Honolulu (2,380 miles).

It was agreed at the outset that I would charter *Sealestial* in Tahiti over Christmas, an arrangement I made with Dr. Papo enthusiastically, in part because I wished to know the Tahitian Islands, in part because I felt psychologically disloyal in failing to be with the *Sealestial* for the entire trip up to our starting point in Hawaii. What I hadn't anticipated was a phone call from Dr. Papo in October, inviting Christopher Little and me to sail from Panama to the Galapagos.

"How long does it take?"

"Oh," said Michael Papo, "three, three and a half days."

This is temperamental with Papo, who if you asked him how long it would take to fly from New York to Los Angeles and he wanted to make you feel good, which is how he wants to make you feel in almost every situation, would answer, "Oh, two or three hours." The distance, Panama–Galapagos, is almost 900 miles, which translates, sailing on *Sealestial*, to between five and six and a half days, depending on the weather. We wouldn't, then—the schedule wouldn't permit it—be able to both sail to the islands and visit them. We elected to visit them, and to sail from island to island aboard the *Sealestial*.

It isn't easy to get there: figure about thirty-six hours. I rather like it that some places should be remote. They "feel" remote. It *ought* to be difficult to reach the Galapagos Islands. One day, one supposes, a cartridge at the neighborhood airport will transport a passenger to the snows of Kilimanjaro nonstop, no fuss. I hope the day is far off, because when one reaches the Galapagos one should feel that a certain amount of exertion went into the effort: requisite mortification of the flesh, so to speak, before reaching the shrine.

Now I confess that I was drawn there primarily because of the combination, *Sealestial*-Galapagos. It makes a great deal of difference, in appreciating the islands, if you are a naturalist or are inclined in that direction. Zoo nuts should go to the Galapagos even before they go to Paris, Rome, or Venice. If zoology is your aphrodisiac, the Galapagos will really turn you on. An example is author Tui De Roy Moore's *Galapagos: Islands Lost in Time*, in which he writes about marine iguanas, which you will see in the Galapagos or not at all: "They [have] long scaly tails, short legs with sharp claws, and thin spiny crests running down their backs. They have been described as utterly hideous, yet in this natural setting they [are] starkly beautiful." Waal . . . Herman Melville didn't think the natural setting in any way alchemical. ("Take five-and-twenty heaps of cinders dumped here and there in an outside city lot, imagine some of them magnified into mountains, and the vacant lot the sea, and you will have a fit idea of the general aspect of the Encantadas [as the Spanish call the islands].") Cruising about in the waters in which Darwin spent nearly a year freights you with the weight of the insight kindled there. His famous paragraph: "Considering the small size of these islands, we feel the more astonished at the number of their aboriginal beings, and at their confined range. Seeing every height crowned with its crater, and the boundaries of most of the lava-streams still distinct, we are led to believe that within a period, geologically recent, the un-

"... the boundaries of most of the lava streams still distinct ..."—Darwin

broken ocean was here spread out. Hence, both in space and time, we seem to be brought somewhat near to that great fact—that mystery of mysteries—the first appearance of new beings on earth."

A few days in the Galapagos are at worst endurable, at best distracting and even engrossing. Still, one wouldn't recommend a week at Bayreuth to people resolutely indifferent to music, and one shouldn't lightly sign on for eight or ten days at the Galapagos unless one is prepared to believe that a marine iguana can be starkly beautiful.

I felt especially aggrieved at my degenerate lack of appreciation of what was spread out for us, given the spectacularly difficult time one has in getting permission to cruise about in the Galapagos. It isn't widely known even to worldly yachtsmen: No vessel is permitted to linger in the islands for more than three days, and these three days must be spent in Academy Bay. What is most expressly forbidden is taking your yacht and helping yourself to the islands, dropping anchor here and there on your own impulse. So that it is a double prohibition: against staying, even in port, longer than is needed to fuel up and provision; and against extemporaneous cruising. In our case a waiver was finally achieved, though we were of course required to travel with a guide.

We bade the captain and his wife and crew goodbye—we would see them in three weeks, in Tahiti, for which they set out, planning a nonstop cruise. Returning, I counseled friends who can face life without a visit to Galapagos at least to have a look at the aforementioned book by Miss Moore. She is all but a native of the islands, her Belgian parents having taken her there at age four to avoid the world war. She grew up, with her younger brother, in the style of Swiss Family Robinson, and one of those recondite genes Charles Darwin occasionally had to wrestle with gave her remarkable powers to express what it is to grow up in perfect harmony with the creatures of Galapagos. Reading that book, and then seeing the islands: or, better, seeing the islands while reading that book, gave me a window on the excitement of the world of the naturalist, much as one supposes a deaf man, reading Tovey, can actually sense what music can do for you. The strayest page will give you words and phrases like opuntia trees and epiphytic lichens and liverworts. You come upon tender clumps of ferns, and explore rain-filled ponds and sphagnum bogs. You are excited by the deep shady spots of yellow-crowned night herons sleeping away the daylight. You see the child on the wide rocky reef where the cone shells live beneath the coral grit, in tide pools where sand-colored blennies nibble at his feet. You see them finding the shiny chocolate-brown cowry shells with the white spots and marvel,

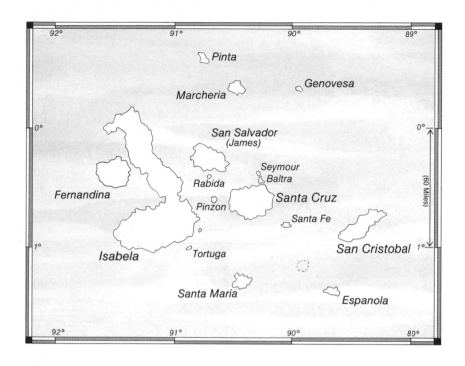

The Galápagos.

when the weather is hot and calm, at myriad microscopic organisms
that glow at night. Before you sleep, you gaze at the tranquil
mangrove-surrounded cove with the flashing blue phosphorescence,
the lightest movement in the water provoking showers of light.
Perhaps, coming home, you will have rowed your small skiff quietly
on moonless nights, every darting fish, every small shark leaving
a sparkling trail like so many shooting stars in a black water sky;
and the green sea turtles are there, outlined in a blue glow, dozens
of meters away . . .

All of that is, for me, better engraved in the memory by reading
about it than by experiencing it; alas, it is so with sailing. There
are those who would rather read about an ocean passage than
endure it.

8

TAHITI

The Tahitian leg of our Christmas Pacific jaunt was ill-fated. The worst of it had to do with the illness of wife Pat. On December 7, Christo was to be ever-so-happily married to Lucy Gregg in Washington. Pat's pain in her right hip, the morning of the wedding, became so intense she had concluded tearfully, at noon, that she would not be able to attend our only child's wedding.

Six Percodans later she made it; but painkillers notwithstanding, we were required to guide her at snail's pace down the aisle of Washington's St. Matthew's Cathedral, where she arrived well ahead of our guests. She made it to the wedding reception, back to New York City and, the following day, to the hospital. Early the next morning she went into surgery. A partial hip replacement, after an earlier operation, had fractured, causing pain all but unbearable. We had planned, before her illness, to leave for Tahiti on December 21. Intensive discussions resulted in Christopher Little and wife Betsy's flying out as scheduled, to begin the scheduled cruise on *Sealestial*. I would spend Christmas with Pat and then, with my sister Priscilla, fly out the following day, meet the *Sealestial* in Bora Bora, whence we would work our way back to Tahiti for what would be left of the two-week charter—about ten days. The auspices of the trip began badly.

At play in the Galapagos.

Sailing away from Terceira, destination Horta.

"... Their separation—by a 10-foot-wide land bridge—caused great sadness, and they continue to weep copiously, his green tears filling the one lake, her blue tears the adjacent lake; lakes that touch each other, even as the boughs of Baucis and Philemon nestle together in the legend."

The mountains of Tahiti.

"... We are led to believe that within a period, geologically recent, the unbroken ocean was here spread out. Hence, both in space and time, we seem to be brought somewhere near to that great fact—that mystery of mysteries—the first appearance of new beings on earth."

A beach at Tahiti.

Aboard PATITO, *sailing across the Sound to Treasure Island in November:*
Danny, WFB.

At anchor. At left Mark Scott, who relates his plans for a solo navigation
beginning in June 1987.

Conversations began cheerfully. "I'd love, to, but I can't. I'll be out of town."

"Where?"

"Tahiti, as a matter of fact."

That exchange had happened a dozen times during the first three weeks in December. It was followed, as often as not, with something like a whistle, or a smile of romantic envy, or a whadda-yaknow, you really get around! kind of look. It didn't surprise because you had tipped your hand that you expected that kind of reaction when you added, after Tahiti, "as a matter of fact." "As a matter of fact" is the idiomatic tip-off to an announcement the theatricality of which you desire to attenuate ("As a matter of fact, I'm getting married that day").

The mere mention of Tahiti tends to do that. It is often spoken of as the most glamorous island in the world. By which no one means that it is the most beautiful, or the most remote, or the most anything other than just that: the most glamorous; vaguely in-accessible, incurably romantic—the nineteenth-century counterpart of King Edward VIII's twentieth-century romance. The Duke of Windsor gave up his throne for Wally, Paul Gauguin gave up his wife and career for Tahiti.

Yes indeed, it was to Tahiti that Gauguin went, as we all know, renouncing the bourgeois world of Paris so that he might devote himself undistractedly to his muse. In his memory there sits, at the far end of the island, thirty miles from the capital and port of Papeete, a nicely organized museum on the site where Gauguin lived and worked. It is scattered with memorabilia, none of them a painting by Gauguin because (nice irony) the Gauguin Museum can't afford a Gauguin. It is recorded, in one of the display cases, how much money changed hands at the last dozen public sales of Gauguin paintings. If poor Gauguin had had just half the proceeds from the posthumous sale of one of those paintings he could have lived the whole of his life in relative luxury.

I thought the whole thing an interesting symbol of modern Tahiti. You can view a reproduction of a Gauguin painting for very little, but it costs a whole lot to buy a Gauguin. You can read about Tahiti, and it is a whole lot less expensive than going there. But people who take the trouble to go seldom regret it. My colleague Bill Rusher, the publisher of *National Review*, has been there eight times; his attorney, seven times. (One sometimes wonders why they don't just stay there.) They are under the irreversible impression that heaven will work, or not work, according as it approaches the atmosphere of Tahiti, inducing the repose of the soul they both find in the area, both especially favoring the island of Bora Bora.

But there are things to watch out for, and we didn't do this. Principal among them is the time of year. Beware. Just as you would not choose the month of December to travel the fjords of Norway, so you must not choose the month of December to sail about in Tahiti. You might strike it lucky—lucky here defined as that uncharacteristically bright, balmy, sunny day, with the wind cooling you and bringing you the fragrance of the island. December is midsummer, so give the month a wide berth.

Arranging to go to Tahiti is not to be compared with flying to the Caribbean. Flying there is expensive, and staying there is expensive. On a chartered yacht much of this can be avoided. But the principal drawback to increased tourist traffic to Tahiti, it seems to me, is the matter of the seasons.

The great itch to get away from America's icy season comes during the winter. That urge, combined with the inclination to festive self-indulgence, means a lot of travel around Christmastime. But this is the bad time in the Society Islands, as Captain Cook designated these islands, occupying the equivalent geographic area of Europe.

Well, Tahiti partisans will tell you, wait until late April or May, if you want to be safe.

Safe from what? Safe from a lot of rain. We had rain ten of the eleven days we spent in the islands, and that eleventh day's sun was as flirtatious as an ecdysiast, showing itself with coquettish reluctance only every couple of hours, after the customers have bought enough drinks. The annual rainfall in Tahiti is 72 inches, and one fifth of that falls during the month of December.

There is the rain, and there is the heat. If the wind is active, the heat is bearable. But sometimes the wind is dormant, or else you are shielded from it, and the temperature then becomes close to intolerable for those carefree Americans who are used to walking about under air-conditioned parasols. I should have given more attention to the problem of *Sealestial* and ventilation, in anticipation of the big month coming up in June. It was in Tahiti that I decided we needed more fans, and as soon as I got back to New York the great search for 12-volt fans and a 24V-12V converter began. I have written elsewhere about my conviction that cruising sailboats that intend to dawdle in hot areas simply need air conditioning—a trivial expense, by the way, when you contemplate the perspective, the expense that goes into a successful cruising sailboat. To forgo air conditioning (if you plan to spend time in tropic areas, here defined as anywhere south of twenty degrees north latitude, from May to September, and its complement on the other side of the equator) is the equivalent of setting a cluster of jewels in tin.

There is air conditioning in the finer hotels, for instance the Tahara'a in Papeete where Priscilla and I rested the evening we arrived (at about three A.M.), but a lot of the fancy hotels that shoot out on stilts over the warm and inviting beaches are without air conditioning.

Captain Cook reached Tahiti in 1769 after eight months at sea. One can appreciate, under the circumstances, that the sail he made from Tahiti to the furthermost Society Island of Bora Bora, a mere one hundred and eighty miles, was for him the equivalent of a trip across Long Island Sound. For the contemporary afternoon sailor, distances between the islands are on the hefty side. Rather like the Antilles contrasted with the Virgins. A typical day's sail in the Society Islands is six to eight hours. But it is an engrossing day at sea, yielding just that vague, stimulating sense of high alert that maintains the keenness of the experience. There are great stalactites under those waters, many of which reach teasingly up to just inches and feet under the surface, so that at one moment your fathometer will show you with a hundred feet of depth, and at the next you will be sitting on top of a coral reef. Never, says the good book wisely, go close to shore when the sun is below twenty-five degrees over the horizon. You need the sun high, to disclose the dangers below. Do as you are told.

Returning to the matter of heat, one can hardly blame the Society Islands for their geographical location. They are situated slightly east of Hawaii, not thousands of miles west as is popularly supposed. But they are way, way south (Latitude 17 degrees), almost as far south of the equator as Hawaii is north of the equator. And it happens that, at about Christmastime, at Latitude seventeen degrees south the sun is, so to speak, overhead. And unlike the Galapagos which, as noted, are right on the equator, the area hasn't the benefit of quirky air currents that bring in coolness.

It is just plain hot. And, of course, when *our* hot and sticky season comes along—summertime—it's perfect weather in French Polynesia: their wintertime, with a climate the equivalent of the Dominican Republic's in December. But the summer itch, among U.S. travelers, is often an itch for relief from the summer heat, which is why American tourists tend to think of Europe, or Canada, or the abnormal cool heights of Mexico City. That, after all, is why the Caribbean and Florida offer off-season rates during the summer. A pity, because French Polynesia is a joy to cruise.

Oh, yes, on the matter of disadvantages one needs to comment on indifferent manners, this being especially the case in Bora Bora where tourists tend to be treated with that languid forbearance that has given a bad name to Nassau and, if things do not one day soon improve, is likely to shut down Antigua. Bad weather, granted, tends to enhance distemper. When you run into a combination of rain, heat, *and* bad manners the cumulative impact is provocative. Even little things. What is a *little* thing? You ask for a morning paper. *"Il n'y a plus."* That ("We're out") is *a world away* from *"Sorry,* we're out." "It is certainly de rigueur," Alistair MacLean comments in his wonderfully readable book *Captain Cook,* "to dwell at sentimental length on the golden people who inhabited this other Eden, the handsome men, the gorgeous girls, their

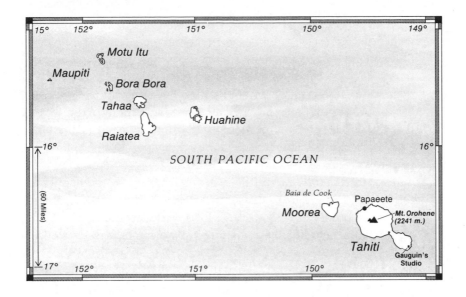

Society Islands.

simple natural form of life, their affectionate natures and, in short, the wholly Utopian nature of their existence. Now, apart from noting in passing that those self-same golden boys and girls were much given to infanticide, ritual murder, the waging of the most bloodily ferocious internecine tribal warfare in Polynesia and indulging in the practice of theft and pickpocketing on a scale and with an expertise that would have made Fagin turn in his union card—apart from that, I say, there is little to be said against this approach."

One acknowledges the mischievous temptation to resist conventional myths. But when all is said and done, this isn't possible in Tahiti, for so simple a reason as that the legend of this paradise is based on substantial reality.

The islands are, on anyone's measure, spectacular visual creations. Why (ever?) try to compete with Herman Melville in such matters? He put it about Tahiti:

Seen from the sea, the prospect is magnificent. It is one mass of
shaded tints of green, from beach to mountaintop; endlessly diversi-
fied with valleys, ridges, glens and cascades. The loftiest peaks cast
their shadows over the ridges and down into the valleys. At the head,
these waterfalls glitter in the sunlight as if pouring through vertical
bowers of verdure. Such an enchanted air breathes over the whole
that it seems a fairyland, fresh and pure from the hand of the Cre-
ator. The picture becomes no less attractive upon nearer approach.
It is no exaggeration to say that a European of any sensibility who
wanders into the valleys for the first time, away from the haunts of
the natives, sees every object as if in a dream, owing to the ineffable
repose and beauty of its landscape; for a while, he almost refuses to
believe that scenes like these should have a commonplace existence.

There now, it has got to be worth it to verify whether a place
so described has that effect on you. As with that poetic Belgian
girl, writing about the Galapagos? What will Bora Bora, or Tahaa
or Raiatea or Huahine, or Moorea or Rangiroa or Tahiti do to you?
Will you be tempted by going there to do as Rupert Brooke did?
*"Tonight we will cut scarlet flowers in our hair and sing strange,
slumberous South Sea songs to the concertina, and drink red French
wine, and dance, and bathe in a soft lagoon by moonlight, and eat
great squelchy tropical fruits."*
You can do all of that in those islands, at the right time of year.
In the postwar age there are conveniences Rupert Brooke could not
have guessed at, including the air conditioning, and the restau-
rants, and the comfortable hotels, with the little individual cottages
that cozy up to what becomes your private beach.
But a hundred years after Melville, and a generation after
Brooke, you travel the distance from the poet to the travel agent.
The Polynesian Magazine for Tourists for October 1984 leads off
with an editorial foreword from Alexander Léontieff, identified as:
"Vice Président du Gouvernement de la Polynésie Française,
Ministre de l'Économie, du Plan, du Tourisme, de la Mer, de
l'Industries, et du Commerce Extérieur," and he puts it this way
about French Polynesia: "If jolts caused by Nature and men occasionally disturb the tranquility of our islands, this is only the price

Sealestial, *stern-to at Papeete. Next stop, Honolulu.*

of life and they cannot alter the deep serenity which dwells in us. The sound of our country offers an unending range of fleeting emotions which are at the same time encounters with Beauty, Truth, and Eternity. Our music and our rivers, our beaches and our legends, our flowers and our festive meals, are yours. Come and meet the men and women of Polynesia, dream in their company with the sound of the guitars, and share our joys, and so perhaps you, too, will feel, when the moment to leave arrives, a lump in your throat: an omen of return."

Fact is, the Littles and the Buckleys didn't feel that lump, though we were glad we had gone. Principally, our problem was that we went to the Louvre wearing dark glasses, to the Metropolitan Opera House wearing earmuffs; to Tahiti in the rain.

Even so we departed on the long trip home in high strategic anticipation. The next time Christopher Little and I would see *Sealestial* would be in Honolulu to begin our Pacific adventure.

Book Two

RACING
THROUGH
PARADISE

9

THE DECISION: SAIL THE PACIFIC

It seems altogether normal, I've always assumed, that one particular day it occurred to Napoleon to invade Russia. I grant there are those deliberate types, who force themselves to sit down one morning at age thirty-five to decide at what age they will retire, and where they will go on to live and die; but I suspect they aren't that numerous. Besides which it is just a little un-American, isn't it? Spontaneity being an American attribute? In any event, I remember exactly when it occurred to me to make the Pacific trip. We were at Treasure Island, as we refer to Eatons Neck on Long Island, on one of those overnight Friday sails, and the talk after dinner turned to ocean cruising, and Danny said he wouldn't want to cross the Atlantic a third time on a sailboat, and the words tumbled from my lips, "How about the Pacific?"

"That's different."

I there and then resolved to sail the Pacific, though I said nothing about it.

The very first thing you ask yourself, once you have reached such a decision, is: Cross the Pacific how, where, when, and, especially, with whom? You acknowledge that any venture of that magnitude with any hope of attracting the subscribers you want along has got to be scheduled at least three years before launching. My chosen list shaped up quickly in my mind.

Danny Merritt, obviously: We have been friends since he was twelve and I almost forty. He was best man at my son Christopher's wedding, he crewed on my boats for ten years during the summers; he lives down the road apiece and is an unending pleasure as a companion on boats, at the tennis court, indeed anywhere. I doubt that a political thought has ever crossed his mind, and I would be the last person to introduce him to that seamy subculture. He was (briefly) unhappily married, while helping to prepare *Cyrano* for our initial crossing. And then, during our second Atlantic crossing, he learned he would be a father. He is now married to Gloria— bright, loving, volatile, a professional nurse and certified alcoholism counselor. They are raising two sons and are regularly visited by the daughter of his first marriage.

Moreover, when I approached him about the trip, Danny was feeling restless. He was unhappy at work, underexploited in the insurance business, the career into which I and his father had prodded him. When I did so, I harbored the illusion that insurance agents, in the 1970s, were the same kind of people-next-door with whom I had grown up: the friendly man in the little office who does everything from insuring your car and camera to insuring your life and limbs and resignedly but cheerfully accepts your collect calls from Paris. What Danny had discovered was the bureaucratization of the insurance business; the banks of computers that suck out all the relevant statistics before anyone can say yes to anything. What the profession had effectively lost in that evolution was what Danny had primarily to offer in his own persona: personal exuberance, a truly sincere desire to help in any situation, a marvelous wit, extraordinary physical adroitness. All of this combines to nothing very much in the Harvard MBA world of insurance. No doubt his restlessness in his job prompted him to agree instantly to sign on for our Pacific passage, though by the time we set out he was enthusiastically launched in a fresh profession, as an advertising salesman for a brand-new magazine, *Power and Motoryacht*.

Christo was also quick to sign on. My son had felt remiss about the second Atlantic trip, but that summer of 1980 was his crucible. He was four years out of college and had met with success as a junior editor at *Esquire*, suddenly finding himself one summer day, following a reshuffle, promoted, at age twenty-five, to managing editor. Then Clay Felker came along, and *Esquire* turned into a fortnightly. Christopher didn't want to try to administer a publication that came out that frequently, electing instead to work for *Esquire* as a roving editor. He was planning a leave of absence to embark on a book, and when *Esquire* changed hands yet again he resolved to take the summer off and complete, in a rented house in Nantucket, his book *Steaming to Bamboola.* In this remarkable (it is the critics here speaking) book he rounded out his extensive experiences on merchant vessels, begun at age seventeen when he went around the world in a tramp steamer, which included a half-dozen wintry passages in the North Atlantic. The very first book most authors find awfully intimidating. Christopher could not even consider an entire month's distraction and I did not push him, though I missed him sorely. But now, having completed his second book, the novel *The White House Mess*, he was ready.

Reggie Stoops of course. We have sailed together since the mid-fifties, sailed everywhere, and since he is self-employed (as a plastics engineer and consultant) and divorced, he is nearly always available. *Nearly* always? You could call Reggie at midnight and ask him if he would accompany you on a six-month safari beginning the day after tomorrow, and the chances would be good he'd be there, in Banana Republic dress. You want him as a friend, as a contemporary, as an accomplished sailor, as a kind and patient omnipresence, and as probably the only sailing friend I have who doesn't have to close his eyes to concentrate before knowing in which direction you turn a screw to tighten it.

Van Galbraith, another old friend and sailing companion, was now ambassador to France, a political appointment in which I had ever so obliquely figured. He had been having a whale of a time unlacing most of the traditional corsets by which diplomats bind themselves into invisibility. When he arrived in Paris he announced to the French community, with a natural and disarming grin made in Toledo, Ohio, and absolutely unchanged by Yale College, the Harvard Law School, Shearman & Sterling, the Morgan Guaranty Trust Company, and Dillon Read, that he was not only a Reagan appointee, he was an *enthusiastic* Reagan appointee, and what's more if anybody wanted to savoir pourquoi, well, all they had to do was ask him—which, astonished, much of Paris proceeded to do, in newspaper interviews, over the radio, on television. It was a quite remarkable performance because although from time to time he was officially chastised (for instance for criticizing the French government for having Communists in the cabinet—why would anyone want in the cabinet of *your* country someone who is loyal to *their* country? he once asked, wide-eyed), he got along, critically aided by his resourceful wife Bootsie, just fine with the socialists who learned at first hand what they had never suspected, namely that just as it is possible to coexist with Communists so, mirabile dictu, is it possible to coexist with a Reaganite. Van said that June 1985 would be just fine: He'd be giving up his post about that time and a sail across the Pacific would be just what he needed to decompress before going back to banking.

Christopher Little had come along on the second Atlantic crossing because I needed a good photographer on board. I had known him slightly, had known his father Stuart, a classmate of my brother, more or less forever. I had carefully vetted him before the 1980 trip, and he passed every test with flying colors. Married, with a picture-pretty little girl, his only concern was that he knew less about sailing than Betsy his wife, but I told him I knew less about sailing than Bus Mosbacher, and he laughed, conceding he knew more about photography than his wife. Yes, he was eager to come.

We had now the full complement of six people, but I invited Dick Clurman anyway. I rejoiced at the prospect of his coming, but did not expect that he would. I had invited him on the 1980 trip and at first he had accepted, but on learning that the other four crewmen would not be Teddy White, John Chancellor, Mortimer Adler, and Isaiah Berlin, declared that he would take only the first leg of the trip. You see, Dick Clurman is an intellectually restless soul, and conversation is his bag. The thought of sustaining

Dan Merritt ("Danny")

Evan Galbraith ("Van")

Christopher Buckley ("Christo,"
"Christopher")

Reginald Stoops ("Reg")

Christopher Little   *Richard Clurman ("Dick")*
("Christopher Little")

for thirty days an analytically constructed and philosophically oriented conversation with Danny, Christo, Reg, Van, and me was
simply implausible, and of course he was quite right. But on the
St. Thomas–Bermuda leg he did get enough ocean sailing under his
belt to confirm that the prospect of an analytically constructed,
philosophically oriented, sustained discussion even with Socrates
aboard an oceangoing sailboat was unlikely to happen; meanwhile
the mysterious magic of blue-water sailing reached out and bit him.
To my astonishment he accepted immediately, even on the understanding that, once aboard, there would be no bailing out. I was to
learn from his journal (at my request they all kept journals, some
more conscientiously than others) that the weight of his commitments (he was writing a big book about why people are angry at

the press) almost caused him to pull out, as late as February. He could have done so without any critical reduction in the size of the crew, though the experience would have been vastly reduced for all of us.

So then, we had the crew.

The next priority was to line up Allan Jouning. We had sailed with Allan when he was the skipper of the *Sealestial,* in the Caribbean at Christmastime. And when I thought to cross the Atlantic in a chartered vessel, I wanted a captain I liked and admired who was accustomed to my own ways aboard ship, and who acknowledged me as the skipper, save (here insurance policies dominate) in any situation (none ever arose) in which I stipulated one course of action, he another expressly invoking the safety of the vessel: in which event, he becomes the commanding officer. Allan is from New Zealand and is the soul of calm, competence, and good humor. He was engaged in an intricate transaction, superintending the construction of Dr. Papo's *Concorde,* described above, of which he was to become the skipper. But he agreed, at a meeting in New York, to carve out the month of June 1985 for me, no matter what he was otherwise doing.

Next came the problem of a vessel.

I tend to think that problems dissipate if only you write the proper letter to the proper person. This one did not. After many inquiries, mostly through Julie Nicholson, yacht charterer, I located only two suitable ships, both lodged in Tahiti. What was in prospect for the owners was a ten-week charter: two weeks to sail from Tahiti to Honolulu. One month with us, from Honolulu to New Guinea; one month back to Tahiti. For two weeks in February 1984 I was at my computer in Switzerland, MCI-ing my messages to Julie, who was doing the brokering. The better of the two boats, after we had outlined a deal, entered a critical qualification: the boat was on the market, and if purchased before June 1985 by someone who didn't want to take on the charter, why, the contract would dissolve!

Such a development, at my end, could only be compared to the Last Days of Pompeii. Accordingly I decided finally on the other

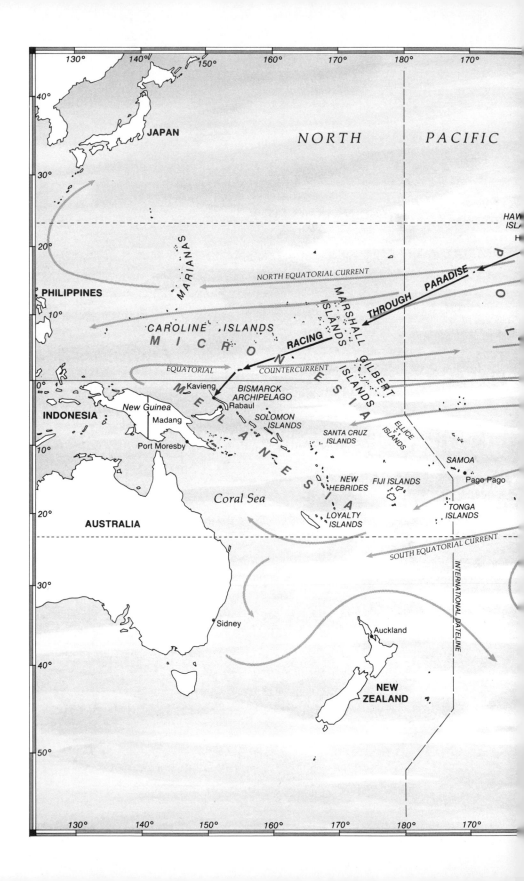

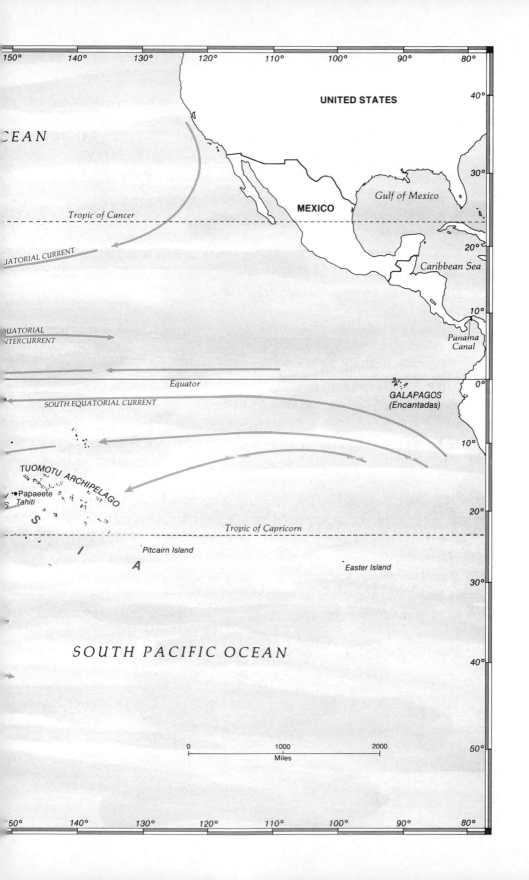

150° 140° 130° 120° 110° 100° 90° 80°

UNITED STATES

40°

30°

Tropic of Cancer

20°

EAN

CEAN

Gulf of Mexico

MEXICO

Caribbean Sea

ATORIAL CURRENT

20°

10°

QUATORIAL
NTERCURRENT

*Panama
Canal*

10°

Equator

0°

GALAPAGOS
(Encantadas)

SOUTH EQUATORIAL CURRENT

10°

TUOMOTU ARCHIPELAGO

Papaeete
Tahiti

20°

Tropic of Capricorn

`Pitcairn Island`

Easter Island

30°

A

SOUTH PACIFIC OCEAN

40°

0   1000   2000
Miles

50°

150° 140° 130° 120° 110° 100° 90° 80°

boat, negotiated the rental figure, and Allan volunteered to sail from Tahiti to Honolulu in order to familiarize himself with it . . .

At which point my old friend Dr. Papo, the owner of *Sealestial*, suddenly announced that he desired to take that boat (he has a fleet of three) to the Pacific, and would concert his plans with mine.

So: we would be back with Allan on a very familiar vessel. There are intricacies in chartering a boat under such unusual circumstances which need not be dilated on, but if you get around to doing the same kind of thing, expect to spend a little time with friendly, and less than absolutely friendly, lawyers and insurance agents—that kind of thing.

I made a composite deal: the *Sealestial* would head for Tahiti to be there in time for Christmas. Instead of our regular Caribbean cruise, as I have noted, we would take two weeks in Tahiti. (The bonus already noted.) In order to sail to Tahiti, it makes sense to go first to the Galapagos. Would I like a cruise in the Galapagos Islands? I would indeed. So then I faced the (short) week in the Galapagos on *Sealestial* just before Thanksgiving, two weeks in Tahiti, both times described above, and a month in June, sailing from Honolulu to New Guinea.

A sizable taste of the Pacific, I thought, until I finally got around to the breathless experience of staring hour after hour at charts of the Pacific and recognizing that there is practically no such thing as a sizable taste of the Pacific in less than, say, a year. You might as well say you have experienced Chinese food after a single dinner in Singapore. But the distances would be immense and if—as has happened to me—you can get into real trouble crossing from the Connecticut shore to Long Island, you can get into trouble sailing four thousand miles of the Pacific.

10

PREPARATIONS

The passage was for me the primary thing, a point ever so important to stress, and perhaps to ponder. The vastness of the Pacific is something known to everyone. The North Atlantic Ocean, courtesy of glacial eccentricities, makes little accommodation for island hopping: You have Bermuda, and you have the Azores, and that is about it. Although the distances between some of the islands in the Pacific are enormous, as we would experience, viewed as a basin, the Pacific is wonderfully hospitable to island hoppers.

But since I wished to *cross* the Pacific rather than to cruise in it, I could reasonably consider only the one starting point—Hawaii, U.S. territory. To have begun the passage in San Francisco or Los Angeles would have added two weeks we didn't have. Start in Honolulu and go where? It occurred to me it would be fine to end the passage in Auckland, in New Zealand, where I have twice been, and the home city of Allan Jouning. Those were the two fixed points I had in mind when I turned to the question of way stations.

I look back with amusement at the first memo I sent out to my companions, at the end of December 1983:

> A route that suggests itself at this point, having done a little work on it with weather charts, will be: Honolulu to the Marshall Islands,

1900 miles, or about the length of the Azores run [on the Atlantic trip: i.e., Bermuda to the Azores], course southerly, winds easterly. Marshall Islands to Samoa, south by west, 600 miles, winds easterly. Samoa to the Fiji group, southwest, 600 miles, winds easterly. Fiji to Auckland, 1400 miles, winds easterly for the first two thirds, then variable. Total distance, 4400 miles, or 200 miles less than the Miami-Marbella run. The objective would be to make the trip in 28 to 30 days, allowing a day or two in the Marshalls, in Samoa, and two or three in Fiji. I propose we leave on the first of June, arriving approximately the 30th in Auckland. This would make it possible for those who desire to do so to come back in time for the Fourth of July. Or to spend that week exploring New Zealand, or hopping back via Tahiti. Much more in due course but the purpose of this memo is to get you all to block out the month of June 1985.

Over the next period I, and in particular Van, who has a penchant for maps and charts and logistics, fanned out the news of the projected trip, asking for advice and information. A few people were startlingly kind, beginning with Roger Hallowell. He is the Executive Director of the Cruising Information Center, a branch of the Peabody Museum in Salem, Massachusetts. He wrote to say that he needed to know first things first, namely were we planning to get the boat as far as possible on a circumnavigation, or to some definite goal; or whether we simply wanted to explore some nice South Pacific islands, as he put it, "a gunkholing cruise."

He then reminded me that the southeast trades "have a southern limit of about 20 deg. South, leaving you with possible head winds for a leg from Fiji, Tonga, or Samoa to New Zealand, roughly 1200–1500 miles.

"If you want to stay in the trades, and if time permits, you might consider a long first leg to Pago Pago (2280 mi.), then to Fiji (660 mi.), New Hebrides (660 mi.), Guadalcanal (550 mi.), then either to Rabaul on New Britain (550 mi.) or to New Guinea–Port Moresby or Madang (780 mi.)." He went on to recommend the (indispensable, we found) Landfalls of Paradise by Earl R. Hinz, from which in a P.S. he quoted the following distances (as the crow flies, and in nautical miles; add 15 percent for statute mile equivalents):

Honolulu to Auckland	3820
" " Guam	3320
" " Nouméa	3370
" " Rabaul	3360
" " Kwajalein	2160
" " Pago Pago–Samoa	2280
" " Suva–Fiji	2780

I thought a first leg of 2300 rather too long a stretch, to be avoided if possible. The balance of the proposed itinerary seemed appealing, but the warning against head winds while going down to New Zealand stuck in my mind, and I began to think in terms of New Guinea as an alternative destination. I returned to the pilot charts and they revealed that head winds, in the New Zealand–Fiji area, were to be expected approximately 25 percent of the time in the month of June (midwinter in that part of the world) . . . I'd continue to think about it.

Mr. Hallowell followed up his note not long later by telling us that one of his "clients" reported that volcanic activity in Rabaul (New Britain . . . I here and hereafter refer to the Bismarck archipelago as simply, "New Guinea." Those who care should distinguish New Ireland, New Britain, and New Guinea as separate political entities) had closed the harbor down to yachts, but that nearby Madang had excellent facilities. "All yachts," he went on to say, "have been complaining about slow passages this summer due to light winds in the trade wind belt. [My client] had to power a good deal . . . His estimate is that you will not have much time to spare with your thirty-day time limit."

I wrote then, in the fall of 1984, to the fabled Captain Irving Johnson, who in his brigantine schooner had circled the globe, with a boatful of young people, four or five times. I told him about the constraints on my time and asked what was the best route to take. I elucidated, "By 'best' I mean most interesting, where we can have a shot at a few pretty islands. A shot is about all we'd get, needing to traverse that distance in that length of time. I have the charts, the books, etc., but what I most covet is information from someone as exhaustively familiar as you with every interesting point in the world."

He could not have replied more conscientiously or more amiably. His first suggestion was that anyone planning a cruise in any remote part of the world sign on as an Associate Member of the Seven Seas Cruising Association (SSCA, P.O. Box 2190, Covington, Louisiana 70434). "You should get three or four years of back issues plus the very necessary geographical index to save time." He said that he had read every word of the Bulletin for the past thirty years.

Having now experienced it, I can see why. It comprises, pure and simple, short (and some long) letters from sailors recounting any singular experience or encounter anywhere in the world: a fine restaurant in Samoa, a good hardware store in Honolulu, a mislabeled buoy in the Antilles. One certainly needs the index if one wishes only information about a particular itinerary. Captain Johnson went on:

> With only a month to spend on such a big ocean as the Pacific and ending your voyage in New Guinea, I wouldn't think of starting from Hawaii. It would be a waste of time. There are three possible places, all connected by air, where you could join the *Sealestial*. The easternmost is Tahiti; in the middle, Rarotonga in the Cook Islands, where the brigantine *Yankee* was wrecked after [Captain Johnson hastened to add] we sold her. She is very visible high up on the reef. The third is Suva in the Fiji Islands where the plane lands at Nadi on the west side of the island.

Voyagers who have experienced particular islands and found them especially pleasurable are generously eager to give out the news.

> To list islands of interest westward bound from Tahiti, first comes Huahine. The next is Bora Bora, but that island is now messed up by tourists. Maupiti has a very exciting entrance and a man should be aloft. There is a real native atmosphere ashore. We have taken *Yankee* in a couple of times, drawing 11 ft. Then on to Suvorov, basically uninhabited but a great story, told in *Man and His Island* by Tom Neal. Then head down to Rarotonga which has English-speaking natives and is a lovely island. Don't miss Palmerston. Various books tell its strange history. There is a bit of it in our first

(1935) book, *Westward Bound in the Schooner Yankee*. The natives will show you where a tiny patch of sand is found on the lee side for anchoring. The pass through the reef is suitable only for outboards, or the natives will take you in. Here hundreds of people have the same last name, Marsters.

Captain Johnson was not through:

Westward to Vavau in the Tongan Group, thence to Tin Can Island (Niuafoo), the northwesternmost of the group. Great stories at all these places. On to the westernmost side of Fiji and take a look at the Awassa Islands. Next come the New Hebrides, now Vanuatu. It is unlikely that you will hit the particular date when the land divers of Pentecost Island dive headlong 78 feet into the ground from their tower of jungle materials with long vines tied around their ankles. Usually the hike inland on Malekula is worthwhile. With a quick stop at Espiritu Santo you can dive on Million Dollar Point and see the *U.S.S. Coolidge* in the bottom of the harbor. I was in many of these places during World War II when I had command of a survey ship, 4,700 tons, with fourteen boats and twenty-four hydrographic engineers making charts after a violent start of the war at Pearl Harbor on the infamous December 7th.

A remote and very interesting island is Utupua in the Santa Cruz group east of the Solomons. Then I would suggest the Marshall Bennetts which were originally coral atolls but were raised 4500 feet and the people now live in the dried-up lagoon. There is a little island in the easternmost Solomons called Santa Ana with an interesting history . . .

The capital of the Solomons is Honiara on Guadalcanal: great stories of World War II. Henderson Field is still in use. Just across Iron Bottom Bay, scene of our greatest defeat in that war, is Port Purvis where beautiful clear water comes out of the side of a mountain and is piped directly aboard with the ship anchored out and stern tied to a dock. Take flashlights and climb up to a cave where the clear, fresh water flows continually. Ask all the way along about any special islands of interest, but watch out for bum information as a lot of people don't understand what you are looking for. Two other islands in that vicinity that might be of interest are Rennell and Tikopia (variously spelled).

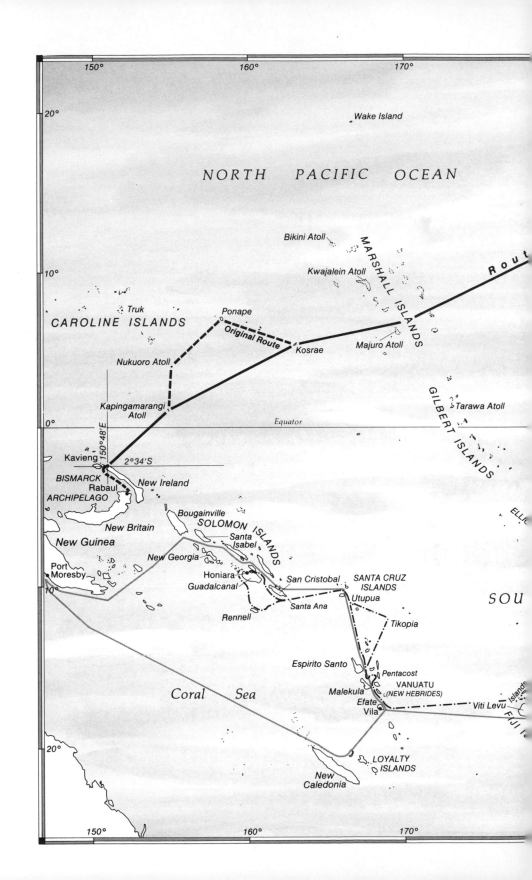

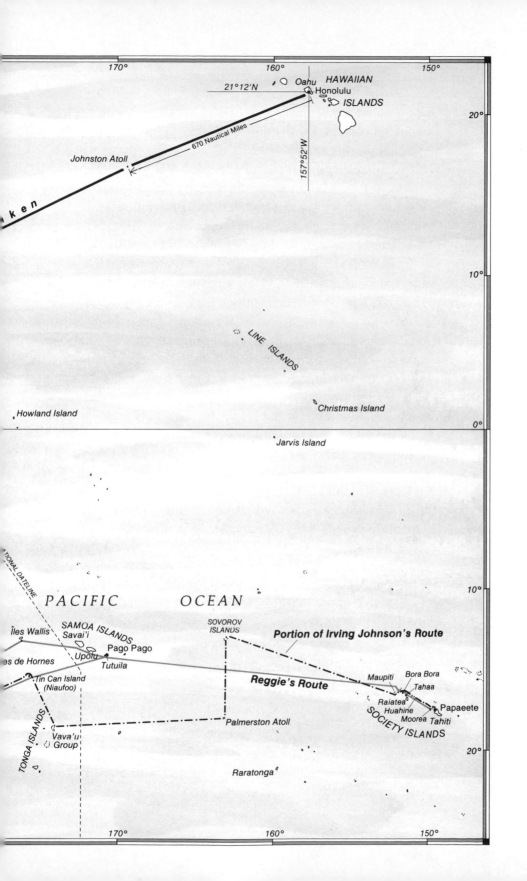

170°

160°

150°

21°12'N
Oahu
Honolulu
HAWAIIAN
ISLANDS

20°

670 Nautical Miles

Johnston Atoll

157°52'W

ken

10°

LINE ISLANDS

Christmas Island

Howland Island

0°

Jarvis Island

NATIONAL DATELINE

PACIFIC   OCEAN

10°

SAMOA ISLANDS
Îles Wallis
Savai'i

SOVOROV
ISLANDS

Portion of Irving Johnson's Route

es de Hornes
Upolu
Pago Pago
Tutuila

Maupiti

Bora Bora
Tahaa

Tin Can Island
(Niaufoo)

Reggie's Route

Raiatea
Huahine

Papaeete

Moorea Tahiti
SOCIETY ISLANDS

TONGA ISLANDS

Palmerston Atoll

Vava'u
Group

20°

Raratonga

170°

160°

150°

Having quoted from only one half of Captain Johnson's letter I am reminded of Dick Clurman's telling me, a year or so ago, that only a journalist can give truly accurate and useful driving instructions. He recalls a friend, internationally renowned for his efficiency as an administrator, who, in giving Dick instructions over the telephone on how to drive to his country place, gave him casually the route number, as though the route began just outside Madison Avenue, where Dick Clurman lives (it began nineteen miles north of New York). "Take it to Sugarloaf Road. And when you take that turn, watch for a great big New England church. Huge white steeple on your left. Now, when you see that church, *ignore it*."

We did not visit a single one of the sites Captain Johnson so effusively recommended, for the reasons originally given—that we were embarked on a passage, the way stations being not unimportant, but not primary in their relevance. But I could not here suppress Captain Johnson's joyous cornucopia, and perhaps before I disintegrate I shall sail on what I'll call the Johnson Cruise, following exactly his itinerary. I should think it appropriate to plan about six months for that one.

In October, in a memo to the gang, I confirmed the decision to substitute New Guinea for Auckland. My thinking was to head from Honolulu to Johnston Atoll, 700 miles southwest and the nearest point of land to Hawaii; then to Majuro in the Marshalls (1300 miles southwest); then to Kosrae in the Carolines (500 miles); then to Ponape (300 miles); then 260 miles south-southwest to Nukuoro; 165 miles south to Kapingamarangi; and 300 miles south-southwest to Kavieng in New Guinea (New Ireland); and, the final leg, 120 miles to Rabaul, assuming the volcanic activity had ceased.

> Now most obviously wrong with this schedule is that it gives us a trip that takes 35 days and this we cannot do. We plan a 30-day trip, with only one day's leeway. We will therefore need to do some fine-tuning. The problem would vanish if we can stay in the westbound current and avoid the countercurrent. I shall be writing to investigate this matter . . .

The winds are (I speak here roughly) behind us for the first quarter of the trip, and off the port quarter for the next half, then abeam. They average Force Three or Four [8 to 18 miles per hour]. On the route we are taking, at the time we are traveling, there is a close to zero chance of hurricanes or typhoons. Now the distances I have shown above total 3,700 miles. If we managed 180 miles per day, we would need 21 days of sailing, which would give us nine days of layover. The currents might permit us as much as 40 miles extra per day on the trade-wind equatorial legs. We have the option of sailing right by the last three of the islands. In short, if we agree on the basic route, there is plenty of improvisation that can cut back the days so as to have us landing on Day 30 in Rabaul.

Oh yes: Depart Honolulu 1600* Sunday, June 2.

I had a spirited reply from Reggie, and I wavered (for a day or so). It was most awfully persuasive, and refreshingly saucy:

I got a Pilot Chart of the South Pacific (Pub 107) yesterday and immediately checked the currents along the route from Tahiti to Port Moresby. You will be pleased to know that they average 13.5 knots right on the tail all the way. The actual range is shown as from 5–10 knots at Tahiti and reaching 10 to 25 knots around Fiji. That means we can *drift* the whole distance in 11 days!

Well, I thought I'd better just check that one out before I passed it on to you, so I called the Navigation Information Branch of the DMA (Defense Mapping Agency) in Washington (202 227-3137) and found that the current figures are not given in knots [nautical miles per hour] as stated, but in *miles per day*. So we will pick up $25 \times 13.5 = 337.5$ miles from the current.

In case you haven't yet been through the fine print, the chart for June also gives the following information for the Tahiti–Moresby route:

Winds: a very steady force 4 (13–18 mph) from the southeast 33 to 65 percent of the time, from the east from 20 to 37 percent of the time, from the south about 10 percent of the time, northeast, 5 percent. It hardly ever blows from other directions and is calm only one percent of the time.

* BWT [Buckley Watch Time]

Air temperature: a steady 26 deg. C. (79 F.).

Water temperature is the same: 79 deg. all the way.

Barometric pressure. We follow a steady high pressure ridge of 1012 to 1015 millibars that stretches right across the Pacific.

Compass variation is from 0 to 4 deg. east and back to 2 deg. east.

Visibility: Never less than two miles.

Gales: the chance of a gale in the area is about .5 percent. Along our route it is about one eighth of one percent.

Tropical cyclones: Have never been reported in June along our course.

Wave height: About 400 miles south of our course wave heights of 12 feet are reached 10 percent of the time in June. I would guess that we might expect one or two days of such seas.

Route: The island groups on the course from Tahiti to Moresby are as follows:

—The Society Islands (Tahiti, Moorea, Bora Bora, Tahaa, and Raiatea, Maupiti and Motu Iti). These are all within 1650 miles of Tahiti.

—Then 1100 miles to Pago Pago in Samoa, where there are three islands: Tutuila, Upolu, and Savaii.

—Wallis Island and Isla de Horne are possible stops but the next big island would be in the Fijis:—Vanua Levu and Vita Levu (Suva). It is 670 miles from Pago Pago to Suva.

—Next stop, Vanuatu (New Hebrides). There are fifteen islands here. Vila Harbor on Efate Island looks like the main port. Vila is 600 miles from Suva.

—At Vila we're 1,360 miles across the Coral Sea from Port Moresby and can either go southwest to New Caledonia and the Loyalty Islands or go north through the New Hebrides chain to the Santa Cruz Islands and then through the Solomon Islands (San Cristobal, Guadalcanal, New Georgia, Santa Isabel, Bougainville).

If we followed this route it would be about 1,560 miles from Vila to Port Moresby or a total of 4,130 nautical miles.

Reggie, who is a precisionist, then had a little fun with me.

A quick check of your memo with the chart in front of me makes me wonder whether we should find a good navigator for the passage.

My chart shows Rabaul on New Britain and Kavieng on New Ireland—neither one on New Guinea. (However, I guess one shouldn't take you literally.) And the distance from Majuro to Kusaie (Kosrae) *can't* be 469 miles. I make it 502. [I had used thumb-to-little-finger measurements, Reggie a pair of dividers.] But then, by your coordinates you've located Honolulu in the middle of Oahu and both Majuro and Kosrae 15 miles east of where they should be. I don't think I'd better check the courses.

And then, characteristically, Reggie puts a soft touch on the subject, a little parachute for my self-esteem:

There's an interesting note at the top of the Pilot Charts. It says they are "founded upon the researches made *in the early part of the nineteenth century* by Matthew Fontaine Maury, while serving as a lieutenant in the United States Navy."

It made a great deal of sense, and the islands en route were more attractive by far than those that lay along the direct route from Hawaii. But the formal point kept yanking at me. *I did not want a cruise, I wanted a passage.* Preposterous to make the point, given that the distances were equivalent. But sailing from Tahiti to New Guinea would be a *cruise* within the Pacific, and I wanted a Pacific *crossing.*

We paid heavily for the distinction.

There were further communications from Roger Hallowell, persistently helpful, enclosing memoranda from voyagers in Micronesia, my favorite being the gentleman who said, "One should plan to spend at least two months or more in the Fiji area."

I decided on the route.

There followed a flurry of memos, mostly dispatched during my six weeks in Switzerland, where every week or so I would pore over the charts with Van, who visited, and with Christo who, with Lucy, spent the time with me in Switzerland, engaged in finishing his novel. I touched on several matters in one memo.

Our first stop will be Johnston Atoll, WSW, approximately five days' travel. It is a mysterious island . . . and the ambassador [Van] is devising means to penetrate it, which should prove much easier to do given the events of last November [the Reagan landslide]. If necessary, we shall have to arrive with gas masks, a responsibility of the Procurement Officer, who will be named before this memorandum is completed.

• I had a pleasant and productive meeting with Allan Jouning, who plans to be in Hawaii four or five days before our departure, rather than the fortnight previously discussed, because: He is going to be a father! Allan will be in close touch with Keith [the *Sealestial*'s regular captain] to check on the boat's physical health. He will also see to it that we have some 12-volt fans for the main cabin, and a 12-volt icemaker, a matter of some importance. [I should have written 24 volts, in both cases.]

• We are pleased to report that Liz Wheeler, familiar to all early patrons of *Sealestial*, agrees to come out of retirement in order to act as chef.

• The following commissions are hereby granted. All perquisites attaching thereto will be fully enjoyed, in usufruct.

—Procurement Officer: Daniel Merritt

—Safety Officer: Reginald Stoops

—Meteorological Officer: Van Galbraith

—Diplomatic Advance Man: Van Galbraith

—Navigation: WFB

—Communications Officer: Richard Clurman

—Surprises-Along-the-Way, including wines, tidbits, biscuits, magazines, firecrackers, surprises, entertainment: Christopher Buckley

—Health and Medical: Reginald Stoops

• I highly recommend the book *Landfalls of Paradise: The Guide to Pacific Islands,* by Earl R. Hinz. Western Marine Enterprises Inc., Ventura, California 93002. If you want this book, call Reggie and ask him to ask his store to send it to you, and remit payment.

• Unhappily, three of us cannot arrive in Honolulu until Saturday night, namely Van, Christopher Buckley, and WFB. Van has 35th anniversary at Yale (as does WFB), followed by commencement address in Utah. Christopher has 10th ann. reunion at Yale. So this is a plea to Clurman, Merritt, Stoops, Little, kindly to try to get to Honolulu two or three days earlier to help get things in order.

And, a month or so later, more memorandums and bulletins . . .

• Here is information of miscellaneous character concerning our forthcoming adventure. Might I, while at it, gently remind you all that the Post Office serves not only to carry communications from me to you, but also from you to me, so that you may feel free to answer questions put to you, for instance: When do you plan to arrive in Hawaii? and other questions as posed by my last communication.

• Ambassador Galbraith has been wonderfully helpful in establishing a number of things, to wit: Our route takes us by several islands, enumerated in the penultimate memo, all of which lie within Micronesia, and are under U.S. protection of some sort or other. This translates into: No visas are needed for the entire passage *until* we arrive in New Guinea.

• On the matter of health. It is required by the relevant authorities (though concededly this is a requirement that is not enforceable) that all members of the crew take precautions against malaria by swallowing Aralen and Fansidar. These are pills which need to be taken beginning X days before we begin the passage, and ending Y days after we complete it. My doctor is looking into dosages, plus any difference in terminology between Frog anti malaria pills and U.S. anti-malaria pills. This information will be forthcoming in another memo. It is further recommended, though not required, that each of us receive an injection of gamma globulin, which helps guard against phlebitis, or gout, or whatever.

• FYI, the rates for the passage Rabaul–New York are: first class, $2460. Club Class $1610. Coach Class $1400. Excursion (which is the same as coach, subject to the requirements mentioned elsewhere) $1008. The committee [WFB] will come through with Excursion fares. Any hedonist who chooses to do so is free to upgrade himself.

• Concerning bunking arrangements:

—WFB and the ambassador will share the owner's cabin.

—Reg and Christopher Little will share guest cabin #1.

—Dick Clurman will have use of cabin #2, except that the top bunk will serve as stowage space for non-hanging articles of Dan Merritt and Christopher Buckley.

—Christopher Buckley and Danny will sleep in the after cockpit. They will bring their own sleeping bags from *Patito*. They will use lockers in WFB's cabin for hanging items (pants, jacket, foul-weather gear) and Clurman's cabin, top bunk, for other gear.

• I am exhausted by this effort, and so bid you a very temporary farewell.

Van raised an interesting question concerning a division of responsibilities, which drew another memo:

Van raised the question of responsibility, allocation of same, as between him and Dick. Thus spake Zarathustra:

Van is the vessel's Meteorological Officer.

Dick is the vessel's Communications Officer.

So then Van has the responsibility for keeping a weather log [never done, I now note], giving us warnings [done splendidly], that kind of thing.

Dick has the responsibility for seeing to it that the vessel is fully equipped to receive all relevant stations, as also to transmit, in the event of emergency, or for social purposes. [See below, extensively.]

In re Dick: we need to establish that the ship has all the radio gear you think we need. Important: there is a publication called *Selected Worldwide Marine Weather Broadcasts*, available from the U.S. Government Printing Office, and probably from a dozen ship supply-store firms in New York. I'd recommend picking one up in the event *Sealestial* doesn't have one. I'd also recommend a check by phone with Judy Papo to make certain that the radios are all in working order. (Can't resist passing along the full name and address of the weather people, to wit: "U.S. Department of Commerce, National Oceanic and Atmospheric Administration and Information Service, National Climatic Data Center, Federal Building, Asheville, North Carolina 28801.")

In re Van: The Weatherfax ought to be in working order, and will save you a lot of work if it is. [It was not.] Second point: In random reading recently I learned that a plain old AM radio, especially when tuned to lower frequencies, will tell you if a thunderstorm is in the area. The louder the static, the closer it is. The same exploration can be done using an RDF, with the dividend that the direction in which the storm lies is ascertained. (The passage I read indicated that there is no way reliably to ascertain whether the storm is ahead or behind the radio's null—the problem, so-called, of reciprocal ambiguity.)

My colleagues finally broke silence, and I heard from them by telephone and correspondence. Reggie applied himself to master the Astro and Navpac programs, usable on a Radio Shack TRS-80 computer, designed to complement the grand navigational plan on which I was spending so very much time with Hugh Kenner, the distinguished critic and my longtime friend. The most memorable item in Reggie's letter was, "I want you to know *I've already started my journal* and plan to shame you all with my eloquence. Look to your laurels, Buckley." That letter was written on April 8, and as I write, a year later, surveying Reggie's completed journal, I think it fair to say that such was his devotion to an early start that by April 8 he had written about 95 percent of his completed journal.

The question of preventive medicine merits the sequel.

> • I promised I would pass along the word on the matter of pre-ventive medicine I got from Van. I needed, having got from him the names of the relevant drugs, to inform myself on the relevant dosages. This required a little doing by my doctor. I hoped also that, having ascertained all of that, I would be able to get enough drugs to supply us all. No go. My M.D. says that he would not want me to pass along the drugs to others, though the probability is high that I could do so without your running any medical risk, or my running a civil risk. But he says you should get a clearance from your own doctors. Perhaps you have special allergies. It is particularly relevant if you have an allergy to sulfa drugs. Anyway, you will need to take, preferably on the same day of the week, the following two drugs: Aralen and Fansidar—for a period of eleven weeks. Beginning one week before we take the passage; during the four weeks of our pas-sage; and for six weeks after the passage is completed. We can pool our supply when we get on board and ask Liz to serve it to us, say on Mondays at noon, with a nice, dry Bordeaux.

But that was superseded by Dick's deeper research to the effect that traveling in malarial country one ought *not* to take Fansidar unless symptoms of malaria (fever, chills, headache) develop. Then take three tablets at one time and continue with your Aralen. Dick sent us all a copy of a learned paper published in the *Morbidity and Mortality Weekly Report*, printed and distributed by the Massachusetts Medical Society, publishers of the *The New England Journal of Medicine*. It is entitled, "Revised Recommendations for Preventing Malaria in Travelers to Areas with Chloroquine-Resistant *Plasmodium falciparum*." It confirmed the anti Fansidar-as-routine prescription.

The procurement of sufficient ice was a paramount objective. *Sealestial* had an icemaker that worked only when the generator was on. Since the generator is on only three or four hours every day, we had no steady icemaker. Moreover, when the generator was on and the ship was heeling, which was practically always, water tended to spill from the ice trays before freezing. The only solution was to buy an icemaker. But since there are none such that run off 24 volts (the ship's electrical supply from the batteries when the generator is off), we needed a converter. Anyone who thinks it is easy to procure a converter for transforming 24-volt DC power to 12-volt should undertake to try to find one. Ours arrived in Honolulu the afternoon before we sailed, and was hastily installed. The wrong fans arrived a week before we sailed, and were replaced by the correct ones the morning we set out.

And of course, wines. Danny calculated that fifty cases of beer was about right, and I got the wine through a merchant in Honolulu: 3 cases of Vintage Selection Cabernet Sauvignon, 3 cases of '82 Kendall Jackson Cabernet Sauvignon, 3 cases of '82 St. Bonnet, Medoc, 3 cases of '83 Fleurie, Barolet, 4 cases of '82 Chablis, Barolet, 1 case of '81 Ch. Gloria, 5 cases of '83 Muscadet Sèvre-et-Maine, 3 cases of '78 Jean Léon Cabernet Sauvignon, 3 cases of '83 Piesporter Michelsberg Kabinett, Reh, 3 cases of Mateus Rosé, 1 case of Freixinet Cordon Negro Brut champagne. The cost was $2,525.74. Liz served approximately one thousand man-meals, so that comes down to $2.50 booze per person per meal; okay as a rough estimate, but there were seven or eight cases left over, which we ended up giving to a church at Kavieng. I note that Captain

Cook, on his bark *Endeavour*, provided, for seventy men at sea for one year, "Beer in Puncheons, 1200 gallons, Spirits 1600 gallons." I haven't the energy to decipher which of the two vessels, *Endeavour*, or *Sealestial*, was the more vinous.

I can't conclude the section on selective preparations without mentioning the matter of The Swedish Crackers.

A friend in Gstaad casually served them at a little lunch a year or so before our passage, and I was overwhelmed—dry, crisp, perfect flavor, incomparable with cheese, peanut butter, ham, butter. I asked Frances Bronson kindly to order me a thirty-day supply for eleven people. This evolved into a country-wide search in which seven or eight people participated—every one was sure that he/she knew of one delicatessen (the one that has *everything*) that would have them. No luck. I sent a cable to the bakery in Sweden. We learned that they were only just now being introduced in America, and could be bought through an agency in Princeton, New Jersey. Three days before sailing, one hundred packets (225 g. each) of Pains Grillés Suedois au Blé Complet arrived, bringing me thirty days of contentment. Ironically, my easily jaded colleagues eventually tired of them, after devouring them hungrily for two or three thousand miles. (The divine crackers are now available from ABA Management and Development, Inc., Research Park, 210 Wall Street, Princeton, NJ 08540.)

11

TO JOHNSTON ATOLL

The morning after our departure from Honolulu we jibed the boat, early in the morning. I figured it would take until about noon before we came back on our rhumb line, that being the great circle line that runs from Honolulu to Johnston Atoll. The wind had lightened, and at one point I turned on the engine—my rule of thumb would be to use power if our speed fell below six knots.

There wasn't, at this point, much to do except to begin, with some seriousness, to take on the business of navigation. I had told my companions that as a matter of self-discipline I would not avail myself of the ship's satellite navigation system (SatNav), which commitment proved easy enough to abide by after Danny, who did look at it within a day or two, pronounced it "at least thirty miles" off our dead reckoning position—i.e., worthless. The excitement, for me, was that we had on board a prototype of Trimble's exciting GPS (Global Positioning System), with which I'd in due course experiment. But the GPS, when and if we got it working, would not yield us a position save for a couple of hours a day, when it happened that the three operational satellites (of the contemplated twenty-six) happened to be in celestial harmony with Trimble's surrealistic little antenna, which squatted, securely strapped down, on the deck above. It was too early to think about GPS. It would be back to the sextant, chronometer, calculator.

There was the safety drill to get done, over which Reg would preside, but we decided to put that off until later in the afternoon. We were, that morning, just a little drugged. Some were recovering from mal de mer, others of us from the jet trip from New York. We were all adjusting to the rhythm of life at sea. There was the feel of "What's the hurry?" Indeed, what *was* the hurry?

Besides, we had a lot to engage us that had nothing to do with sailing the Pacific. Van had written the first draft of a journal of his four years as ambassador to France. Dick Clurman had the first lengthy two chapters of his magnum opus on the press, focusing on the hectic rise in libel activity, the ambiguities of the libel law, the evasive strictures of the First Amendment, and the public unrest with the behavior of the press. Christo had just finished copy-reading his comic novel *The White House Mess*, and I had with me the first draft of a novel I would need to give a final reading to immediately after landing back in the States.

Christo was taking seriously his duties as Entertainment Officer. After lunch, a notice in big black crayon appeared, attached by Scotch Tape to the mirror on the port side of the companionway, alongside the watch schedule:

TO ALL HANDS
TONIGHT'S MOVIE:
The Wackiest Ship in the Army
Starring Jack Lemmon, Tab Hunter
*   *   *

Place: Odeon *Sealestial*
Time: Following the star sights
(GooGoo bars will be served)

The GooGoo bar is a confection I discovered in a catalogue last fall. A wonderful catalogue!—offering the consumer a thousand different edibles, with emphasis on foods available only from Mom-and-Pop outfits who ply their business by mail. It was sent to me because among the items offered was the brand of peanut butter I especially covet (Red Wing), publicized there alongside my published dithyramb to it. Leafing through its pages the preceding November, I had sent a few people a basket of sorts for Christmas, based on the seductive descriptions in the catalogue. When I read the description of GooGoo Clusters, made in Nashville, Tennessee, I instantly added them to the list. And lo, I had cast bread upon the waters, because the GooGoo people were so pleased by the order to a half-dozen people that they added my own name to the list, sending me a complimentary package. The result was revelation, and in a pre-passage memo to Christopher I had urged him to add GooGoo bars to the delicacies which, as Entertainment Officer, he would be procuring for his shipmates. Such is the pride of the manufacturers in their product—which contains chocolate, peanuts, corn syrup, sugar, creamed coconut, milk, whey, starch, butter, salt, gelatine, egg whites, hydrogenated vegetable oil, and artificial flavoring—that every GooGoo bar carries the notice, "Guarantee of satisfaction: Your GooGoo Cluster should be fresh and in good condition. If not, we will replace it. Just return the unused portion and tell us where and when you bought it." A safe offer, granted, made to GooGoo consumers en route, in a sailboat, from one end of the Pacific to another.

Christo had taken his commission with comic seriousness. His log records the "entertainments" he had brought along, in addition to 28 full-length movies. To wit:

1 model of the *Titanic*, to be collectively assembled.
1 cribbage board.
1 Risk game.
1 Trivial Pursuit (Genus II edition).
1 electronic battleship game.
1 checkers set.
1 lifeboat game.
3 Gary Larson "Far Side" books.
1 jumping rope.
2 tapes of David Niven reading from his memoirs.
1 copy, *The Hunt for Red October*.

1 Ruger M-14 rifle ("also has survival aspect").
1 .410 shotgun and case of clay pigeons.
1 Ping-Pong table (miniature size) and equipment.

That morning I read the first two or three chapters of Van's memoirs. They were not in professional shape, far from it. He began the book by reprinting a long and excellently written profile of him published in a Greenwich, Connecticut, magazine on the eve of his departure for Paris. Van's point in doing so, he explained, was that this would save him the trouble of telling the reader what the reader would want to know about his background, and he reminded me that, by way of a prologue to one of my books (*Cruising Speed*), I had reproduced my entry in *Who's Who*. True, but I reminded Van that bare-bones information in the telegraphic style of *Who's Who* is different from a ten-page profile. And I added that one reason for my having done what I did was to tease *Who's Who*, which had stuffily declined, in the entry for that year, to include among my organizational achievements my proffered, "Founder, Nat. Com. to Horsewhip Drew Pearson, 1967," which I had inserted into the boilerplate *Who's Who* entry in *Cruising Speed*.

Van has written only a single book, twenty years ago—a technical book with a coauthor—and he will need, if the balance of the book is as shaky as the first few chapters, to put in a vast amount of work before the book is publishable. Van will be surprised by this evaluation, in part because he simply assumes that his natural wit and fluency make their way into his prose, which they do not. Dick Clurman, picking up the manuscript after I had set it down to do the noon sights, was similarly distressed by its vulnerabilities and summoned me below to share his misgivings. We agreed that our own counsel, together with ambient pressure from others who read the manuscript, would persuade Van, one of the wittiest and most refreshing men in the world, not to rush into print with a premature draft.

At lunch Van teased Dick about his helmsmanship, the beginning of relentless corporate amusement over Dick's towering in-

Van at work on his manuscript, an ambassador's memoirs.

competence on board a boat which never provoked in Dick anything
but a delighted amusement, either that or else heated denials of
maladroitness, though this was never easy to demonstrate when,
e.g., while engaged in professions of general competence he would
coincidentally spill his coffee over two or three of us, or absent-
mindedly put out his cigarette in Christo's ice cream.

In the early afternoon, after plotting our noon sight, I read the first chapter of Dick's book. He had followed closely the libel trials of General Sharon against Time Inc., and of General Westmoreland against CBS. His account slowly, methodically, masterfully, fleshed out the theoretical questions the two contests had reified: *Time* magazine had been judged not guilty of libel in law, but was certainly guilty of sloppy journalism in practice. What does that mean? What does that say about the purposes of litigation? General Westmoreland was believed (including by the jurors) to have been unfairly treated by CBS, but CBS had won: What does *that* mean, and in what direction ought libel law to go, in order to conciliate the understandable hunger for self-justification, the growing ire of a public tendentiously deceived, and the healthy appetite of a pluralist society for candor, however tendentious?

Dick had worked for *Time* magazine, serving as its chief of correspondents for many years. He was, notwithstanding his personal loyalties, remarkably judicious in assessing the merits of *Sharon* v. *Time*. I told him I had had an account, over the telephone in Honolulu, of the party *Time* Editor-in-Chief Henry Grunwald, a good friend of us both, had given while we were en route to Honolulu, in honor of Clare Boothe Luce, a party Dick and I had both been invited to. Clare had been characteristically amusing over the phone to me. "This," she said, "is the first time *Time* Inc. has acknowledged my existence since Harry died. I suppose they figured I had to die pretty soon and they'd better do something soon."

An invitation had been issued to the President, and he had accepted. One of his speechwriters had asked my advice on what the President might say, and I suggested he have a little fun and combine it with a tribute to Henry Luce. The speech draft was written, and along the way the White House bureaucracy decided that the President should limit his participation to a simple toast to Mrs. Luce. But the speechwriter had contrived to get his draft to the President through back channels; Mr. Reagan had read it, decided he liked it and would deliver it, and gave word that he wanted a podium. And so the speech was given. Clare had responded to it by saying that what she liked best about this particular President was that, in office, he had retained his sense of humor. And she closed by saying, with oblique reference to her own age and the President's, "He who laughs, lasts."

Almost always, except when the weather was sour or when our preoccupations with wind and waves interdicted such satisfactions, there was music in the cockpit, as also below when we dined. I had with me a hundred cassettes, about 80 percent classical, the balance jazz, mostly jazz piano, including all of Dick Wellstood, if there is such a thing as all of Dick Wellstood this side of the Green Pastures. The *Sealestial*'s musical inventory included a half hundred of the usual things, one part rock, one part schmaltz. Every time I cruise I manage to forget antecedent disappointments in the matter of trying to communicate to others, including Christo, my enthusiasms in music. I thought to try to engage the particular attention of those in the cockpit one afternoon by sheer journalistic blackmail. I said, Had anyone noticed the rave reviews given to the Bach Goldberg, as performed by Andras Schiff, in *New York* magabine by Peter Davis, three whole pages? I managed to get Christo and Dick quite excited by what I reported Davis had said, and the great moment came when I would put on the tape, which I did. Within five minutes they were talking to each other. It hadn't worked.

It doesn't work. A few days later I tried again. Would they like to hear Judith Norell performing the harpsichord at my house, the first of the series of celebratory House Concerts, so called, in which, during the tricentennial year (1685–1985), she had performed the entire repertory of Bach's music at private homes? Dick had been there for that particular concert, and had been present at one or two others given by friends. I put on the cassette, the reproduction was superb, the sun beneficient, the wind a gentle accompaniment.

Once again, after about three or four minutes, their attention was diverted . . . they simply did not want to listen.

I predict, sadly, they will never voluntarily sit down and listen— *listen*—to such music, except as external circumstances require. I noticed, too, how different it is when the music is of another's choice. Christopher put on a Beatles cassette one night when we were below, and when he saw that his companions were not sitting there silent, taking it in, he made the altogether appropriate gesture. He took the cassette off the main machine, stuck it into his Walkman, and listened reverentially, by himself.

I don't blame him. But I continue, and always will, to suffer the disappointment I feel that others don't share with me the pleasure, the elation "my" music gives me. When Tom Wendel was aboard, on *Patito* and on *Sealestial*, it truly made a difference, for instance, in diminishing the tedium of the watches, to listen together. A good case can be made for reserving one berth, on a cruise such as this, for someone who can share music with you.

Everyone—always—arrives at these cruises with volumes of wonderful-opportunity-to-get-read books, and the bright idea is almost always a failure. For one thing there are the interruptions, primary among them the tendency to drop off to sleep. Christopher complained in his journal that he didn't get three minutes' reading done before dropping off to sleep. Occasionally one gets a head of steam while in the cockpit on a sleepy daytime watch, or in the saloon off duty, but with startling infrequency. Dick has always been the exception, in part because he reads at such phenomenal speed he doesn't have time to get sleepy or distracted. I'd guess he raced through twenty books on this trip. I read about one third of David Landes's wonderful history of the timepiece, *Revolution in Time*; Tom Clancy's *The Hunt for Red October* (everyone read that); Van's book and parts of Dick's, and the new novel by Louis Auchincloss, which I had in galleys, featuring Ivy League dramatis personae with a hardboiled protagonist who, while an undergraduate at Yale, regularly frequented a bordello in New York on weekends, an extracurricular activity unlisted in the pages of Yale literature one tends to run across. How wonderfully Auchincloss spins his tales. But I was alarmed by the profusion of exclamation points, and relayed that misgiving to him from the first port of call, though his judgment in these matters is better than mine.

It has over and over again been demonstrated that a blue-water cruise is not an occasion conducive to catching up on one's reading, but always one tries. After all, how different is this resolution from the habit of going back and back to sea, never mind one's resolutions at sea, so frequently made in blood, *never* to submit to this kind of thing again?

It was time for the safety drill. "My affection for Reggie," Dick wrote in his journal, "has overcome my constitutional impatience. It took me a while but I can now grin and wait as Reg meanders to the resolution of whatever task he undertakes, or answers the question he has been asked."

This time around, Dick, who is highly automated (he brings along a half-dozen radios, each with its manifold support system), thought covertly to record Reggie's safety briefing.

> **Dick Clurman.** All eleven of us are on deck, crowded around the cockpit table, our sundown drinks in hand. As Reggie begins, his pauses fill more time than his instructions. It is supposed to be deadly serious stuff. Not exaggerating—our lives could depend on it. But Reggie's creeping languor is too much even for my relaxed boatmates. His long pauses invite leavening . . .
>
> REGGIE: "Okay, let's do the sinking scenario first. Case A is where we have about two minutes to grab the stuff and go." [He vaguely starts to describe the buddy system and the allocation of the two life rafts. He starts to assign us by name.]
>
> DICK: "But Captain Allan's going down with the ship."
>
> ALLAN: "That was a long time ago. I get off first now."
>
> REGGIE: "The lifeboat captains are Bill and Reg."
>
> DANNY: "What happens if one of them dies?"
>
> CHRISTO: "You designate a successor with your dying words."
>
> VAN: "I'll be in charge of cannibalism."
>
> CHRISTO: "Which raft gets the GooGoo bars?"
>
> CHRISTOPHER LITTLE: "What are we supposed to wear?"
>
> CHRISTO: "The latest."
>
> ALLAN: "If someone doesn't have a knife [to cut the painter] when the boat goes down, the raft will go down with it."
>
> BILL: "Is there a knife attached?"
>
> ALLAN: "No."
>
> REGGIE: [to no one in particular] "Make a note of that."
>
> [Reggie mentions the Emergency Locator Beacon. Nobody knows where it is until Noddy comes to the rescue.]

BILL: "Okay, go ahead, Reg. Let's go. Anything else on the life rafts?"

CHRISTO: "Movies. I'll get the movies."

DICK: "What about ice?"

VAN: "Danny, will you bring the ice machine? Who's got the skeet gun? We can shoot birds."

CHRISTO: "What about wine? I'm particularly fond of that Muscadet '67. Will we be able to spend some time looking for it?"

DICK: "In the ten-minute scenario we could have Liz make a picnic lunch."

BILL: "Okay, go ahead, Reg."

REGGIE: "Situation B is a ten-minute sinking. If we get hit by a submarine, a whale, or something like that, pick up the grab bag."

BILL: "Where is it?"

REGGIE: "Wherever it is."

BILL: "Is that a state secret?"

CHRISTO: "On a strictly need-to-know basis."

REGGIE: "We'll have to have another meeting to resolve some of these things. One of the things we have to do is make up a grab bag with provisions, fresh water, and so forth."

BILL: "Before the emergency? Make a decision, Reg!"

REGGIE: "Okay, in the event that it's a slow sinking—"

CHRISTO: "Let's hope."

REGGIE: "One thing I left out is the flares and rockets. Well, we'll have another meeting and, well, then we'll seriously assign some of these things. Then we'll have a man-overboard drill."

BILL: "Give us the man-overboard drill now."

CHRISTO: "Are you finished with the sinking scenario?"

REGGIE: "Pretty much so."

DICK: "The ambassador gets no special consideration in any of these?"

CHRISTOPHER LITTLE: "He should grab the flag and wave it."

REGGIE: "Now this foghorn. If anyone sounds it, that means all hands on deck."

BILL: "Go ahead, next?"

REGGIE: "Okay, throw the man-overboard pole over, detach the line, then—"

BILL: "Stop: You'd need three arms to do all that."

REGGIE: "First of all the guy that goes over shouldn't try to swim to the boat. Just look for the strobe light."

BILL: "Okay, Reg. By the way, where *are* the life jackets?"

REGGIE: "I think they've all been put in the aft cabin. I'll check on that."

BILL: "Reggie, move. Let's go."

REGGIE: "Okay, now in case of fire—"

VAN: "Wait a minute. Where *are* the life jackets?"

DANNY: "They're in the hanging lockers."

DICK: "I've got ginger ale cans in mine."

DANNY: "Well. Drink the ginger ale quickly."

DICK: "Serious question. Where are the life jackets?"

BILL: "Where the hell *are* they, Reg? Can you say where the life jackets and fire extinguishers are located?"

REGGIE: "Not now, but we'll get a list of that and tell you at the next meeting."

Bill spotted his first star and suddenly asked for his sextant and computer.

CHRISTO: "Is that about it?"

REGGIE: "Oh no."

Then Reggie began a life jacket demonstration so halting that it would have lasted from New York to Bermuda if a flight attendant gave it. The meeting was starting to splinter off.

DANNY: "Is Bill's star notebook up here?"

As Reg droned on, Bill was now standing, braced against the mast on the afterdeck trying to get a star sight, but he couldn't find his book, and couldn't find double AA batteries for his computer.

CHRISTOPHER LITTLE: "We put the batteries in with the suntan lotion."

REGGIE: "Okay, that concludes the first meeting."

There never was a second.

[Dick adds in his journal]: "Incidentally, two grab bags, meticulously filled with survival supplies, were finally put together, and placed on deck in green garbage bags. Nobody told me, so with my constant desire to keep things shipshape I was on the rail about to dispose of the 'garbage' overboard when an aroused Reggie spotted me and shouted: *'Don't do that!'* "

Lots of fun. But not quite, quite fair. I have a (non-neurotic) respect for the man-overboard emergency. It doesn't go quite as far as Roy Disney's, who told me he keeps portable urinals in the center of the cockpit to deter his young sons from leaning over the side at night. But the problem is never far from the mind. It was only the year before that Reg had had an experience. He was sailing *Patito* up Fishers Island Sound at ten in the morning, the spinnaker up. A young man was up forward and was in the process of dropping the spinnaker when a puff caught it and the sudden lurch threw him into the water.

"The hell of it"—Reggie was telling me about it a few days later—"was that it took, I swear, damn near seven or eight minutes before we could turn *Patito* around. There were only two of us left on board. We had to bring in the spinnaker, which had gone overboard, before we could start the engine without fouling the propeller." When the boat was finally turned around, 180 degrees, and powered back on a reciprocal course, the two survivors looking about desperately for the man overboard, it transpired (the man overboard, picked up by a passing fisherman after about fifteen minutes, was both shaken and angry when he reported this) that *Patito* had slid right by the flailing crew member, fifty yards to starboard, without spotting him in the bright water between the sun and the boat.

Reggie and I, in the calm of the not-quite-post-mortem, resolved to burn it into our memories that step one in case of man overboard would always be, in the case of *Patito*, the release the dinghy we regularly trailed. Step two would be to throw overboard, at intervals of fifteen seconds, the half-dozen cushions (they double as life preservers) lying about the deck, as also, of course, the man-overboard pole, with its high red flag. Then you take as long as you need calmly to bring down the sails. Moreover, the Trimble Loran has that stop button, previously described, that freezes the location where the accident took place. I went further and created what I still call, in memory of the incident, a Stoops Preventer: a 10-foot ⅜-inch line with huge snaphooks on either end. If the wind is as much as one degree aft of the beam (jibes take place when you are sailing downwind), I secure the boom by snapping one hook through one of those steel bails that run under the boom, the second onto the genoa track. There are holes in the genoa track every half inch or so, so that a snap hook can clasp onto the track without any need for adjustment: simply reach down ten feet to the appropriate ring.

Several months before we set out, I had a letter from Reg:

A few of us serious sailors were having a serious discussion at Trader Vic's saloon, down Atlanta way, a few weeks ago when the subject of safety at sea somehow arose through the fog. Specifically, the best way to deal with the man-overboard problem. We were able to agree that trailing a long line overboard with a few floats on it would be a good idea, even though it would slow the boat down a little bit—perhaps 0.1 knots. I thought in our somewhat sorry state we were unable—even if we had had the inclination and fortitude to try—to pull together all the necessary numbers, estimates, intelligence, and logic necessary to solve the knotty problem of what effect the trailing line would have on our time en route. Several days later, I got a letter from Lars Steib dealing with the problem in some detail. [Reg enclosed a wonderfully amusing letter tracing efforts by a mainframe computer to solve the problem, but requiring of Steib knowledge of the exact shape of *Sealestial*'s hull and keel he didn't have: ". . . the head of the (Naval) department suggested that I speak to his teenage son, who had some special arrangement with the Navy, whereby he was able to use their primary computer, which is secretly hidden under some mountain in Nevada. I spoke to the kid in English, he spoke to me in computerese. He could hardly understand me and I understood absolutely nothing he said but he agreed to write me a letter, or actually have his computer write my computer a letter. This is what I received: 'Think of it this way, pretend there are two identical boats leaving point A at the same time for point B, 4700 miles away. Boat #1 moves at 6 mph and Boat #2 at 5.9 mph. Boat #1 covers the 4700 miles in 783 hours while Boat #2 covers the same distance in 796 hours.'"] I thought—no, I was *sure*—you would be intrigued with the answer, to say nothing of the weighty philosophical implications that naturally follow: i.e., whether the possibility of losing a man overboard is worth adding thirteen hours to an already tight schedule. After all, if you fall overboard, it's your own fault. Right? On the other hand, one must consider the prospect of spending more than thirteen (there has to be some reasonable limit, right?) hours looking for a former shipmate.

There will be no jibes anymore. I reviewed an extraordinary novel, Hank Searls's *Overboard*, for the *Washington Post* in 1977, the tale of a skipper who wakes to find his only crew member—his wife—not present in their 40-foot ketch. The book deals with his agonized effort to retrace a boat's path in search of a live body that might have fallen overboard as long ago as four hours. The hero is desperate when finally, after adroit calculations, he spots her, immobilizes the boat, and dives into the water for the rescue. But . . . "*Linda Lee* [his ketch] was hobby-horsing, pitching at each swell. The jib had eased from its furlings and was filling with wind at each crest. The jib sheet was fouled. As the sail bellied, it began to climb magically up the headstay . . ." *Linda Lee* sailed off, unmanned.

One has to be fatalistic, but only up to a point. There are seas, and we experienced many of them, in which man overboard would have meant man drowned. But we knew what to do in the event of an emergency, *pace* Dick; and when at night the seas were rough, anyone going forward did not go alone, or without a lifeline—at least not when I was on deck, nor (I had their assurances) when the other watch captains (Reg, Christo, Danny) were in charge.

Still, when I read Tom Watson I am mortified over the differences in *modi operandi*. He wrote, in his *Logbook for Helen*, an enchanting account of his Pacific sail:

> . . . we established a firm rule that nightwatch members stay within the cockpit at all times and that everyone wear a safety belt clipped to a strong part of the ship while on deck at night. In addition, since the new *Palawan* was a center-cockpit boat, which made it difficult to get a life ring overboard promptly, we added a device I had first used on the last racing *Palawan*. Long tubes were welded into the stern, inside of which were emergency buoys with ten-foot

plastic masts, topped with large red flags. The buoys were hooked in turn to life rings fastened to the stern rail in stainless rod cages also containing whistles, dye markers and strobe lights. The entire contraption was rigged so that if someone in the cockpit spotted or heard a man go over, he could pull a ring nearby, which released the life ring, pulled a buoy out of its tube, and activated the light.

Among other things, that tells a lot about his success with IBM.

Christopher.   While having a midday swim in mid-ocean the other day, a fantasy occurred which I have been unable to drive from my mind. It is this:

A sun-dappled day. Noon. *Sealestial* is stopped. All are over the side swimming, crew and guests—all except Dick. The sails are set, but we are hove to for the swim. Dick has been asked to "mind the helm."

We gambol and disport in the blue waves, and suddenly we observe that *Sealestial* has started to . . . sail away.

"Dick!" we yell. We observe him turning the helm—the wrong way.

"Starboard, Dick! To the starboard!"

At this Dick begins executing the helm to port, as *Sealestial* sails calmly farther on.

"To the right, Dick! Right!"

But he continues to turn the wheel to the left, in great earnest.

As the ship moves out of sight, the Pacific sky is rent with cries of "Dick! Diiiiick!"

At this point I awake, feverish, murmuring:

"The horror, the horror!"

We listened, during the cocktail hour, for the first time to twenty minutes of David Niven, reading from his two autobiographies. He had been an intimate friend of three of us. Listening became a habit, twenty odd minutes (one episode), just before sundown. And Allan, usually reclusive, would sit behind the cockpit, beer in hand; he didn't miss a single episode.

"Do you know," I whispered to Van, after listening for a few minutes, "David sounds as if he had had a couple of snorts." We

Niven Hour. Do Not Disturb.

both reflected on this, in the first place because David Niven was a notoriously light drinker, in the second, because his professionalism was so disciplined he wouldn't permit himself so much as a glass of wine before a professional engagement. *But there was something there in the voice,* a suggestion of an imperfect control of the odd syllable . . .

Of course. Van and I both nodded at the same time, having seen him through the period of his tribulation. We reconstructed that his awful disease (amyotrophic lateral sclerosis) had hit him, and it is just faintly detectable in the reading. The dying actor, giving a great performance; an eternal theme, eternally inspiring.

David began his autobiography by reciting the events of his boyhood—on the whole, dismal—days: He had lost his father and acquired a cruel stepfather, was turned over to sadistic schoolteachers, but ended finally at a public [private] school where, except for a major scrape, he was happy. His ebullience always broke through, as when, discussing his four years in the military, he came to their ending, after a course on something or other taught by a major general martinet. "He was going on about fields of fire, close support, trajectories . . . Finally he closed his notes. Any questions, gentlemen? My hand went up. I will never know what prompted me to do it. Four years' frustration, I suppose, but I opened my mouth and heard myself say, 'Could you tell me the time, please? I have to catch a train.' " Not long after, he was off to New York— and to Hollywood.

I wish I could say I remembered the evening's movie, *The Wackiest Ship in the Army,* but the first day at sea is a long day, and most of the audience slumbered, while dreamily congratulating the Entertainment Officer on his enterprise. The midnight watch, defined as beginning at the end of the evening's movie and going until one A.M., mobilized, relieving Allan and Noddy, whose single watch took place during dinner and the movie. The wind was permitting us to hold within twenty degrees of course, and the moon was full, the following, silvered seas patronizing as they slid us along our own fleeted way.

12

THE MAGIC OF GPS

In my book *Airborne* I undertook in one chapter to appease my frustration over the language in which celestial navigation is characteristically taught by attempting to say it plain, in layman's language. But I am a practicing editor and felt, under the circumstances, the need to acknowledge that some readers are simply uninterested in reading anything at all about celestial navigation (I understand; I furtively skipped Melville's chapter on cetology in *Moby Dick*).

It was a dilemma. On the one hand I wished to demonstrate the penetrability of celestial navigation, on the other hand I shrank from the didactic imposition . . . So I said to the reader, with some pain, that if said reader was absolutely uninterested in the subject, he could bounce over to page "X", where, the navigational lectures concluded, the sailing narrative resumed. I was on the one hand chagrined by readers who applauded (and took advantage of) my contingent concern for their attention (they were not interested in navigation, c.n.), and on the other hand heartened by readers who took pain to advise me that they found the chapter rewarding (I happily record that the chapter in question has been reproduced, in print and video). Here I haven't the identical problem (more people are interested in the ramifications of GPS [see page 142], which will be serviceable on land as well as on sea, than in the techniques of c.n.); but, following precedent, I advise, with some reluctance, that the Pacific narrative continues on page 155.

Twenty years ago (Reg and Van were along), racing to Bermuda from Newport, we heard over the boat's radio a voice struggling to sound all-American, but for all the speaker's effort, undisguisedly British. Probably the wretched skipper (wretched, because the mere use of his radio telephone meant automatic disqualification as a contender) reasoned that his humiliation over being lost at sea ought not to compromise the presumptive claim of Britannia to ruling the waves. But it might as well have been Robert Morley attempting to sound like Humphrey Bogart. He said: *"This is the Yacht* Merlo *calling Bermuda Radio. We need to know: Are we east or west of the island?"* That was before Loran was efficient, and in any event, its use wasn't permitted by the Race Committee: only celestial navigation, plus a radio direction finder, an instrument too primitive in those days to tell you reliably whether you were heading toward or away from your objective. That quandary would accost us, every now and again, on the Bermuda race: A vessel might slide right by the island uncertain it was doing so, like the poor Brit; and so the skipper would agonize over whether to continue on his southeasterly course, or to make a U-turn and look for Bermuda back there in the general direction he came from. (It transpired that the yacht in question, in the heavy seas and overcast weather, had indeed slid by the island. Ask not why he didn't notice, with his radio direction finder, that he was passing by the island when he was abreast of it. These things happen at sea.)

In October 1958, on *The Panic*, my first ocean boat, we were battered by one substantial hurricane, which was followed by a second mini-hurricane. Twice we had hove to. We hadn't had a celestial sight for three days and were well out of range of the radio direction finder. If my Guardian Angel had suddenly—indulgently —appeared, smiled at my chart and, wordlessly, implanted a little X on it to indicate where I *actually* was, I would not have been surprised if my position had been as much as eighty miles off, north, east, south, or west of Bermuda. Those are times when you remind yourself there are 600 wrecks in the vicinity of Bermuda.

With the advent of the Loran, about which I have sung my love song above, it is no longer such deadly serious stuff. But it was well after my introduction to Trimble Loran that I learned what was soon coming. There are sailors who will object to the very idea of a definitive navigational all-weather device, on the grounds that no man-made contrivance can ever replace the predictable movements of the sun and stars captured by (all but) unbreakable sextants, inerrant timepieces, and incorruptible almanacs. I readily grant them these presumptions, having three times crossed oceans, needing on every one of those passages to rely exclusively on a sextant (with the aid, on two occasions, of radar, which however is useful only if you are a dozen miles or so away from your objective and if, per impossible, the radar is actually working).

Electronic gadgets can go wrong. And so can engineering gadgets go wrong. Reggie points out that when you step into your automobile to drive to New York from New Jersey you cannot absolutely count on the motor's continuing to operate during the whole of the necessary driving hour. But in fact you *do* count on getting there. And appointments are never hedged on the contingency that providence, in protest against your presumption, might clear its throat and cause your motor to stop in the middle of the highway. So you drive comfortably along, the journey undertaken with sufficient confidence to sedate even your insurance company, which will give you fifty thousand to one that your airplane, leaving JFK, will land in Los Angeles, not on a mountain peak in between.

I quickly discovered, as I noted earlier, on charting the present course, that Loran would be of no use to me in the Pacific. The required radio transmitters for Loran don't cover most of the Pacific. Loran coverage is not available worldwide for two reasons, the first being that Loran radio signals are limited by the radio wave spectrum in the area they travel. Accordingly, the availability of Loran tends to reflect the density of user traffic. In wide ocean areas, the Pacific being the primary example, the investment in

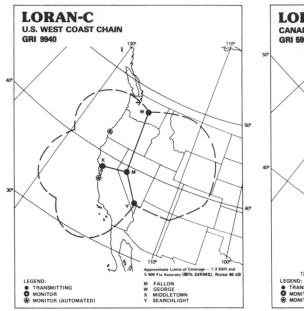

LORAN-C
U.S. WEST COAST CHAIN
GRI 9940

LEGEND:
● TRANSMITTING
◎ MONITOR
⊛ MONITOR (AUTOMATED)

M   FALLON
W   GEORGE
X   MIDDLETOWN
Y   SEARCHLIGHT

Approximate Limits of Coverage — 1:3 SNR and
¼ NM Fix Accuracy (95% 2dRMS), Noise 46 dB

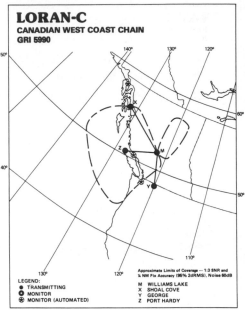

LORAN-C
CANADIAN WEST COAST CHAIN
GRI 5990

LEGEND:
● TRANSMITTING
◎ MONITOR
⊛ MONITOR (AUTOMATED)

M   WILLIAMS LAKE
X   SHOAL COVE
Y   GEORGE
Z   PORT HARDY

Approximate Limits of Coverage — 1:3 SNR and
¼ NM Fix Accuracy (95% 2dRMS), Noise 60dB

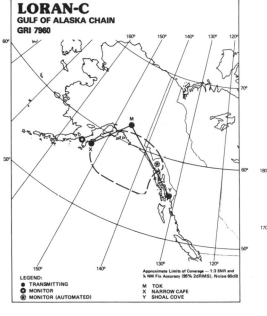

LORAN-C
GULF OF ALASKA CHAIN
GRI 7960

LEGEND:
● TRANSMITTING
◎ MONITOR
⊛ MONITOR (AUTOMATED)

M   TOK
X   NARROW CAPE
Y   SHOAL COVE

Approximate Limits of Coverage — 1:3 SNR and
¼ NM Fix Accuracy (95% 2dRMS), Noise 60dB

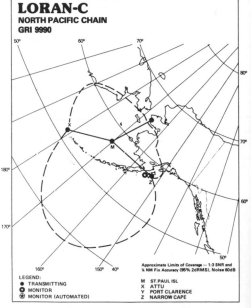

LORAN-C
NORTH PACIFIC CHAIN
GRI 9990

LEGEND:
● TRANSMITTING
◎ MONITOR
⊛ MONITOR (AUTOMATED)

M   ST.PAUL ISL
X   ATTU
Y   PORT CLARENCE
Z   NARROW CAPE

Approximate Limits of Coverage — 1:3 SNR and
¼ NM Fix Accuracy (95% 2dRMS), Noise 60dB

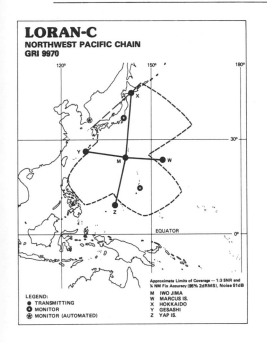

LORAN-C
NORTHWEST PACIFIC CHAIN
GRI 9970

Approximate Limits of Coverage — 1:3 SNR and ¼ NM Fix Accuracy (95% 2dRMS), Noise 51dB

LEGEND:
● TRANSMITTING
◉ MONITOR
⊛ MONITOR (AUTOMATED)

M IWO JIMA
W MARCUS IS.
X HOKKAIDO
Y GESASHI
Z YAP IS.

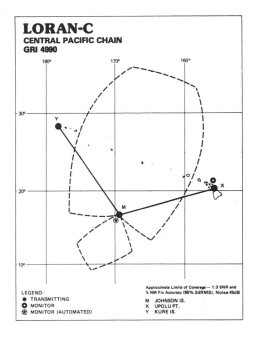

LORAN-C
CENTRAL PACIFIC CHAIN
GRI 4990

Approximate Limits of Coverage — 1:3 SNR and ¼ NM Fix Accuracy (95% 2dRMS), Noise 45dB

LEGEND:
● TRANSMITTING
◉ MONITOR
⊛ MONITOR (AUTOMATED)

M JOHNSON IS.
X UPOLU PT.
Y KURE IS.

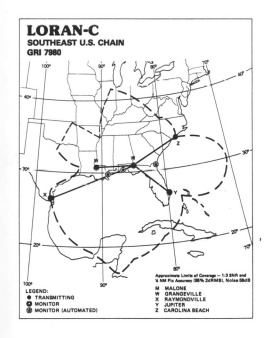

LORAN-C
SOUTHEAST U.S. CHAIN
GRI 7980

Approximate Limits of Coverage — 1:3 SNR and ¼ NM Fix Accuracy (95% 2dRMS), Noise 58dB

LEGEND:
● TRANSMITTING
◉ MONITOR
⊛ MONITOR (AUTOMATED)

M MALONE
W GRANGEVILLE
X RAYMONDVILLE
Y JUPITER
Z CAROLINA BEACH

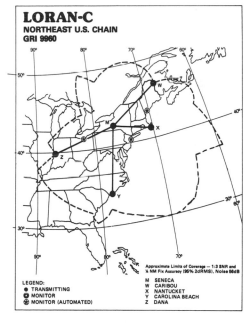

LORAN-C
NORTHEAST U.S. CHAIN
GRI 9960

Approximate Limits of Coverage — 1:3 SNR and ¼ NM Fix Accuracy (95% 2dRMS), Noise 56dB

LEGEND:
● TRANSMITTING
◉ MONITOR
⊛ MONITOR (AUTOMATED)

M SENECA
W CARIBOU
X NANTUCKET
Y CAROLINA BEACH
Z DANA

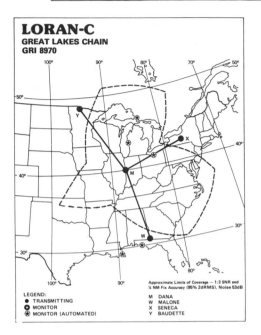

LORAN-C
GREAT LAKES CHAIN
GRI 8970

Approximate Limits of Coverage — 1:3 SNR and
¼ NM Fix Accuracy (95% 2dRMS), Noise 53dB

LEGEND:
● TRANSMITTING
◎ MONITOR
✪ MONITOR (AUTOMATED)

M DANA
W MALONE
X SENECA
Y BAUDETTE

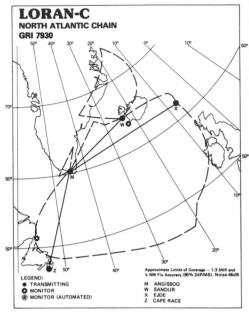

LORAN-C
NORTH ATLANTIC CHAIN
GRI 7930

Approximate Limits of Coverage — 1:3 SNR and
¼ NM Fix Accuracy (95% 2dRMS), Noise 46dB

LEGEND:
● TRANSMITTING
◎ MONITOR
✪ MONITOR (AUTOMATED)

M ANGISSOQ
W SANDUR
X EJDE
Z CAPE RACE

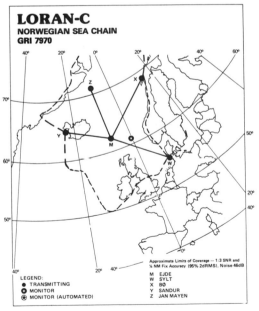

LORAN-C
NORWEGIAN SEA CHAIN
GRI 7970

Approximate Limits of Coverage — 1:3 SNR and
¼ NM Fix Accuracy (95% 2dRMS), Noise 46dB

LEGEND:
● TRANSMITTING
◎ MONITOR
✪ MONITOR (AUTOMATED)

M EJDE
W SYLT
X BØ
Y SANDUR
Z JAN MAYEN

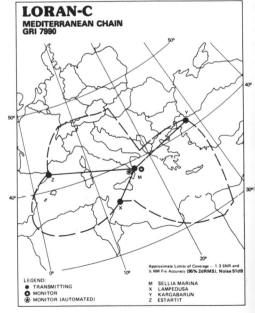

LORAN-C
MEDITERRANEAN CHAIN
GRI 7990

Approximate Limits of Coverage — 1:3 SNR and
¼ NM Fix Accuracy (95% 2dRMS), Noise 51dB

LEGEND:
● TRANSMITTING
◎ MONITOR
✪ MONITOR (AUTOMATED)

M SELLIA MARINA
X LAMPEDUSA
Y KARGABARUN
Z ESTARTIT

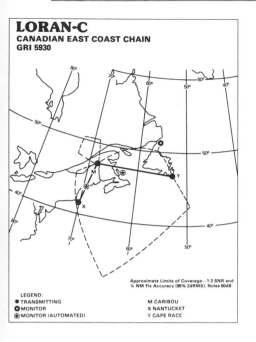

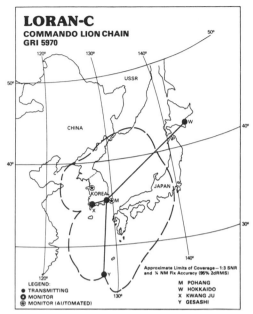

necessary transmission sites outweighs customer demand. Add to this the technicians' knowledge that an electronic miracle is around the corner.

It was with a certain wistfulness in my voice that, in conversation with Charles Trimble, the head of Trimble Navigation, I told him over the phone that in June 1985 I would need to depend yet again on celestial navigation. That was when I first heard the magic acronym:

"It's too bad you'll be just a little too early for GPS."

"What is GPS?" I asked.

I thought I heard a low moan at the end of the line. I was probably mistaken, because Charles Trimble is too polite to manifest dismay at others' ignorance; and besides, since the time of that exchange (July 1984), I have thirty times casually (*"I was talking the other day with a navigator about the new GPS system . . ."*) and as many times studiedly (*"Wait a minute! Have you never heard of something called GPS?"*) brought up GPS to boating people, and not once has anyone I was addressing shown any familiarity with the term or the revolution it stands for. For a yachtsman who has wrestled with the problem of finding out where he is, on occasions that range from nonchalant curiosity to desperate need-to-know, that ignorance is on the order of a farmer's not knowing that the means to control the rainfall are at hand and will be operational in three or four years. Even so, whenever I mention GPS I continue to feel like a hot news ticker.

A few weeks after my first conversation with Charles Trimble he gave me the sensational news: He would lend me, for my Pacific trip, an experimental model. It would be the first ever used aboard a sailing boat. Danny, who is frequently on the West Coast on behalf of *Power and Motoryacht*, arranged to pick up the unit, receive instructions in how to operate it, and bring it with him to Hawaii. By the time I arrived it was sitting in my stateroom, an instrument about twice the size of a videotape recorder, its cable running through the cockpit ceiling to the crucial antenna above.

When two-dimensional GPS is thoroughly established (late in 1987—the three-dimensional mode, designed for airplanes, is scheduled for a year later), ships at sea, or ships groping for an alien harbor—or for a cut, or for a buoy, or for a fairway marker—will know, at any moment of the day or night, where they are, give or take fifty yards. When coming into major ports they will know where they are within two or three yards. Airplanes, in the days immediately ahead, will substantially increase the running knowledge of exactly where they are, and blind landings—which not all that long ago featured Clark Gable with a flyer's helmet, a wing, a prayer, and a deeply furrowed brow—will be effortless. Helicopter pilots will be able to fly sideways between palm trees at night, assuming no one has moved the palm trees during the day. Surveyors, oil drillers, dredgers, pipeline layers, cartographers, fleet owners, police, ambulances, all will depend on GPS. And not inconceivably the fancier car models of 1989 could offer, for a thousand dollars, hardware that will exactly locate your car's position, and software that, when you grope to find 322 Beacon Street in Boston, will lead you there quietly, authoritatively, via a little screen on the dashboard directing you where to turn, or a voice synthesizer advising you when to do so. I suppose MicroSoft will provide a version that will describe historical curios en route. What's going on?

I need to pause in my exuberance to disclose the single item of what may be secret information that I picked up at Johnston Atoll, though I will not reveal from whom. It turns out that GPS will be so accurate, the Defense Department is suddenly wondering whether or not it will vouchsafe that accuracy to mere civilians. Mere civilians translates to: the Soviet Union. Their instruments of terror are quite accurate enough as it is, without giving them satellite signals, via GPS, which would permit them to plop their missiles right into our silos. But that is an unsettled question; we focus now on what is theoretically scheduled to happen in a couple of years *

* Several weeks after our return, my attention was called to an article in *Electronics Week* (May 27, 1985). "The view from the Institute of Electrical and Electronics Engineers Vehicular Technology Conference held in Boulder, Colorado, last week was that the Department of Defense still won't make the most accurate signals from its growing network of global positioning satellites available to civilians. Indeed, even the military version of the Global Positioning System will not permit motorists to simply scroll an on-board electronic map and know what street they're on.

"This view flies in the face of some of the glowing predictions from makers of optical discs, who seek to sell their product as a storage medium for digitized maps in GPS navigation. But according to Air Force Colonel Phil J. Baker, 'the highest GPS accuracy we could provide without jeopardizing national security is 100 meters of true geodetic position.' (Some 95% of the positioning information falls within two standard deviations, which is the civilian standard.) The Pentagon believes that by providing civilians with Mil-Spec GPS receivers (accurate to within 10 m of true geodetic position), some would inevitably fall into the hands of a potential enemy, thereby vitiating an important advantage for U.S. and allied troops.

"Two navigation services are involved in GPS: the Standard Positioning

It comes down, of course, to navigating by satellite. Now this is not a new experience. During the sixties, we launched satellites used to guide our Polaris underwater fleet. Those satellites, which in 1967 the Department of Defense extended to the general public permission to home in on, gave birth to a satellite navigational system called Transit. From Transit, which a boat owner can purchase for about twenty-five hundred dollars, you can learn roughly where you are a number of times per day. But these revelations do not come in at regular intervals. Depending on where you are and where the satellites are on which you are relying, as much as eight hours can go by before you get a reliable fix; and even then that fix is accurate only to five hundred yards. I pause to remark that five hundred yards is all you need if visibility is abundant. But five hundred yards is not enough in fog, or in the dark, where navigational lights are scarce or nonexistent, as is the case in so many parts of the Caribbean, and everywhere we traveled in the Pacific. It was just that, the lack of precision measured in terms of a hundred feet, that would delay our arrivals in Majuro and Kosrae.

But research was continuing under formal (DoD) and informal (Hewlett-Packard) auspices. Brad Parkinson, a Stanford astrophysicist, had been the director of the GPS program while working with the Air Force Space Division between 1972 and 1978. The Defense Department had positioned six satellites, and was using them to give us continuous global coverage of nuclear explosions, the better to keep our eyes on the machinations of the big bear. (That is the kind of thing Disarmament Folk mean when they speak of "verifiable" agreements.) That subsystem's flotilla, called the Integrated Operational Nuclear Detonation Detection System (IONDS),

---

Service, whose main civilian market will be aviation, where 100-m accuracy is perfectly adequate for aircraft except when approaching the runway; and the Precision Positioning System for the military. In implementing SPS, the DoD plans to encrypt the PPS signal and intentionally degrade its accuracy for unclassified users—that is, car and truck drivers. Thus, a driver using a GPS receiver might derive some advantage from it on an open road, but it would be worthless in a city."

Sextant maintenance.

roams the skies systematically and comprehensively. Any detonation of the nuclear family alerts it; whereupon, through its constel-
lation, it reports the treacherous event to a ground station. There
are those who credit Parkinson as the principal technical architect
of GPS. Someday Tom Wolfe will write a book starring Brad
Parkinson, Charles Trimble, and Ralph Eschenbach.

Eschenbach was a young scientist quietly at work for the aggres-
sive computer firm of Hewlett-Packard. At H-P, standard operating
procedure encourages off-duty activity of a speculative kind, and
one summer day Eschenbach, in the Midwest on vacation, found
himself wondering whether it could be established, within say one
meter, where those navigational satellites actually were at any given
moment. Now the satellites travel eleven thousand miles high at

a speed of about eight thousand miles per hour, but if you think that question awesome under the circumstances, consider this: Signals received from those satellites travel at approximately one foot per one *billionth* of a second. Ralph Eschenbach made his calculations and thought to conceive a GPS receiver and antenna that could measure signal transit time to within a few billionths of a second.

The idea took root. The Defense Department was working on a similar idea and had, of course, first access to the technology needed to implement a GPS system. Hewlett-Packard, beginning in 1976, assembled a full-scale effort to prove the feasibility of a low-cost land navigation receiver. In 1978 Charles Trimble, then age thirty-seven, who had been fourteen years with the computer company, bought up its Loran data and founded his own research company. Hewlett-Packard decided to get out of the commercial navigational business altogether in 1982, and Trimble bought up the GPS data and hired Parkinson and Eschenbach. What he had in mind was the development of a receiver at once reliable and relatively inexpensive, a receiver that would bring in satellite signals and transform the information into a beautiful, three-dimensional navigational fix. Its full name is the Navstar Global Positioning System, but us-types call it just plain GPS.

Brad Parkinson likes to tell the story . . .

At about the time all this was going on, in the southwest Pacific the Navy was conducting a war game, the Blue Fleet vs. the Red Fleet. The weather was bad. Transit signals were infrequent and therefore unreliable. At one point the commander of the Blue Fleet espied a vessel by radar, and the big question was whether the vessel was a friendly Blue or a hostile Red. This could be established only by knowing its location exactly and checking out that location against the friendly fleet's known deployment. Rapid calculations were made, based on all available navigational knowledge. Upon which the vessel was proclaimed a part of the enemy fleet, and solemnly condemned to death. The hypothetical torpedo was dispatched and many were there when the great ship went down with all hands.

However, the wretched vessel in question, it transpired, was all the time *a perfectly friendly Blue*. Moreover, *it* knew exactly where it was—because it had on board a MANPAC, an experimental receiver based on GPS navigation. The Navy was so impressed by the resulting certitudes that a jolt shot into the Department of Defense, which thereupon authorized full speed ahead in the development of GPS satellites.

So there were six of them in space as we wended our way across the Pacific on *Sealestial*. More will rise via the space shuttle until, in 1989, an entire 21-satellite working complement is in place. The shuttle disaster (January 1986), followed in such rapid succession by failures of a Titan from Vandenberg and a Thor Delta from Cape Kennedy, left planning for the U.S. space program in disarray. The failure of the French Ariane, during the same season, compounded the problem. There is much jockeying for position among available launch dates. But the word is that GPS satellites are near the top of the priority list for launch dates. Three different NASA launch schedules show that under the unfriendliest scheduling, the next GPS launch would come in February 1988. That launch would complete two-dimensional coverage by the summer of 1989, which is all that a boat needs, unless it is sinking. There is, moreover, a possibility that the priorities might be improved. There is talk within the Joint Program Office of the next shuttle's carrying two GPS satellites into space.

Meanwhile, Trimble—relying only on existing (1985) GPS—has, for $20,000 (competing with Texas Instrument's equivalent, designed and made for the Defense Mapping Agency and costing about $150,000), come up with a receiver that weighs thirty-five pounds and an antenna that weighs three pounds. The receiver, as I have said, is anything but outsized. Its antenna is six inches high and has a diameter of seven inches. The description of that antenna by Ralph Eschenbach and Roger Helkey of Trimble Navigation will perhaps help you envision it. It does very little for me, but the very sequence of words and syllables, so lasciviously arranged, communicates excitement . . . "[*The*] *simple antenna that meets these criteria consists of two half-turn bifilar helices fed in phase quadra-*

ture. One of the turns is subminiature rigid coax." That little bugger will bring in and measure satellite signal propagation time in billionths of a second.

What in fact is going on that is understandable to an amateur? I asked Charles Trimble, and he put me on to some plain English from Robert P. Denaro of the TAU Corporation in California: "Knowing the range of one satellite establishes a sphere around the satellite upon which the user must reside. Knowing the range to two satellites determines a circle. A third satellite range reduces this to two points, one of which can be rejected as unreasonable."

Oh, all right. Imagine it is the sun you are working with. If you know that you are exactly one million miles from the center of the sun, then you could be anywhere on a sphere of which the sun is the center (yes, including one million miles higher than the sun). If then you know that at the same moment you are ten thousand miles from the moon, you will know that you are at some point on a circle described by the two spheres' intersection. If then you know that you are also one billion miles from Vega, you will know that you are either in Cuba or in North Korea, and common sense will need to inform you which of the two is right, which "unreasonable." And then, if you have your exact altitude, or the exact time, or a signal from a fourth satellite, you will have a handle on a fourth dimension that permits you to locate yourself in space. It is that fourth dimension that absolutely situates you, providing no hypothetical alternative where you could otherwise be at that moment. For such lapidary fixes, airplane pilots, in critical situations, would pay over the gold in Fort Knox.

Now the final accuracy of your position, in existing (1986) arrangements, depends on the geometry of the satellites at the moment you take in your signal. The GPS satellites are not geosynchronous—i.e., they do not squat perpetually over the same spot on earth. That arrangement sounds neat, and satellites can be launched and directed into geosynchronous orbit. But doing so requires that they glide approximately twenty thousand miles above the surface of the earth. And to transmit signals from that further distance uses up a lot of satellite power. Moreover, if one satellite failed, a sector of the globe would be left without coverage, whereas the failure of one of the lower, revolving GPS satellites would cause merely a momentary lapse, and in a matter of minutes the successor satellite would heave in, filling in the vacuum pending the replacement of the failed instrument. (There is a redundancy factor built into the projected twenty-one GPS satellites which will permit the failure of as many as three.) Moreover, it is easier from a single spot on earth to "upload" all the revolving satellites, which twice a day fly overhead and receive sequentially up-to-the-billionth-of-a-second corrections, as required to make them perform exactly as specified.

The enemy of the truly perfect fix goes by the name of the GDOP, or the Geometric Dilution Of Position. The primary cause of a large GDOP (bad) is the configuration of the satellites viewed from the position of the observer. The wider the angles between the vessel and individual satellites (good), the greater the accuracy. GDOPs can be reduced, leaving you with two- to three-yard accuracy, by the expedient of constructing a transmitter in a fixed and known location, whose signal yields the factor on the basis of which correlative corrections automatically ensue. These transmitters need to be line-of-sight, so that to make them useful to airplanes landing, or ships coming into a harbor, one has to take close account of the surrounding terrain.

When we set out from Honolulu with the borrowed GPS I figured that for approximately four hours every day we would know exactly where we were by using the satellites already up there in orbit. Now if the America's Cup people, using exactly what we had, had erected two "pseudolites," as they call fixed-position transmitters, they could have done so at a cost of about $250,000, negligible stuff by the spending standards of the affluent contenders for the Cup. These transmitters would need to have been situated not more than fifty miles from Perth. With these additional signals supplementing the signals of the satellites that will be in orbit, Greater Perth would have finished GPS navigational certitude to the racing yachts during all the hours they were at sea competing.

But certainly before the next race in 1990, all sailing vessels and powerboats that wander about the islands and coves of Maine or, as we were doing, the coral atolls of the Pacific, or the sandy beaches of the Caribbean or the Aegean; that struggle through fog in the English Channel, or are days without having seen land or stars while crossing the Indian Ocean, will know exactly where they are.

Think big. Schedule a rendezvous with another yacht somewhere in the Bay of Fundy on a foggy day—the GPS version of the Star Wars' hitting a bullet with a bullet.*

---

* I must share a letter from Dexter Olsson of Bethlehem Steel, a personal friend who on hearing my reference to such a rendezvous wrote me: "About twenty years ago, Dan Strohmier and I performed exactly that feat on the Block Island Race. From about eight miles away at night in the densest fog I've ever seen we successfully located the buoy off Newport which must be observed before rounding Block Island. The fog was so dense we had to suddenly alter course to avoid the buoy. In the process, as the only 'engineers' on board, we were subject to quite a bit of ridicule. This was followed by a very long period of silence after our near collision with the buoy (the method and principles we used are the same as the Japanese have used in their quality improvement efforts and the ones we're using now to try to better them).

"Our equipment was an old fashioned RDF, a chart, and a piece of tissue paper. We plotted a scatter band of hundreds of RDF fixes, no one of which is accurate within a hundred yards. The resultant accuracy was pinpoint.

"There are many applications of variability theory to navigation. Any time that you have a system which permits multiple readings, these methods can be used. Having quantified the variability of your navigational measurement system, you can then identify subsequent readings as:

"1. *Within normal variation* (hold your course).

"2. *Significant trends* (alter course).

"3. *Outside of expected variability* (review measurement and calculations).

"We are using these same methods to begin to control our processes in making steel. Variability in chemical composition, physical dimensions, and other properties is now quantified mathematically. When things are within the expected variation of the process we don't make adjustments unless clear trends develop. The old-fashioned habit of adjusting because things are not exactly on target actually increases variability. Analogously, constant minor course corrections actually result in a longer sail."

GPS will make that possible; has already made it possible, if only for a few hours every day, with expensive hardware which, however, is projected to reduce in cost by 90 percent.

The sailor is free to indulge himself his moment's nostalgia. And in the months and years ahead—and not inconceivably in the millennia ahead—some sailors will continue to use the sextant and the tables and the watch, in part because the exercise of a skill the learning of which requires a certain application is not nonchalantly abandoned, else why would Boy Scouts continue to learn to make fire from friction, or—sublime example—why didn't the outboard motor anachronize the oar? What is likeliest to happen is that skippers with the least intimation of the romance of celestial navigation will continue to use the sun and the stars; not only they, but also that hardy breed (I am not among them, but I am addicted to a sextant) of skippers who never *quite* trust technology. There are pilots all around who are required to land airplanes and satellites and whatever on the dogmatic assumption that the signals they receive are reliable. But yachtsmen operating within more generous intervals of time will probably continue to use the primitive instruments, or better, instruments deemed primitive, but instruments which, assuming a global electronic blackout, will still locate a recondite coral atoll in the mid-Pacific. I *am* one of this breed, and the instinct is more easily explained away, I suppose, by reflecting that I am in other respects also a reactionary.

Danny and I did considerable sweating with the GPS. The first of our problems was soon solved by Reggie. The unit was, of course, wired to run off 110 volts. But that voltage, on *Sealestial*, is only yours when the generator is on, which meant that every time Dan and I wished to check in with GPS we needed to turn on the generator. And, of course, when the generator was off, the clock within the unit stopped working, which meant that start-up time was greatly increased. Four or five days of this, and Reggie rewired the unit to operate from our 24-volt system, so that it was always on.

But the most vexing problem was to get it to pick up its satellites when we knew them (by consulting a special almanac) to be in line

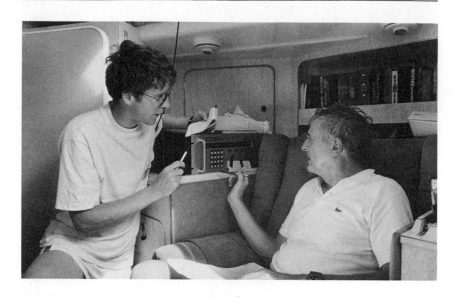

Studying the control panel: Where are those satellites?

of sight. In order to pick them up, you needed to feed your actual
position into the unit within (the manual said) thirty miles. (We
found that the requirement was closer, in fact, to fifteen miles.)
And since it happened that, typically, the machine was satellite-
operative in midmorning, generally before the noon sight, and
many hours after the preceding night's star sights, fishing around
for the correct position required much trial and error. We wrote to
Charlie Trimble a note making several suggestions for the model
that will eventually retail to the sailor.

But on two occasions, one at sea, one at land, we could check
each other out. It is of course silly to check a GPS: It is by definition accurate. Really, we were amusing ourselves when at Kosrae,
anchored between two coral reefs, we coincided. This time it was
very early in the morning, within GPS's functioning period. It
placed us (the position on the GPS receiver is given to you in ten

thousandths of a minute—i.e., roughly six inches) as exactly as we could place ourselves on a large-scale detail map.

> **Danny.** The time, we know, is accurate to one billionth of a second, thanks to IBM's uploading the satellite. What accuracy! WFB took a noon sight as I took down the last reading from GPS. I did not tell him the position, but wrote it on a blue card and stuck it in *Red October*, terrific book by Tom Clancy.
>
> After another wonderful lunch, Bill worked out the sight and said, "I like this fix." So . . . I compared our positions:

	WFB	GPS
LAT	12° 55′	12° 54′
LONG	174° 44′	174° 45′
TIME	0001:30	0001:29
DIFF	+ − negligible	

A month before setting out, I traveled to Silicon Valley. Trimble Navigation, a Silicon Valley computer enterprise, is right out of Disney's seven dwarfs' workshop. It is only a few sheds, a few dozen informal and busy and terribly bright people; packages, computers, a warehouse, microchips, and high enthusiasm. Javad Ashjaee had been head of the computer engineering department of the University of Teheran and had been minding his own scientific business up to the moment when he thought to protest the seizure of the American hostages in 1979, and that brought him Instant Exile. His eyes were shining bright as he led me to view the work he had done the day before. He had put a Trimble 4000A GPS in the trunk of his car and driven about the streets of San Francisco, having instructed the machine to record on a computer the car's location every ten seconds during his journey.

So now I see a dot imprinted on a piece of paper, and then successive dots, tracing the golden voyage of that car. I see the needle-stitching dot moving down a line that exactly duplicates a street on a map of San Francisco I am looking at alongside. I see the dot stop its vertical journey and replicate itself four, five times. What is going on?

"Stoplight!" Ashjaee beams.

Then the dots suddenly start back in the opposite direction, but a millimeter separated from the first line of dots. Huh?

"U-turn!" he smiles.

All the travelers in the world will smile when GPS is finally, completely, here, whether we travel on the ocean, or on land, or in the air. It would be fine to come up with a spiritual counterpart to the GPS, but that fix will remain inscrutable, while precious little else any longer is.

13

AT SEA

It usually isn't until Day 2 or even Day 3 that one has the feeling that Life at Sea is truly under way. This involves a lot that is routine and, usually, a certain amount of what isn't quite routine. It is perhaps true that more of the latter tends to happen on passages skippered by me than on passages skippered by others, though even seasoned admirals record unusual experiences. These, however, usually fade from memory unless there was something that thumbtacks them to mind, such as a great event in the mid-fifties. The Air Force and the Navy were bitterly feuding over whether more money should be spent on bombers or on aircraft carriers. Senate hearings were going on and one poor admiral chose that most delicate moment accidentally to run his aircraft carrier into a sandy shoal somewhere off Chesapeake Bay. A photograph of the stranded carrier appeared on the front page of the paper the morning the chief of staff of the Air Force was called to testify. He began his testimony by volunteering to deploy a half-dozen B-52s to tow the aircraft carrier off the shoals.

I combine an endless interest in navigation with a preternatural clerical clumsiness. I rely on a fitful memory that, for reasons I'll never be able to trace, will jolt me, at any time of day or night, to ask, Why had I done this? or, Why had I not done that? Inevitably, when you have not navigated celestially for a season or two, it requires time to get rehabituated to the protocols. I had a flying license while at college and, when I became engaged, promised my bride-to-be that I would quit flying, but kept two fingers crossed behind my back. But along the line, an old air salt (he must have been at least thirty) told me that unless you fly ten hours per month, you really *should* give up flying, his point being that with less than ten hours' monthly calisthenics, that which you have, under instruction, trained yourself to do instinctively eases out of the reflexive memory. In an airplane often there isn't time for navigational ratiocination. In a sailing boat there is. You can spend hours on a star sight or two, reflecting on this or that facet of what it was that might have given you an anomalous reading.

I set out after literally months of work, mostly done on the shoulders of Hugh Kenner. He is, as I say, a great literary critic who also disposes of the special skills you need to become an accomplished and inventive computer programmer. We worked on something we called WhatStar. Six months earlier I had said to myself: Why isn't it possible, by the process of exclusion, to ascertain what celestial body you are actually looking at, through your sextant, at any given moment? Why—to look at the question from the other end—can't a computer tell *you* that the star you were looking at had to be Vega, in place of *your* having to tell *the computer* that the star you were looking at was Vega?

Hundreds of hours were spent equipping me with a program according to my specifications, and here now I had it to use, for the first time at sea, programmed into my Epson lap computer, the PX-80.

My responsibility? To feed the computer: 1. the time of day (in Greenwich, of course), 2. the date, 3. the altitude of the observed body, 4. the azimuth at which it was sighted (i.e., its bearing on the ship's compass) within thirty degrees, 5. the assumed position of the vessel (accurate within thirty miles).

"*Wait now . . . Matter of seconds, Danny* [Danny was the assistant navigational officer], *THERE!*"

"Vega," the Epson should read, followed by an "intercept" and

Grappling with "WhatStar" and lesser enterprises.

an azimuth, with which you plot your line of position (LOP). This (an LOP) is a straight line, drawn at right angles to the azimuth, at a stipulated distance (the intercept) from that position. For instance, if your assumed position was at Point X, and your Epson told you you had a negative intercept of ten miles at an azimuth of 270 degrees, you would draw a line from Point X due east (negative —090 degrees) for ten miles, and then draw a line at right angles to your intercept, in this case a north-south line. The sight would have told you that your vessel was somewhere on that line. A second sight, with a different azimuth (ideal: an azimuth ninety degrees different from your first azimuth), would give you a second LOP. Where Number One LOP crosses Number Two LOP is where your vessel actually was when you shot those sights.

WhatStar would do this for me, including what they call the fix—i.e., yielding me the latitude and longitude of where sight one on Vega crosses sight two on Spica.

The theory was—is—marvelous. But I wrestled for four nights between Honolulu and Johnston, and little by little discovered what the problems were, concerning which problems more in due course. As so often has happened, I was subsequently reduced to taking sun sights, and one or two star sights where I already knew the names of the stars I was looking at. My fumbling at the mechanical level reached the high point of coordinated clumsiness when Danny and I, each one of whom had an identical watch-chronometer in hand, managed more or less simultaneously to abort the watch time by depressing the wrong button after putting the watches into a stop-watch mode.

The vessel's latent resources, little by little, were drawn on. When the going was calm, Christo set up his miniature Ping-Pong table. The second day was for the most part windless, and so we proceeded under power, making it possible to place the table on the foredeck where a tournament was begun. At noon we paused to swim, and this became the moment to initiate our new Ruger .223 stainless steel rifle, an acquisition purchased primarily as a shark watcher. (One person sat aft, looking over the swimmers' heads, in the event

The Ambassador and the Entertainment Officer at play
(the Engineer at work).

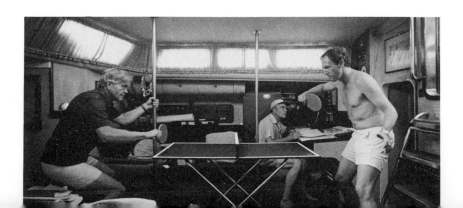

Shark watching and swimming. They go together.

a fin should glide in our direction. None ever did, but it can happen.) Danny and Christopher then did a little target shooting. It is a loud bloody thing, sufficient to scare off anything this side of kamikaze sharks, or other warm-blooded, cold-blooded predators.

Almost everyone was now prepared to eat lunch, and we began one of a series of lunches and dinners prepared by Liz which, had they been served to us in the Four Seasons in New York, would have left us gasping with admiration. In his engrossing book on his own Pacific trip, Tom Watson, Jr., writes that "shipboard morale is directly affected by the quality of provisions on board and the way they are prepared," quoting a Major Tilghman, identified as "a renowned mountain climber and long-distance sailor." He wrote, "Fate cannot touch me today; I have eaten well." About the food, Van recorded: "Yesterday we had fresh yellow, firm tuna, marinated and poached, plus a salade niçoise, avocado sauce, sliced eggs, followed by a cheese tray and sliced apples. Today we had ham-and-celery salad with gruyère cheese plus an eggplant relish plus cold lamb salad with chutney and pineapple. Tomorrow we are having a Mexican lunch—guacamole, shredded chicken, red kidney beans, grated cheddar, pickled Maui onions. All served up on tortillas according to one's own taste."

We were well fed and still under power, but there were indications that the wind was picking up. I gave a course that would in a few hours compensate for the southerly drift required by the starboard tack of the evening before.

Below, in the master cabin, is a chair for the construction of which I blessed Dr. Papo as frequently as I cursed him for the lack of air conditioning. To begin with, it is comfortable. More, it is so situated that on a starboard heel you simply ease more securely into the armchair's back. On a port heel, your rubber-soled foot travels easily onto an aluminum hand-bar, giving you all the leverage you need.

I had several bulging briefcases of unattended mail, and so I tucked in; there was nothing at the moment that needed doing on deck. I had just begun when Christo came in, shoving a *New Yorker* cartoon under my nose, so amused was he by it. It was by James

Liz Wheeler, alchemist.

Stevenson, to whom, coincidentally, I had assigned a column when editor of the *Yale Daily News*. Stevenson was a freshman in college, but already a senior humorist. The cartoon: She, in bed. He, sitting on the edge of the bed, dazed and sleepless. She: "Do you have to decide this *minute* between George Bush and Jack Kemp?"

The struggle between the two politicians engages us both at several levels, ideological and personal. Christopher was speech writer for Bush for a year and a half; his first cousin, John Buckley, is press spokesman for Kemp; and I had invited both of them to speak at the forthcoming *National Review* thirtieth birthday party (we got Reagan and Kemp).

To the mail. James Jackson Kilpatrick is not only a wonderful columnist, but also a precisionist. Two years ago he published his superb book, *The Writer's Art*, to which I wrote the introduction.

Over a period of twenty years—perhaps once a year, or twice—we clip specimens of each other's current work when we spot in it any solecism (God help us) or awkwardness. His notes read simply, "Tsk tsk," and clipped from one of my columns is a paragraph containing the sentence, "It is a cliché that true equality is only exhibited when you permit yourself to get as mad at a minority member as you would at a fellow fraternity member." He correctly inverted the words so as to make it read, "exhibited only . . ."

One gets all kinds of letters that are routine, even formulaic, in sentiment, construction, or tendency, but sometimes the spontaneity is as refreshing as—well, as refreshing, I could only think right now, as a ship's air conditioner. Mrs. Laurel Walter of Portsmouth, New Hampshire, writes me:

"I see by the papers that you're going to do it again—cross the ocean, that is. This time it is ostensibly to test some new navigational system, but my guess is that is not really the reason. You just can't wait to get out there. I sometimes wonder if you know how fortunate you are to be able to do what you do." (So far, my serial answer, under oath, to these assertions would be: 1. Right. 2. Wrong [I would test a new navigational system, but I never suggested that testing it was the purpose of my trip]. 3. Right. 4. Right.) She continued:

"But at this moment in time I find it not so fascinating, and I suppose that is why I am finally writing a letter to you after some years of saying: I must write to that man, about one thing or the other. I have a thirty-four-year-old son who has suddenly (well, maybe not so suddenly) decided that he will, in due course, quit his perfectly decent job, sell his house, buy a boat, and sail solo around the Caribbean. Or maybe the Greek Islands. Or the world. Which would be a valid decision had he any sailing experience at all. I think he crewed two races in the Great South Bay of Amityville where he grew up. He is taking an eight-day sailing course in the Bahamas this June, and presumably thinks that will be enough. I can only hope that he is so seasick he will give up the idea. But obviously he is not committed to idiocy. The Pacific? For crying out loud, Buckley, that's a BIG ocean! . . .

"And now Buckley says, 'What does this crazy woman think she's doing, writing to ME about this?' Pay me no never mind, dear. It's Sunday, it's raining, the processor is running, and it seems like a good time to write you a letter. Good luck, break a leg, or whatever you say to someone about to set sail in a pea green boat, wooden shoe, or whatever fragile thing you've dreamed up." Obviously a super woman, and I write and tell her so.

Miriam Siolberberg, on the other hand, writes studiedly, Madison Avenue style, "Do you like adventure? [Answer: It depends.] I am inviting you to take part in a very special historic expedition. If you join us you will experience more adventure than you ever thought possible. I promise you will live to tell the tale. [Always reassuring.] I represent three Polish explorers. In May 1981 they became the first explorers of Colca Canyon in Peru. Colca is twice as deep as Grand Canyon (at one point the walls are 2.5 miles high). It has extremely difficult rapids, including Class VI. [Tops is Class X.] Once in, the only way out and back to civilization is by shooting the rapids by kayak and raft. These three explorers charted and navigated the formerly uncharted white waters of the Colca River."

Anyway, the Polish gentlemen are apparently going to do it again. "You are cordially invited to join one of our expeditions in the summer of 1986. I must emphasize, this is a thrilling adventure, but it is not suicidal. All your expenses would be paid in return for your endorsing and/or writing about the trip. I will be in touch with you . . ."

I remember, as a boy, being greatly amused when my father told me of the Englishman at a bar in London. He picked up *The Times* and focused, in the classified advertisements, on a request for volunteers to join in a two-year, mosquito-ridden, alligator-infested expedition up the Congo into cannibal territory. The patron read and reread the ad as he filled and refilled his glass, his indignation mounting steadily. He stumbled finally to the telephone, dialed the number given in the ad, got the expedition's secretary, and said slowly but clearly, "My name is Jeremiah W. Wilson, my address is 28 Walton Street, and I wish you to know that I am *not* volunteering for your expedition!"

It happens that I am unmoved by rapids life, though I have done a bit of it. I thank her . . .

A doctor from Dallas, Texas, writes charmingly. Our liaison is curious. After reading *Atlantic High,* he resolved, with five other professional men in Dallas, doctors and lawyers, all of them sail enthusiasts, to do exactly as we had done: to charter a boat and sail across the Atlantic. We were in regular touch; the big trip did not materialize, but a shorter version of it finally did—a cruise down through New England waters, and I met the five men for dinner at the New York Yacht Club. He writes to thank me. He says his cosmopolitan companions had wondered how the dinner with a stranger would go. No need to have worried about it, he says; it went just fine. "Sometimes too much analysis disturbs relationships, so perhaps it is best left unanswered. Meanwhile allow us to sense a kindred spirit. Daniel Levinson, in his book *The Seasons of a Man's Life,* notes the absence of close male friendship in America today. This sailing trip has allowed a few of us to grow closer, in a healthy and supportive manner. It is a project we will continue to nurture. I perceive that you might be doing the same with your own friends and sailings."

There were one or two letters from correspondents who had also seen the reference to my forthcoming Pacific voyage, volunteering to accompany me. And a letter from David Cadogan, master of the *Scarlett O'Hara,* with whom I had sailed in the Azores. I reflected on a conversation we had had, and a plan I had explored . . .

How many times, I asked David one night after dinner, had he at that point crossed the Atlantic in a sailboat? Answer: eight times. Did he have aboard only professional crew? Answer: Yes.

I told him that my two books about sailing across the Atlantic had elicited a large number of letters, like those I had now on my lap. Those here relevant were from men (of all ages) and women (fewer, but also of all ages) imploring to be signed on as members of the crew if at any time in the future I thought to cross the ocean again.

Probably the most concentrated lot were from young men. They would begin by telling me how much experience they had had as sailors: some of them as lake sailors, some who had had some ocean sailing or Great Lakes sailing, several of whom had acted as crew on races to Bermuda. But what they wanted most was—an Atlantic crossing.

The second lot came from men in their forties and fifties. They too recounted their experiences at sea, mostly with coastal work; again, a few of them having made a race to Bermuda, or to Halifax. They dreamed of an Atlantic crossing, and now that they are well settled in their work—I remember a few doctors, lawyers, airline pilots—they could easily arrange a thirty-day furlough from work, and would be ever so happy to make the voyage.

And then there were youngish (twenty to twenty-five-year-old) girls, and a few women in their forties. Since ocean sailing is as of this writing still a male-dominated enterprise, more often than not they would volunteer to sign on as cooks, or as stewardesses—or, a few would say forthrightly, as seapersons ("I am as handy at the wheel or handling sails as my son, and he won the junior championship on our Snipe last summer").

I needed to say, in every case, Thanks very much, but I do not commute across the Atlantic, and if ever I were to traverse it again, I would elect to take with me—intending nothing unfriendly—a crew with whom I was very well acquainted, since the personal experience of a crossing is very important to me . . . that kind of thing.

I had asked David about the phenomenon of the great number of individual sailors who yearn for a transatlantic experience, and the complementary phenomenon of fifty-odd pleasure boats that set out every spring from the Caribbean to the Mediterranean, there to take on charters; and the same fleet which, in September–October, scratches about for supplementary crew to make the voyage from the Mediterranean to the Caribbean, in time for the winter charter season.

David said it was correct to assume that at least fifty boats, in a typical summer, undertook the transatlantic voyages; and that fifty boats, accordingly, needed to hire a few hands to help with the long hours of watches on a trip of approximately 3500 nautical miles if you are taking the shortest course from, say, St. Thomas in the Virgin Islands to Gibraltar.

What catches the eye, of course, is the flotilla moving with paid hands across the Atlantic while, in the United States, there are young men—and young women—and older men—and older women —perfectly capable of supplementing the regular crew of an ocean-going charter boat who are sitting at home writing letters to book authors, against the fantasy that one of them will one day telephone and say, "Are you free to crew across the Atlantic with me next June?"

And so, extemporizing as we went, David and I began to fine-tune. I had begun by asking him about the economics of the idea.

Question. What does it cost an owner to hire a hand to help on a transatlantic passage?

Answer. The wages are modest, and of course they vary. But you can think in terms of $750 per hand, which would include wages, the cost of his food, and his return fare.

Question. If a vessel were to take on four guest hands, could the arrangement be something on the order of a quasi-charter? Is it feasible to treat them as guest hands, expected to do full duty as sailors, who however would not be expected to attend to the maintenance of the vessel—the regular crew cooking the food, washing the dishes, making the beds?

Answer. No problem. The regular crew of the boat, so to speak its cadre, would include a cook-stewardess and a hand, and between the two the extra duty could be performed, making the trip more attractive especially to the older, paying guest hands. Needless to say, the regular captain would be totally in command of the ship, with formal authority over the guest hands.

Question. Suppose that, in order to make the passage more alluring, more adventurous, more exotic, the direct route—St. Thomas-Azores-Gibraltar—were to be altered, so that the vessel would now go St. Thomas Bermuda-Azores-Gibraltar: How much overhead would that add to the owner's burden?

Answer (after considerable meditation). Probably not more than eight hundred to one thousand dollars if the entire passage were stretched out by no more than one week.

Question. Would the guest hands need to have had extensive experience in ocean sailing?

Answer. No. The guest hands would have to be competent sailors, and experienced on the water. But they would not, for example, have to list on their application forms evidence of having crewed in a Bermuda race, or anything comparable.

The conversation turned to the question: What would be the appropriate sum of money to charge one person who desired to make such a crossing? But first, a careful definition of what *he* does, and what is done *for* him.

The guest hand takes a watch—four hours on, eight hours off. During his off-hours he is, of course, on call for emergency work. He needs to know how to steer the vessel, how to trim sails, how to hoist and how to strike them. He must be temperate, but not necessarily abstemious. He will need to supply references, so that the enterprise's coordinator can pass on his qualifications for the owner and skipper.

In return: The permanent crew will feed him, make his bunk, dawdle in Bermuda for two or three days during which he and his fellow guest hands can visit and tuck in their psyches for the next 1900 mile run, to the Azores. There they will stop for a day at Horta, run over to Pico for an afternoon en route to San Miguel, stay there for two and one half days; push on one thousand miles to Marbella, just past Gibraltar. There the guest hands will sign off, and fly back directly to New York from Malaga, or go on about Europe, as they prefer.

How much?

It has got to be worth the owner's attention, and the skipper's trouble, and the figure David arrived at was $2,000 per head. That would mean $300 (15 percent) for the coordinator, who puts the two parties in touch with each other, $1700 for the owner. On the one hand the owner is out $750 for the detour in Bermuda; but he is plus $750, money he now does not need to pay out for cross-ocean deckhands. So he is approximately $2,000 ahead for one hand, $4,750 if he takes two, and $7,700 if he takes three. This money he would share with the captain and the crew, according to whatever formula he (they) agreed upon.

So who is going to come up with $2,000 for the passage?

Here, I think, pleasant thoughts are catalyzed. We should immediately dismiss the objection that not everyone has two thousand dollars to spare. Not everyone has two hundred dollars to spare. Clearly the opportunity is available only to a minority. But if fifty boats each take on four $2,000 guest hands, you have got a built-in limit of two hundred in the spring, eastbound, passage; two hundread in the fall, westbound, passage. Four hundred per year. There are more than four hundred Americans per year who can afford to spend two thousand dollars a year on one of the singular experiences on earth.

My guess, I had said to David, and my mail now confirmed, was that you would find patrons for Atlantic Bound, Inc.—yes, that is what I suggested to David as a suitable name for the enterprise; and yes, the title is meant to suggest a little of what Outward Bound has come to suggest, tied to adventure and sport, but designed to beef the voyager up, physically and mentally, suggesting even the possibility of lifelong benefits, whether viewed as memory, or growth, or experience. Primarily from the quite young, and the not-quite old. I see it as the gift a parent or godparent might make to a graduating college senior before he goes on to work; or perhaps after he has graduated from law school, or medical school.

And at the other end, I see it as the gift a father (and perhaps a mother) makes to himself after his son or daughter has graduated and the school bills are finally paid. I can imagine a situation in which three or four children join to make a gift of such a passage to their parents on, say, their thirtieth wedding anniversary.

Would an individual sign on alone? Not if there are alternatives —persuading your sailing friend to go with you, if he can find the cash. More likely those who sign on as individuals would be the young men or women accustomed to finding themselves in the company of those with whom they are unacquainted; it is so, during the school years, in situation after situation. As we grow older we are more fussy about the company we keep, and probably the father will not sign on unless he can bring his wife, or a friend—or perhaps three friends with whom he has sailed. That way they would make up the whole non-professional company of a vessel crossing the Atlantic.

Would there be trouble with the professional crew? David Cadogan smiled. Don't you understand?—Captains of charter vessels are precisely trained to get along with all kinds of people; and boys and girls, men and women, who know that for part of the time they are on full duty are likely to be much easier to get along with than the totally self-indulgent charterer who arrives in the Caribbean expecting only to be attended to, to be fed suntan oil, floating island desserts, and frozen daiquiris. Is there the possibility of tension among the shipmates? Yes, there is the possibility of such tension. There is the possibility of tension at home, but the Atlantic Bound Cruises last for only thirty days.

Crossing the ocean, there are the high moments and the low moments. The four hours in a violent squall when you are drenched, tired, perhaps a little sick, perhaps scared. There are the other moments when you are moving with only the sound of water parting under the majestic momentum of a thirty-ton sailing vessel traveling five miles above the ocean floor at ten knots. And you wonder whether, on earth, there is another experience to match it.

Atlantic Bound wouldn't seek converts. Those who would write in expressing cautiously, or impulsively, or obsessively, an interest in the enterprise would know enough about sailing to know what it is to ride the seas, wondering only what is the distinctive fascination of crossing the Atlantic Ocean, from one end to another; a part of their experience, and probably a part of their life.

Well. It sounded like a fine idea to both of us, and we did a little corresponding on the subject, but David now writes to say he could not himself administer the project as his life is too peripatetic. It seems to me something for which there are willing sellers, and willing buyers, always the best combination . . . I told my correspondents, whose letters were now six weeks old, that I apologized for the delay in answering them, that I was already under way in the Pacific passage, and that perhaps one day I would energize a plan that might make it possible for them to cross the Atlantic.

. . . My doctor-correspondent from Dallas had promised at dinner to give me an embellishment on the now-standard seasickness preventive, scopolamine, which now he passes along, to wit: "Scopolamine gr/150 (the 'patch' may be substituted); Bonine 25 mg.;

Dextroamphetamine 2.5 mg." The above, I quickly add, requires a doctor's prescription . . .

And, speaking of medical problems, there is one on deck. I am needed. Or, more accurately, my dental kit is needed.

One half of one of Reggie's rear teeth has broken off, and Christo has volunteered to administer to the problem, and records in his journal:

> WFB got his emergency tooth kit. Started reading the directions: "Thoroughly clean the tooth, then apply the epoxy and the restorative." WFB awfully anxious for me to help poor Reg here, but I was more concerned that I might succeed in cementing Reg's jaw shut for the next thirty days. Can't you just see us spoon-feeding him apple sauce and pressing bananas through the gap in his front teeth? So we laid him down, cottoned his sore lip, mirror-pressed his tongue and glopped epoxy on his bicuspid. Our first surgery! Last, too, I hope.

The whole thing, Van remembered from the wheel, reminded him of the hunter bitten in his privatest part by a rattlesnake. He explained hysterically to his companion what the companion now needed to do, what act he needed to perform to draw out the venom and save the victim's life. His companion said nothing. The poisoned man shook him on the shoulder and demanded that he respond. He finally did. "George," he said, "you're going to die."

The wind has picked up enough to hoist the large genoa, which permits us to hold closer to course than the spinnaker. I make a notation on the log, and while perusing it remark the utter austerity of the antecedent entries—for instance (from the preceding watch): "*Sailing/motoring as before. Stoops and Clurman relieved by Merritt and Galbraith.*" I scribble into the log, "*I would appreciate it if the logbook recorders would stop being so gabby—WFB.*" Logbook provocations are legendary at sea and, of course, a few hours later Christo, coming off watch, would write, "*Holding course of 200 deg. Winds steady, speed under 6 knots. This watch captain wishes to enter a formal complaint against the previous watch's use of the log for poetical purposes.*"

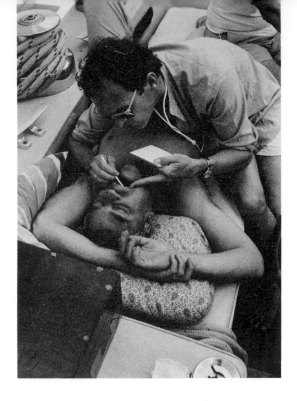

"George," he said, "you're going to die."

And, after his next watch, making reference to Dick Clurman's playful assignment—that we were each to write and submit for him to read aloud at cocktail hour that day one hundred words on "The Owls of Finland"—Christopher completed his log entry, "*I say, to hell with owls. I repeat my question to Him Who Is: Why am I on every other watch? Oh, by the way, winds diminishing to 8 knots, holding 265 deg.*" Under which I wrote, "*Him Who Is seeks from time to time to document that He is not Infallible. Attempts to do this are inevitably clumsy.*"

I had thought, on this passage, to assign non-abstruse designations to the watches. Accordingly, the watch from the end of the movie (usually about 10 P.M.) until 1 A.M. I called the Midnight Watch. Followed by the Post-Midnight Watch (1 A.M. to 5 A.M.), followed by the Early Morning Watch (5 to 9 A.M.), the Late Morning Watch (9 to 1), the Early Afternoon Watch (1 to 5), and, you guessed it, the Late Afternoon Watch, 5 to 9. Christopher Little pondered the question of watch services in his journal:

> Clurman called for a survey at lunch today, as he is wont to do. He polled us on our least favorite watch. For me there is no question: It's the 1 A.M. to 5 A.M. It's hard to sleep beforehand (unless you skip Entertainment Director Christo's film), and you don't have the pleasure of watching the sunrise. I was surprised to be the only one who felt that way. Some said the 5 A.M. to 9 A.M., others one of the daytime watches. *¿Quién sabe?*

Making out a watch roster is not something you can turn over to a computer. We had four chiefs: me, Reg, Christo, Dan; and three Indians: Christopher, Van, and Dick. The trick, apart from excluding me from post-midnight and early morning watches (half perk, half in acknowledgment of strange hours during which I needed to navigate) was to effect some social rotation, so that the same chief was not always on duty with the same Indian. This meant that, occasionally, watch officers would succeed themselves with only four hours off duty. But I was able finally to document to my paranoid son that, over the ten-day stretch at the end of which the roster was repeated, he had had only one more watch to stand than his brethren, though I was never certain he accepted my arithmetic, which, happily, he is intellectually incapable of checking on.

Christo's complaints against life at sea were wonderfully externalized in his journal.

> **Christopher.** Slept . . . 20 minutes at a time, but conclusively, at least. Trouble with the after cockpit is that with the wind coming over the stern, so too come the diesel fumes. Danny says he blew his nose this morning and it came out brown. I suggested the brown might be nicotine, whereupon he suggested I perform a quaint anatomical impossibility. [Christo is a reformed cigarette smoker, and the godfather of two of Danny's children. The combination, he is convinced, mandates a paternalistic crusade to get Danny to quit smoking and save himself from early death.]

Had the post-movie watch last night with Van. Just after taking the helm I heard a flapping noise on the seat beside me. Thought it was the wind flapping a GooGoo bar wrapper at first, but it kept up in a sort of animate way. Flashed on the light and there was a flying fish in the starboard gunwale, eyes wide and uncomprehending at the calamity. Van tossed it back in.

"He'll have a story to tell his grandchildren," Van said. Van is awful good company, you know.

It's 10:30 now. Dick is on his tenth or so Benson & Hedges of the day, underlining the *New Yorker* in red, tossing *Commentary* into the Pacific, reading the *Orientation Manual on Johnston Atoll*, telling us it's apparently "rad safe," which I take to be very good news, though that alone does not recommend Johnston Atoll for permanent mention in Fodor's.

Was coming out of the head after brushing my teeth. Opened the door, which immediately swished back with a smart *Klockk* on my forehead. Hmm, I thought, that must be some swell. Turned out not to be a wave at all, but WFB barrel-assing down the passageway.

"Oh," he said, as I reeled dizzily, "sorry."

Came up on deck, where Dan and Reg were trying to figure out star sights.

"If you need a star sight," I said, still reeling, "just aim the sextant at my eyes."

At four that morning I had slept not at all. My energy had been consumed in trying to stay in my top bunk athwart the pitch of an insensitive but exuberant sea. I ran out of energy. I couldn't remember where, on the *Sealestial*, the leeboards were stowed, and didn't want to wake Allan up to ask him. So I thought to go on deck and advise the watch that, inasmuch as I had already decreed that a jibe should be executed at 5 A.M., kindly advance that hour to 4 A.M., so that I would be able to sleep on the leeward side of my bunk. Christo relates the story of what happened then:

Christopher. A most interesting evening, beginning with an astonishing incident-less spinnaker run. As Danny and I were getting ready to catch our customary ten minutes of sleep, Dan says to me,

"I think you should tell Himself it'd be a good idea to take down the spinnaker." No argument from me, no sir. I was soon to go on a four-hour watch with Dick. It is not uncommon to come back to the helm after sixty seconds to find Dick steering a course of 300 degrees, a mere 100 degrees off course. Van said this afternoon, "In my hypothetical ship in hell—you know, where the English are the cooks, the Germans the police, the Swiss lovers?—Dick is the helmsman." All this being said, at the same time adding Dick is a swell guy, I figured it would be a very good idea to get the spinnaker down before Dick got within ten feet of the wheel. So we all schlepped forward, leaving Reggie at the foreguy in his pajamas. Instead of something being lifted off the deck by a popped sheet or concussed by an errant spinnaker pole, we actually managed to fist the fucker and get it onto the deck. Sweatily, heavily—perhaps I shouldn't have eaten the *entire* Toblerone—but after that, I crawled off to sleep in the after cockpit. I'm getting proficient at this skill (for skill it certainly is). The trick is to train your arms to curl over the cockpit coaming, so that when you are pitched onto the deck, your arm—by now asleep and locked into a kind of rigor mortis—catches you. I am now working on a method whereby it is not necessary to fold your arm behind your back at a 35-degree angle.

At any rate, Dick and I turned to at 0100. Dark, moonless, seas around 10 feet, I'd say—following seas. Squalls moved in, but it was pleasant and cozy in the cockpit. Not desiring to take broadsides, or worse, I politely demurred every time Dick politely offered to take the helm.

About mid-watch, when the rain had abated to a heavy drizzle, Dick and I received a shock. Very clearly, we heard an "Ooooh" astern. I jumped to the life rail, almost stepping on a small bird, which I hadn't seen up to now.

"Did you hear that?"

"Yeah. What *was* it?"

There it was again. A low moan. I scrambled back over the deck of the after cabin so's not to step on the bird. The thought was in my mind that we'd just passed someone afloat in the water. *Possible out here?* And what a mess if there were someone. Twenty seconds or more had passed since the first noise. We'd have to come about and retrace our course in the rain. Already I felt a certain moral culpability for not having gone through the steps the instant after hearing the cry: jacket over, strobe/pole over, countdown, repeated blasts on the air horn to wake everyone. I felt that very first pang of panic. By now I'd reached the after cockpit and shined the light down into Van and Pup's cabin. There was Van. I held the beam on him. Then he waved.

"I must have said something in my sleep," he said. "It's okay."

Thank God. That, apart from a premonition of diarrhea, was the unhighlight of last night's one-to-five watch. Soon it was four o'clock, and our watch looked like it would pass without incident. It was at this point that Himself appeared at the companionway, in boxer shorts, to say he was having a hard time sleeping, not being able to find the leeboards. He said that maybe this would be the time to jibe. "I don't want to have to wake Allan to find the leeboards."

Five minutes later we had managed to wrap the genoa so tightly around the forestay I thought we'd need KY jelly to get it back down. We had also managed to wrap the windward sheet one and one-half times around the propeller.

Well, needless to say, it *was* necessary to awaken Allan. In fact he woke all on his own, the sounds on the deck now clearly panic-tonal. He and I brought in the genoa, pondered the propeller-bound sheet, and persuaded WFB that it would be best to wait until light to raise the second genny. WFB was surprisingly docile to our argument, needing no pressing, perhaps out of a sense of complicity for our present state. What's wrong with our new tack—if it could be called that—was that if sleep was difficult before, it was surely impossible now, what with the 12-foot following swells and Dick at the helm.

So it went. We'd have done better—with a crew inexperienced in handling this particular boat—to have brought the ship's bow up into the wind, instead of jibing. The following morning, soon after daylight, Allan put on scuba equipment and, in his habitual self-effacing way, dived below and untwined the line that, in the chaos, had knotted itself about the propeller.

Christo was otherwise disturbed, I would learn:

"Pup is ensconced in his Bach-and-correspondence environment. I'm worried he's not finding this trip what it should be for him.

Maybe, like me, he's making the B.O. comparisons: [B.O., the Big One, as we had come to designate our first Atlantic crossing in 1975] no Auntie Bill [aboard], no Augustino,* no sense of *crossing*, no Bermuda to look forward to, just a 7-foot-high 'rad safe' rock bristling with military-industrial complex gear . . . Well, there's Majuro and Ponape to look forward to, but those rascals are sixteen days away. For an Entertainment Officer this presents a problem. Maybe I'll have to start slipping Valium into their Sanka."

Danny, it turned out, was thinking the same thing. "I think Bill is adrift. He seems not yet relaxed, the usual animated self. Christo senses the same. Perhaps something more serious is haunting him." And, characteristically: "I'll ask later this afternoon. Bill will never answer directly a question that is hyper-personal but he does one hell of a good job going round and round as if he did. I hope it's an illusion on my part."

It was, mostly. Yes, there was an accumulation of discrete vexations—deteriorating sails, problems with WhatStar, cranky winds and weather, the heat. But what we had come all this way for was, however slowly, crystallizing. Christo had written on the second night out, "A most beautiful sail. The moon sliding in and out of rain clouds, silver swells cresting and overtaking us—big ones, 10-footers. Tried to keep our ass into them, with a bit of success. Every third one would pivot us into a 30-degree heel. Whenever that happens I brace for a clatter of pans and the hundred-odd loose items we've not secured on all the boats we've owned. I remember WFB's obsessions with shock cord [elastic line] on the B.O., telling Danny he wanted enough of the stuff on board to suspend our schooner *Cyrano* from Jupiter." I was beginning to get the feel of a Pacific passage, quite unaware that I struck Christo and Danny as comparatively listless. I tend to fight low spirits to a standstill, generally succeed, and so usually go better than mere stalemate. My own journal records a steady internal barometer.

---

* "Bill"—Kathleen Finucane—was Christopher's maternal aunt, who greatly enlivened our first Atlantic crossing. Augustino is an Argentine-American who acted as steward, and was beloved of all.

On watch.

Off watch.

Lunch in the main cockpit, Bimini overhead,
wind steady, sea stable, food fine.

14

AT JOHNSTON

The night before a landfall is always spirited. The movie that night, as it happened, was lousy (*The Caine Mutiny*; some movies on classical themes work thirty years later, some don't. The play *The Caine Mutiny Court-Martial*, which I saw live in Washington a year later, was spirited, engrossing). The sailing continued fine as it had for three days now, and we were doing eight knots, right on course, wing-and-wing [the headsail set on the opposite side of the mainsail] with the large genoa.

The following evening began with Allan's every-other-day attempt to reach his wife by radio. We were all becoming apprehensive. Dick Clurman wrote about it, with the help of his recording machine. The great moment, and the struggle to realize it . . .

Dick Clurman. Even the unflappable Allan, after six unsuccessful tries, now really wants to get through on the radio. A man's scratchy voice comes back. "Roger on that, how do you read?" The sound is weak, barely audible. It will have to do. "I'd like to make a call to England. Area code 0752, number 668-080, extension 4212."

"Who do you wish to speak to?"

"Name of the person I wish to speak to is Mrs. Jouning, Juliet Oscar Uniform November India November Golf," he repeats three

times. The voice comes back, "How are you going to bill this call?"
Allan gives him all twelve digits from my credit card, repeating them
several times. "Stand by, *Sealestial*." Then a cheery British female
voice chirps over the speaker, "Hello," and fades away. Allan: "High
Seas—*Sealestial*—I cannot understand what the person's saying." It
turns out to be a wrong number. Allan goes through the whole
alphabet sequence again. "High Seas to *Sealestial*, stand by." With
rising exasperation Allan replies, "I am standing by." Finally,
"Hello, Allan," then the voice fades away.

ALLAN: "Hello, is that you, Daphne?"

Nothing. Now Allan is bellowing. "Is that you, Daphne?"

FEMALE VOICE: "Hi . . ." and fades away.

He goes through the whole spell-out and numbers game one more
time, while we crowd around the chart table in the darkened saloon.

ALLAN: "Hello, who is that talking? High Seas—*Sealestial*" Nothing. "High Seas—*Sealestial*. Yes, who was talking? Is there someone
on the line?"

FEMALE: Undecipherable chirp chirp.

ALLAN: "Yes, High Seas, this *is Sealestial*. The call is for Mrs.
Jouning, Juliet, Oscar," etc. "Okay?"

OPERATOR: "Pronounce the name."

ALLAN: "Jouning, Jouning," and he spells it again. "Juliet—over."

OPERATOR: "High Seas to the *Sealestial* one moment."

ALLAN: "Yes, High Seas, I read you."

OPERATOR: "She's on the line, go ahead."

ALLAN: "Hello, can you hear me okay?" Nothing. "Hello. Daphne,
can you hear me okay?"

FEMALE VOICE: "Is it Allan?"

ALLAN: "Yes it is, how are you?"

DAPHNE: "Great. How are you?"

ALLAN: (ever direct) "Fine, what's happening?"

DAPHNE: "You have a daughter. Eight pounds."

We all break into cheers, with much shaking of hands and em-
bracing, and out pops the champagne. Bill asks, "Do we have a
name for her?" Someone shouts, "We don't, but he does, 'Jessica.' "
Danny's characteristically upbeat assessment: "She sounded great."
(She barely sounded at all.) Allan guesses that his wife just had the
baby, may still be in the delivery room. Christopher raises his glass:
"Way to go, Poppa."

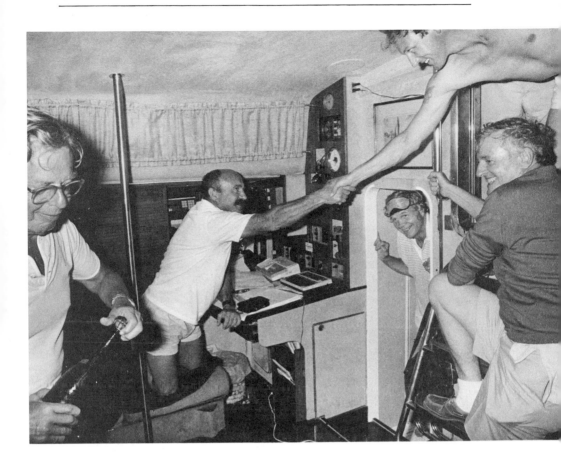

For unto us a child was born.

For unto us a child was born. Poor Allan. There is no privacy on a ship's telephone. Christopher Little's picture is utterly memorable. We were at Latitude 17° N, 4′ W, as best as this navigator could calculate, which best can be pretty good when the muses are in harmony. Jessica was 6,865 miles away, on a heading of 80.3 degrees.

Christo bet Dick that he, Christo, would spot Johnston Atoll before Clurman, and they made the bet in the gravest seaman's tender: one full hour of watch time.

> **Christopher.** *At 1330 I saw it: a low, boxy rectangle.* I let rip with a lusty "Land ho-o-o-o!" Dick was not altogether agreeable to this state of affairs and demanded, with a Time Inc.-ish air, that my "Land ho" be corroborated.

I, the navigator, skipper, and impresario of this whole extravaganza, volunteered the definitive scientific corroboration, and invited a moment's silence to honor my locating these wretched 600 acres of land after 600 miles of downwind tacking. I greatly fear I am being taken for granted.

I have noted elsewhere that it is a psychological constant aboard a sailing vessel that the time between spotting land and reaching it is always about five times what one expects. Having spotted the atoll at 1330, anticipating that we would reach it in an hour or two, we would not in fact sail into the little harbor at Mysterious Johnston until 1800.

Plenty of time in between to do this and that.

Even from fifteen or twenty miles away, one sensed the heavy placidity of the place. We would learn that the highest differential in temperature ever recorded at Johnston was 27 degrees. Before the Second World War, Johnston Atoll was a mere 60-odd acres. It was placed under the U.S. Navy in 1934 by Franklin Delano Roosevelt, an early reaction to Japanese aggressiveness. It became the central control point for atomic testing in 1958 and again in 1962, having come under the command of Joint Task Force Seven. It is (one is not *quite* permitted to gather) the place where unused supplies of poison gas are stored, in the event these should be needed for retaliatory or deterrent purposes: and one supposes, because of the heavy secrecy that shrouds the area, that there are other things going on at Johnston Atoll that go unpublicized.

Never mind. Van's naval attaché in Paris had seen to it all, and we had word that the Secretary of the Navy, John Lehman, a friend of Van's and mine, had passed along the word that we were not a

water-borne cadre of Ban-the-Bombers. We looked forward eagerly
to a night on shore, though not at all to a night of formal social
activity. I raised the point concretely with Christopher and Van,
seated in the cockpit. It is inevitable, I speculated from years'
experience, that we will be invited to have dinner with the brass.
Christo asked whether we could beg off, using whatever excuse.
Van, and I concurred, said no, not really; we would simply need to
go along. Who knows, perhaps it would even be interesting. We
could in any event look forward to walking about—oh! *The gas
masks!*

I went below, fished about in the hanging locker for the critical
paraphernalia purchased last month in New York at an Army-Navy
store—protective devices without which, we had been told, one
was not permitted to land on that mephitic island. I had used gas
masks in training in the infantry, but that wasn't the first time I
had worn a gas mask. Two sisters, a governess, and I stepped off the
Europa at Southampton in October of 1938, bound for British
schools, and were issued gas masks at the docks—the Czech-
Sudetenland crisis was on. (Two days later, escorting us to schools
at Old Windsor and Ascot, my father noticed the commotion of
cars and press at the London airport and told the driver to veer

Arriving in Southampton. Munich crisis, October 1938.
Mlle. Bouchex, WFB (12), Jane (14), Patricia (11) Buckley.

over to have a look. We saw Mr. Neville Chamberlain descend
from his airplane with his umbrella, and heard him bringing us
"peace in our time.")

We resigned ourselves to the probability of a little formal socializing, but it was in any case refreshing to contemplate a full night's
stable bed rest, either at anchor or at the dock.

Allan came up. He had raised the Johnston authorities on 8294.2
KHz and they were on the line. They were expecting us and had
asked how much fuel and ice did we desire (Allan gave the figures:
two hundred pounds of ice, one hundred gallons of fuel), and how
had we planned on reimbursement? Allan asked me. I hadn't
thought deeply about it, and told him to say either by credit card,
personal check, traveler's check, or cash.

Johnston Radio did not there and then specify its preference.
The transmission ended, and we sailed closer and closer.

I went below for an hour. Toward the end of which, Christo
records, "With some effort we fisted in the genoa. WFB came up
and decided we would *sail* into the harbor, thus within two minutes
of lowering the genoa we found ourselves raising it again. And
then lowering the wretched thing within oh, three minutes. Ah,
yes, it's all coming back to me from ten years ago: 'Okay, let's
raise the gollywobbler!' " My son, I recall from many years' experience, exaggerates, and sometimes inclines, at sea, to sloth.
Sometimes inclines to sloth when not at sea, come to think of it.
Of *course* we would sail in. What would all those generals and
admirals think of us if, since we needed to come in under non-
nuclear power, we settled for less than what power we disposed of?

Inside the cut we were hailed, and I brought the *Sealestial* alongside the indicated dock. Van and I jumped ashore and extended a
hand of greeting to a lieutenant colonel, a trim gentleman in his
early forties who turned out to be the base commander, and to the
two civilian aides by his side. We exchanged a few pleasantries.
Allan, Noddy, and Reg were tying up the bow, stern, and spring
lines when I asked our host whether this was the slip where the
Sealestial would be spending the night. This, it became obvious,
was the colonel's big moment.

Throwing out an unwanted line at Johnston Atoll.

The colonel forces a smile of greeting.

The colonel says No.

"No, sir. You can't spend the night here."

Van's smile ended. "I thought you knew we were coming?" he said.

"Yes sir, Mr. Ambassador, but you can't stay. In fact, we intended to bring you the fuel and the ice offshore, but the winds were too heavy."

"When," I asked slowly, "are we expected to leave?"

"Preferably before nightfall, sir."

I signaled to Van and we wandered briefly out of earshot.

He was truly astonished. There was no penetrable security problem. We had our gas masks aboard (though none of the dozen civilians we saw walking about were wearing them), prearrangements had been carefully made . . . Worth making a scene?

No, I said; and Van agreed: the hell with Johnston Atoll.

But there were a few amenities reasonably to be requested. I returned to the colonel and told him that, besides the fuel and ice, we would appreciate some fruit and fresh vegetables.

The colonel nodded, an aide taking notes.

And we would need to make telephone calls.

He said that the telephone was not entirely reliable, dependent as it was on Hawaiian traffic, but that we could go to the recreation quarters (he pointed to the second floor of a barracks-type building nearby).

And we needed a doctor: Noddy's hand should be checked, Christo's dentistry was failing inside Reggie's mouth, and Van had an infection on his forehead where he had had a skin cancer removed in Paris.

The colonel would direct them to the clinic.

And finally, I said, we would like the opportunity to shower; the colonel pointed to a building alongside.

We passed the word shipboard, and there was a low moan of disappointment, followed by the *Sealestial* Stiff Upper Lip.

We succeeded in getting through brief personal calls, ascertaining, in order of importance, three things. The first was that Vice President Bush's advance man earnestly hoped that Van would be back in Paris in time to be with the Vice President on the second of July, when Mr. Bush would be spending the night at Van's residence. The second, that Pat had not left on a trip, as planned for the night before, because Nancy Reagan had called. The conversation had evidently gone about as follows: NANCY. You know, dear, I can't stay at the Waldorf because of the strike. [The New York hotel workers were on strike.] PAT. Ah, but you can stay at the Plaza Athénée—the employees there aren't union! NANCY. Dear, I *can't* stay at a non-union hotel when there's a strike on. (Pause.) PAT. Do you want to stay at our place? NANCY. Would that really be convenient? ... So Pat's trip to Turkey was delayed a day while she prepared our apartment for the First Lady.

The third item of interest was a notice on the bulletin board, spotted by Christopher Little while he was waiting to use what had become, in effect, a public telephone (there was no booth, and therefore no privacy). On the sheet of paper was typed, "SEALESTIAL DUE AT 1700/PERHAPS. MAJOR WILL DECIDE." From this we deduced that there had been an intramural struggle: Would we be permitted to spend the night at a security island, or would we not?

The whole thing, in context, was a *locus classicus* of the kind of intellectual anemia brought on by bureaucratic inbreeding. Simultaneously, 1) strict exclusionary security rules were being applied against 2) a crew two members of which were simultaneously engaged in adjusting their schedules to accommodate the Vice President and the wife of the Commander in Chief. Late that evening the boys would hoot a little over the piquancies.

Now I reported to Christopher Little that Frances Bronson, in my office, having been sworn to secrecy, had been told by a knowledgeable informant that Christopher Little had been "severely wounded" while leaving Honolulu, but that his wife Betsy *must not know of this!* (Some helpful soul in Honolulu had evidently reported Noddy's accident as having happened to Christopher Little.)

After phoning and showering, I invited the colonel on board, but he continued to stand, always with his aides, rather stiffly on the dock, as if o'er the ramparts to watch. It was only when, a few minutes later, I thought to ask him if he and his aides would care to come below, look at our vessel, *and have a Diet Coke,* that he stepped down onto our deck from his dock. With the offer of Diet Coke I had come up with something which could never be confused with the tender of subornation. Van, back from the clinic (where the doctor ascertained that Van's doctor in Paris had left a part of the suture in his skin), joined us, and asked conversationally how long was a tour of duty on Johnston Atoll, to which the answer was, one year.

"No breaks?" Van asked.

"Yes, sir. They go back to Honolulu for stress seminars."

"For what?"

"Stress seminars."

These, he explained, were conducted under the leadership of

chaplains. My mind wandered back to my old friend and sometime employer, William Bradford Huie, and to his novel *The Revolt of Mamie Stover*, a graphic story of supply-side treatment of G.I. stress by an enterprising young woman in Honolulu. "In the future," Christo wrote in his journal, "I plan to take no more vacations, only 'stress seminars.'" Christo, having joined us after his shower, told the colonel that we had on board a formidable baby shotgun with which to defend ourselves. The colonel ho-ho-hoed over that one, and said modestly that in any firefight between the resources of *Sealestial* and the resources of Johnston Island, he would bet on the latter, you bet.

We were all aboard. I paid the bill, and the commissary officer winked and said he was not going to charge me for the sweet rolls and the squash and fruit, and I thanked him.

Suddenly the prospect of going back out to sea palpably disappointed no one, in fact exhilarated most of us. I decided to depart smartly. I maneuvered the boat away from the dock, we hoisted the mainsail and, rounding the channel buoy, raised the genoa, sailing briskly away. Drinks were served and we listened to twenty minutes of David Niven. Today David has landed his first job in the movies, given to him by the "boy genius" Irving Thalberg, who decided that David would do well as "one of the non-speaking mutineers" in *Mutiny on the Bounty*. He was dispatched to the intimidating Sam Goldwyn, who gave David one of those verbal contracts not worth the ink it was written on. "In a year or so if you are any good, I might give you a role." That role turned out to be in *Wuthering Heights*, directed by the cranky, gifted, unsparing William Wyler. "Even Laurence Olivier, after being made to repeat a scene twenty or thirty times, finally confronted him and asked, 'What do you want me to do?' Wyler considered: 'Just be better.' It became one of the all-time classics." David Niven had achieved his professional gait, and so, we felt, sailing confidently out to sea at hull speed, had we.

Dick Clurman, after the Niven interlude, thought it would be amusing to examine hypothetical alternatives at Johnston. He

Back at sea. Who needs Johnston A.?

listed them methodically. Suppose, just to begin, that we had politely declined to leave. Just stayed there at the dock. What in fact would they have done?

Dick upped the stakes. Suppose, he said, that I had put in a call to the President of the United States? (Here Dick had me confused with the late L. B. Mayer.) Third possibility: Suppose we had shoved off the dock, gone, pouting, out into the channel a couple of hundred yards—then dropped anchor and started cooking a steak on the outdoor grill. What in fact would they have done? Poison-gassed us? Notwithstanding our gas masks?

We laughed. I told them about a social act of desperation of my own, back in the early seventies. I was sailing on *Cyrano* with Pat and a few friends, heading south in Key Biscayne, only to discover that a bridge I had intended to pass under was one foot lower than the height of my mast, requiring that we head back up the bay and out to sea, toward a southerly harbor twenty miles down the line. It was becoming dark and the wind was approaching a menacing velocity, so I studied the chart and said, Ah, here is something called the Ocean Reef Club—toward which I forthwith maneuvered my schooner.

But on arriving, we were informed by the dockmaster that this was a private club.

I asked to see the manager, to whom I was taken. Might I please see a list of members? I asked.

No, he said, that was forbidden: Who exactly was my host?

I took a deep breath and said: "Bebe Rebozo." (Surely yachtsman Rebozo would belong to the yachting clubs in his home area, I thought?)

Well, I was told, they would need to hear directly from Mr. Rebozo.

I had got to first base—Bebe was evidently a member.

"I will need your telephone," I said, hoping to be shown to a booth. Not at all: I would use the manager's own phone, right there and then. Having not the slightest idea where to reach Bebe Rebozo, whom I had met only once, I gave the operator my credit card number and the number of the White House.

The operators of the White House are legendary in their pertinacity and ingenuity, as is widely known. I gave my name and said that I wished to speak with Mr. Rebozo. Within four or five minutes he was on the line, and I said, with just the right accent on just the right syllables, "Bebe, you *remember* you told me *last time we visited* you wanted me to get to see the *Ocean Reef Club?* Well, I am *here* right *this minute,* and I think it's terrific, only *the manager* wants to speak to you." He caught on instantly, spoke to the manager who nodded, beamed, made us comfortable at dockside overnight, and the following month sent me an invitation to join the club.

But there was no adaptation of that formula that would have worked on Johnston, Van opined. "They knew we were coming and they knew who we knew. Obviously my naval attaché should have made the concrete point that we might want to spend the night." *Tant pis.*

For a few hours the wind and the boat would perform like troupers. Christopher wrote: "Thus de-sutured and re-veged, we set off again after our two-hour R & R among the nerve warfare guys. The odd thing was how good it felt to be back on the road again. We set our sails wing-and-wing for Majuro, 1300 miles away, and crested the twilight swells, and pretty soon Johnston was just a yellow glow sinking under the horizon."

> **Christopher.**   I went aft to the after cockpit. I lay back for another four hours. All the stars were there, plus Jupiter, the blue mother planet. I really can't discern the mythological beasts in these constellations: to me, Leo might as well be a giant spider or a Midas muffler. Resolve to start designating some of my own constellations. I suggested to Dick we start with C.E.O., pronounced, "see-oh." . . . I think we may be onto something here. We should have a Herpes Constellation, incidentally.
>
> [Christopher was in the mood to give Dick his due.] As a matter of fact, Dick was steering a tolerably good course, "tolerably good," in Dick's case, being less than fifty degrees off course. But after a half hour of this exemplary helmsmanship—he got bored; and soon we were doing Turns and Immelmanns in the troughs of the increasingly frothy seas. This causing Danny's and my heads to bash repeatedly against the cockpit coaming.
>
> "Reg," I snarled from my cockpit bunk aft, "would you please take the helm?"
>
> After three hours of bracing myself and trying various Houdini-combinations, I drifted into something very much like sleep.
>
> Sweet dreams? . . .

At 3:30 A.M. the massive, proud genoa surrendered. Surrendered totally. This was done in style. In a matter of moments it was a mass of chaotic ribbons. The huge headsail became a register of xylophonic sounding boards, bringing a half dozen of us on deck. I headed toward the helm, looked up and saw, dismayed, the moon through a slit in the mainsail above a seam, on top of the spreader. The split had not yet reached the leech. If it did so we would face 1300 miles without a mainsail. A conference with Allan, and the decision to leave the sail up there until morning, rigidly set, on a port tack . . . Danny and Reg were officially on duty when it happened. "It blew," Danny had shouted to Christopher. "I need you forward."

> **Christopher.** *Yes*, I thought, *but pants. Gotta have my pants. Don't relish having my goodies sheared off by an amok weather sheet.* Finally found them.
>
> Allan and I and Christopher Little spent the next 45 minutes doing an inverted Iwo Jima on the genoa. The deck was tossing, and in these seas falling overboard is not recommended. Then we batter-rammed the spinnaker pole out of its fitting. By the time we got back to the cockpit we were good and beat, but at least we'd gotten the remains of the genoa in, without major incident. As we were reflecting on our good fortune, WFB looked up at the mainsail. "Oh, God!"
>
> At spreader level the sail was ripped from luff to leach. It wouldn't have been smart to try to bring it down at night in these seas, but it would have been equally imprudent to jibe with the sail in that condition. It might well sever completely at the rip line, causing a whole lot of unfortunateness. For the rest of the night we would try to keep the wind on the port quarter to avoid the jibe. Trouble was that so doing caused a night of guaranteed roller-coastering.
>
> I left Dan and Christopher Little to return to the after cockpit, nicely awake and heated up. I heard a loud crash from down below and came back forward to see what had happened, though by the sound of it I figured a dinner service for twelve had just been propelled to the deck. I shone my flashlight down below. Its beam caught Maureen hunched over the galley floor. I have to hand it to Maureen: she smiles amidst the most trying circumstances. She explained, squatting there among the shards, that the large serving tray platter had entered the galley steeplechase and not made it past the first jump.

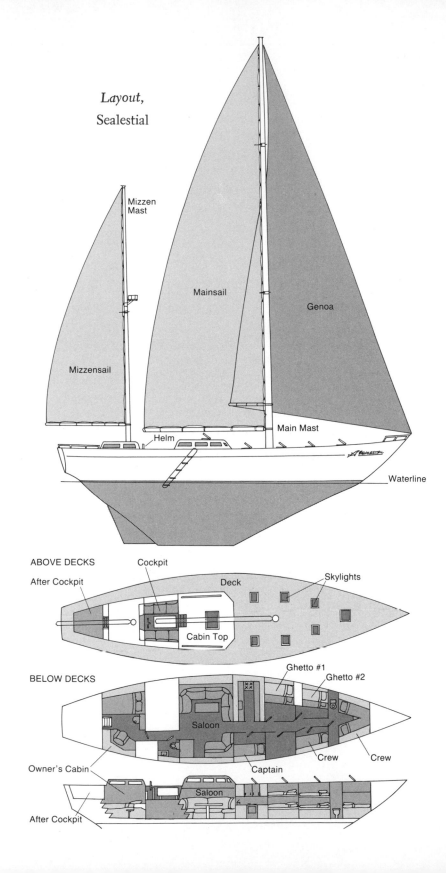

Layout,
Sealestial

Mizzen
Mast

Mainsail

Genoa

Mizzensail

Main Mast

Helm

Waterline

ABOVE DECKS

Cockpit

After Cockpit

Deck

Skylights

Cabin Top

BELOW DECKS

Ghetto #1

Ghetto #2

Saloon

Owner's Cabin

Captain

Crew

Crew

After Cockpit

Saloon

I returned once again to the after cockpit. My sleeping bag was now even more moist. I slammed myself in and looked up at the stars again. They looked less detached than they had before, as if they shared in these events. As if they were culpable. Nonsense—but then the transom dipped into the ocean and with one efficient *slurp* the aft deck was under eight inches of sea.

Oh now, come *on*, I said to myself, hunching behind the rim of the cockpit. *Why isn't it draining?*

The water coursed around my cockpit, slurping and swishing. Nothing I can do here, I said. At which point it began to rain. When the water had finally run out of the gunwales, there was that flopping noise. And the (goddam) flying fish. I mean, these things are wearing out their welcome here. Two nights earlier I'd bean-poled myself into Reggie's hot bunk and was lying there trying to excise the waves from my brainpan when there was this flash through the hatch cover two feet from my head, followed by the telltale smell (kind of like a bucket of fish scales) and that mad flapping. I've been playing St. Francis to these oceanic nuisances for almost a week now and let me tell you, it's getting old.

Anyway, the flapping stopped, and I went back to Lolly-columning myself into the after cockpit. At ten to five I got up and went forward to get my blue jeans.

And that's when I found the bloodstain. I'd tiptoed through the passageway, not wishing to locate the remaining slivers of china with my footsoles. Approaching our cabin, I noticed the entire passageway and cabin floor had been re-linoleumed with Cadbury bars, Reese's peanut butter cups, M & Ms, and Toblerones. It was while I stood there, braced against the bulkhead, that I saw this . . . smear of blood on the cabin door. This was no driplet from a skinned elbow: it looked as if Alfred Hitchcock and Brian De Palma had just shot a scene in there. I checked Dick for vital signs. Light snoring.

I sausaged my legs into my damp Calvins and went aft to take the helm, asking the retiring watch if anyone's arm had recently been amputated.

Dan said that Dick had had a spectacular, face-first deck dive on his way to the ice cooler. Well, I thought, he's going to be a hurt frog when he rolls back his eyelids in the morning.

It was a good watch. (Watches with Van are always so.) But dicey, on account of the 4-foot-long gash in the main. One jibe and we might find ourselves with zero sails. The only recourse was to steer a Mr. Toad's Wild Ride course through these 10-foot seas, keeping our bum to the following seas. It was a no-sleeper course, 35-degree heels every four, five minutes. I asked Van if he'd slept.

"A bit," he said. "I woke up twice. First time because there was a lot of noise. It sounded pretty far advanced so I didn't do anything about it. Second time I was being walked on. I thought I was in Japan. It was your father, attaching the leeboards."

The sun rose, obscuring C.E.O. and Herpes and the others. The moon hung in there while the sky bleached itself pale.

Another evening in our luxury cruise across the Pacific, I thought, lying on my bunk, attempting sleep. It wasn't easy, even in the master cabin, which is one of the two that have fans. The sheer number of things that needed now to be fixed . . . We were without a genoa, and the mainsail was crippled. The mind boggled.

Was the sextant damaged? The timepieces? In the incoherence of drugged somnambulism I found myself giving orders. *Christo, I said solemnly, I think we are without watches! Start counting! Right now! One Mississippi, Two Mississippi, Three Mississippi—and tell me exactly what time it is*—never mind your other duties as Entertainment Officer—*every time I'm with the sextant and say: Mark!*

But, in my dream, somehow I couldn't engage his attention. Christo just sat there in the saloon, writing away in his journal, hour after hour, day after day, and now, suddenly, he was a small child, six years old, back in Stamford, and I was telling him in his playroom that "How now, brown cow" was the first English sentence I had ever learned, and could *he* write it out? and he said, looking up, clearly skeptical that I had ever engaged in an endeavor so primitive, Of course he could write *How now, brown cow*, why, he could write *The quick brown fox jumped over the lazy dog*, and I embraced him, and he embraced me, and it hasn't, really, changed between us in the years since.

15

TO MAJURO

It was a sweaty business, the morning after Johnston Asshole, as the boys now persistently referred to it in their journals. Traces of the genoa, clinging to the mast, and related chaos needed to be attended to. The mainsail had to be taken down, the two splits sewn together. After this, the spreaders needed to be insulated in some way, so as not to aggravate the chafing problem.

> **Christopher.** At 7:30 Allan appeared and said let's do it. WFB at the wheel, we spent the next hour and a half uncranking the genoa, perched on the pulpit above a school of dolphin whose dorsals suggested what else might be under there, sawing away at the leech with my knife. That sail was *wrapped,* let me tell you. We hauled in the Yankee, hoisted a #3 genny the thickness of flagstone (good —harder to blow). There were the usual screwups, in this case a sheet wound around a stay. I coffee-grinded until my arms started to feel like rigatoni. Getting the damaged main down was trickier, but it was while doing this, hugging the boom with my legs, high above the deck, swinging madly, grunting the sail down its track, that I had a little epiphany: *"This is it,"* the voice said, *"this is the point of it."*

Yes. In a sense Christopher was right, because if such points aren't chanced, neither is that impalpable other thing assured, about which Christopher would in due course sing most sweetly, though never innocently: the pains of childbirth remain painful, and they have a safe-deposit box in the memory.

The electric sail-stitching machine of course wasn't working; or, rather, wasn't strong enough to penetrate the tough Dacron of the mainsail. Which meant that Allan Jouning, assisted by Reggie, spent upward of eight hours, half inch by half inch, sailor's palm and needle in hand, working on the sail. The preliminaries done, the wind was blowing at almost twenty knots, so that we reefed the mainsail, intending to reduce the strain against the spreaders at the sensitive seams. Danny spent a half hour suspended at the spreaders, fastening tapes and emollients of various kinds—anything that would cushion the sail's sawing against the wood. Late in the afternoon we were sailing fully again, and speaking of epiphanies, what I now experienced was one.

The large genoa had given us a good ride, wing-and-wing, but the sail was always too large for the spinnaker pole, making the belly too concave. The Yankee, half the genoa's area, was *exactly* right. The mainsail, slightly reduced in area by the reef, was, in turn, just the right amount of sail. The boom was tightly vanged down (i.e., held rigid), the jibe-preventer secure, and what then happened was quite remarkable: We didn't deviate from course by more than a swing of five or six degrees. Even incipient jibes quickly corrected themselves. And I saw now, for the first time in an oceangoing boat, what a proper whisker pole (designed to do to a jib what a spinnaker pole does for a spinnaker—hold it staid, firm, to windward), with which I was so familiar as a boy, sailing and racing a 17-foot boat, would actually do at sea. It had never worked, the two or three times I tried, on *Cyrano*, to wing-and-wing, using the main staysail swung over to windward. In a schooner the mainmast is situated well aft, and my impression is that because of its location it is harder to guard downwind balance, the leverage being wrong. On a ketch, when the sails are well measured and absolutely secure on either side, the boat's own tendency is self-righting, with or without the mizzen sail. The final test came when, trying out the autopilot, we used it with total

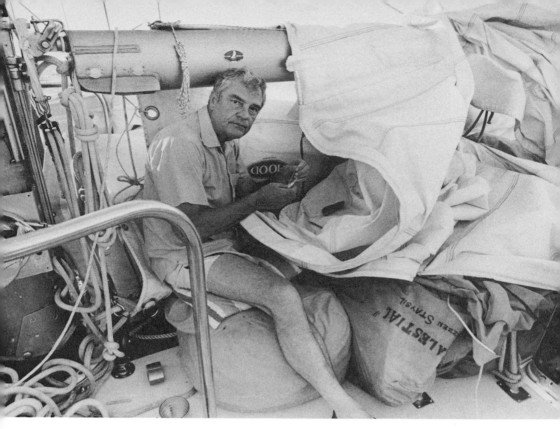

Reggie at the mainsail. Operation 2,001 stitches.

Danny at the spreaders. Operation Anti-Chafe.

The triumphant wing-and-wing rig.

success. The autopilot is not recommended when the wind is fractious, or becomes too strong. But up to a point, one which we had not yet overrun, it is entirely reliable, and indeed less likely to accommodate or to protract a jibe than is a helmsman who has been at the wheel for an hour and whose attention flags, however momentarily. We were doing just fine, and a sense of honed tightness in the vessel, notwithstanding the attrition (no more genoa, a fragile main), gave the impression of a tight ship well aimed, sailing in total harmony with the wind, transcending the curse of downwind waywardness.

I was plagued, during that run, with navigational anomalies. On one occasion, my late afternoon sun sight gave me a longitude by computer that was suspicious, so I worked it out by hand and got a difference of twelve miles. That kind of thing. WhatStar continued to flaunt its conceptual imperfections. Foremost of these, I now knew surely, was the requirement that, in order to identify the star I was shooting, I must correctly assume our position within thirty miles. One evening I shot six stars, and not one of them identified itself on the little screen of the Epson computer. But you see, I had taken an assumed position that was convenient, one where the coordinates crossed, north-south, east-west, for ease of plotting. But this estranged the vessel from the thirty-mile area of operational usefulness.

I redid all the calculations, this time taking an estimated position (where I really thought we ought to be), as distinguished from an assumed position (where I might conveniently assume we were): and four of the stars were forthwith acknowledged by the computer, three of them yielding me a satisfactory fix. But the plotting then became cumbersome. Moreover, WhatStar did not make provisions for bringing in the sun. Nor did it yield a fix by taking, and crossing, two lines of position: and all of this meant more time—sometimes measured in well over an hour—sweating over plotting sheets with dividers, protractors, and parallel rules, with varying assumed positions, to accommodate the computer.

Exactly the kind of thing the computer is supposed to relieve

you of. I find at sea, in my various passages, that I am satisfied with
my celestial navigation to the extent that I successfully pursue the
goal of having it require less and less time to execute. Given computer technology at sea, you shouldn't need to spend more than
fifteen minutes four times a day to wrest from the skies above your
location confidently enough to commission the helmsman's course.
If you spend two or three hours a day at it, you are using your
time inefficiently. Granted, I was conducting an experiment with
WhatStar, and this self-sacrificial, scientist's pose relieved me of
frustration by accounting for the excess labor. But as navigator, I
had other surprises ahead.

After the movie, on the night he had worked so hard on the
mainsail, Allan, relieved of the helm, walked forward on deck to
have a bottle of beer. It was warm, but the wind was sufficiently
brisker than our own hull speed to give us a little net ventilation.
We talked about recent developments in his own life, notably the
advent of Jessica. I talked to him reassuringly about all the women
I knew whose babies were late in coming, and recommended that
by the time Daphne became professional about having children,
she learn from what my own mother did when I (the sixth child)
was late in coming. My mother took two heavy suitcases and walked
up and down in her New York apartment; then went with my
father to the opera, left after the second act, and bore me before
the applause had died down on Act III. Allan laughed, and we
ruminated about his new assignment as captain for William Simon,
the sometime Secretary of the Treasury, whose boat was now being
built in Italy.

I had been involved in this enterprise, however tangentially,
from the beginning. Bill Simon is an old friend, and he scheduled
a lunch with me in the fall of 1983, not revealing his agenda.

He came pretty quickly to the point, spending a mere ten
minutes (something of a record in benign neglect) on the mal-
administration of the economy by Congress, the Fed, the Executive, and the Supreme Court. He wanted to talk about a sailboat.
"I don't mind telling you that what I want isn't exactly conventional. I want the *best*. I want room to move around in. I want to

At the movies. Van and Christo.

be able to live in that sailboat. And I want to *sail* in that sailboat, not putter around."

He was actually asking me for advice. I told him that I had reduced my own ambitions and now owned only my little 36-foot *Patito*. Never mind. He had read my books and he knew that I liked as much comfort afloat as a true sailing boat can get. "I want that, plus."

We met a few times on the subject, and as inevitably happens anytime two sailors sit down to talk about a project, what materializes is: a list. This list went on at considerable length. The boat would be ("What would you think of one hundred and fifty feet?") a thoroughly modern vessel, everything in it that one could want for a long, comfortable life at sea and in port.

For the first time the subject of cost came up, and he wondered what it would require to maintain such a boat as he had in mind. I asked him, Did he know the law of Rusher's Gap, one of the laws formulated by my colleague Bill Rusher, the publisher of *National Review*? No? Well, I said, it's easier to explain *a posteriori* —by giving an example:

You want to build a swimming pool, see, and the pool company's agent makes a few calculations and tells you he figures it will cost ten thousand dollars. But you are a man of the world; you do not get deceived by these perfunctory improvisations. *You* know perfectly well it will cost more. You figure it will end up costing thirteen thousand dollars. Rusher's Gap is the difference between thirteen thousand dollars and what it actually ends up costing.

At which point, trying to act like a man of the world (though come to think of it, in respect of a knowledge of the expense of maintaining boats, I guess I qualify as one), I said: "Put it this way. I'd figure it will come to about the same as maintaining a Learjet."

He liked that. He has a Learjet (as I remember).

Allan laughed for a good ten seconds, which is twice as long as he usually permits himself to laugh. "Fohnny thing. That's just the way 'e put it to me last month. 'Ah figger, Allan, it will cust just about what it custs to keep a Learjet in the air.' "

I recommended Sparkman & Stephens as designers and gave Bill Allan Jouning's name, designating him as the finest sailing captain I had ever been to sea with, specifying only that if they liked each other and made a deal, my captain would not be available during the month of June 1985—"we're going to cross the Pacific together."

Allan spoke now of the exciting new boat whose construction he was supervising. I asked how many crew would be needed to sail the 124-foot beauty (that was the over-all length S & S persuaded Simon was right for the boat he wished), and the astonishing reply to that question tells most eloquently the story of the modernization of sailing craft. Answer: Five.

If he had said fifteen I wouldn't have been surprised. Sailboats become demanding by exponential curve as they increase in size: in cost, in maintenance, in personnel required. Here we were, eleven of us, working about as many hours as one can be expected to work on a protracted day-and-night sea voyage, and providing, from the galley, gourmet fare, less than which the Simons were not likely to settle for. And Simon's *Freedom* would be two thirds again as large as the *Sealestial*—yet it is contemplated that five people will be able to run her, even on long, twenty-four-hour-per-day passages. Racing *The Panic* and *Suzy Wong*, forty-footers, around the clock required eight people (allowing one to be seasick). My 60-foot schooner *Cyrano*, offering tender loving care to charterers, required a crew of four, and that was putting in every night at port. The world had changed: *Freedom* would sail with one captain, one engineer, one mate, one steward, one cook. They would take *Freedom* anywhere in the world, Allan said, itemizing the projected itinerary from the Mediterranean, around the west coast of Africa to Capetown, whence to Perth (4700 miles); up over northern Australia to Hawaii, then to Alaska; eventually south, through the Canal to New England waters; all of this in about two years.

"The most automated bugger," Allan classified it, he had ever imagined, let alone laid eyes on. Aluminum hull, two 56-KW generators, nine sets of 12-volt cells (3700 pounds of batteries for over 2000 amp hours), 4500 gallons of fuel—figure 25 gallons an hour for engine plus generators (they'd be needed for charging only four hours per day). At this rate you have two hundred hours of running time at 10.5 knots; roughly the distance, L.A. to Honolulu. But it's a *sailboat*, which means you don't have to worry, really, about fuel shortage, going anywhere from anywhere. You're going to get wind.

Of course, Allan said, every couple of months he would need to bring people in at port to do heavy-duty revarnishing, that kind of thing. "There's going to be a lot of wood on *Freedom*, and you'll need outside help just to take care of things like that." But at sea, just *five* people. "That's all." The engineer, he explained, would have spent a week or more at each of the special firms they're buying the big big units from: the engine, the refrigeration, the electronics, the generators. "We'll be pretty much self-sustaining,"

William Simon's Freedom . . .

. . . abuilding, in Viareggio, Italy.

Allan said matter-of-factly. Allan does not exaggerate about any-thing.

I asked him, late the next afternoon when we were getting ready for David Niven time, to tell my companions something about the boat we had discussed the night before. "Tell them about the sails, Allan."

Well, he said, put it this way: To get any of the sails to do any-thing—to go up, or come down; to contract in size to exactly the desired area, or to expand—"all you'll have to do on *Freedom* is press a button." Danny, sipping a beer and wearing dark glasses to mute his insolence, observed, "What's so new about that? Press a button is all Bill ever has to do to get sails changed on this boat." I unhappily recorded that everybody found this puerile comment quite funny, Christopher in particular.

> **Dick Clurman.** Danny and Christopher are like two porpoises cavorting, on deck and below. Danny is truly *sui generis*. Although he held our all-time record for sleeping and quaffing gallons of beer in his skin-and-bones frame, he bounds out of a deep sleep with such eternal good cheer that you can count on him for any mission. Up the mast in the bosun's chair with the mast swaying in the wind, he'll spring down below to answer even the slightest suggestion of a request.
>
> It's hard to believe he is thirty-five, a determined entrepreneur who wants to make it for himself and his family. Hard to think of him as anything but the youthful bouncing ball he always is. I can't envision a fifty-year-old Danny, despite his keen intelligence, raven-ous appetite to learn, and devotion to the Buckleys, who unfailingly return that affection. I think he looks slightly askance at me (al-though he would never betray it for a moment), perhaps because I have a hard time being one of the Buckley gang—or any gang, for that matter.

In *Bring on the Empty Horses*, David Niven was now estab-lished as a Hollywood figure. He spoke of Hollywood as a village. "Everybody knew everybody's weaknesses, leanings. There was much camaraderie, a minimum of bitchiness, much college humor."

The "village" was however tyrannized by the two scorpions, Louella Parsons and Hedda Hopper. One of them, David explained, was a strict moralist. She had been married three times and was now wed to a doctor who specialized in venereal diseases. The two ladies had in common only the fact that they "loathed each other." We could understand the notion of a very small village, and of camaraderie, and even of college humor, but it was hard, with the wind playing as it was and the seas so accommodating, to loathe anyone that afternoon, except possibly the sailmaker who had stitched our genoa. Let's celebrate tonight by not drinking to him, I thought, and wondered what full-time malice-mongers eat and drink to feed their bile.

In the course of satisfying my curiosity about Bill Simon's new boat and what it portended, I visited, when I got back, with William Langan, the principal designer at Sparkman & Stephens in New York, and asked him to explain the paradox that soon after the time sailboats ceased to be utilitarian, the most rapid progress was made in their design.

There is an explanation for this, he said. For one thing you have the extraordinary rate of improvement in mechanical and electronic devices. Granted these are of primary concern in powerboats, but they figure also in sailboats. A sailboat designed for cruising (as distinguished from one that is designed only for day racing) profits from many of the developments primarily designed for powerboats.

And, of course, there is the rise in the middle class and the corresponding demand for recreational activity. Utilitarian boats were the instruments of people who mostly worked for a living, and worked most of the time. The abundance of boats is a measure of relative affluence, and with that abundance came competition and the struggle for improvement.

"It has a lot to do," said Langan, who at thirty presides over a staff of fourteen designers, succeeding the legendary Olin Stephens, "with the huge change in materials." Both fiberglass and aluminum make for lighter boats than wood. The advent of Dacron, as a replacement for heavy cotton, made sailboats far less labor-intensive. And, of course, the development of the roller furling gear changed sailing forever. Roller furling permits you, on a sailboat, to activate your genoa by simply winching out the sheet. The roller furling device, at cockpit level forward, unwinds on a cable as you let out correspondingly. The entire big, ballooning genoa floats out into the breeze; when you want to bring it in, you merely rewind the roller furling device, using the winch if necessary. Note that you can arrest the process halfway—and half your genoa is exposed. To sail smartly you would want to relead the clew of the sail, running it forward to get your sail to set properly. But for all intents and purposes your headstay becomes the repository of the genoa, and this is very different from the kind of thing one needs to do on *Sealestial*, say, and needed to do on every sailboat up until a few years ago— dropping the entire sail, bagging it, and putting it away each time after hoisting a different sail. On the hot racing boats they don't tolerate that tiny sag in the headstay intrinsic to roller furling, which doesn't permit the rodlike stiffness of the racing headstay. But for cruising boats, the forfeited incremental speed is exiguous. *Sealestial* would greatly profit from one.

And now they have the open masts that accommodate, winding around a slot, a portion of the mainsail or the whole of it, re-quiring one man only to loosen the clew backhaul, another to pre-side over the furling mainsail; that's all. And the advancement of hydraulics, Langan added, is critical. Electric motors have never been as reliable as they now are. Insulating materials—talk about comfort at sea—are more and more refined. "Modern designers know to look out for disharmonious coefficients, how to watch the mounting blocks, to put up sound boxes. Exhaust systems are care-fully analyzed and properly muffled, engineered with special acoustic materials, combinations of foam. If somebody says he won't tolerate more noise than 40 DB [decibels] at cruising speed, you may need to re-engineer the whole boat."

Freedom is designed as a battery-dependent, rather than generator-dependent, vessel; and stress is placed on water makers. These days a gallon of fuel will produce ten of water, the irony being that here and there fuel is easier to find than water, let alone good water—for instance, in the Virgin Islands.

Communications? Bill Simon considered, but finally rejected, the forty-thousand-dollar SatCom. This is a colossus sheathed by a huge, unsightly dome within which gyroscopic compasses are trained on the relevant satellite. True, the results are miraculous: you get to use your telephone aboard as you would the phone in your home or office. *Freedom* will settle for the conventional single side band—like *Sealestial*'s only better, I confidently assume—plus of course teletypes (great energy consumers, by the way), and, around the corner, there is the GPS I have crooned about.

If the desire is to sail grandly and the resources are there, it does not do today, any more than during the golden age of the huge J-Boats, to count with progressive dismay the dollars spent. The miracle is that—always excepting those cosmic distempers of the sea, which when they come at you simply take over, brushing modern technology out of the way as one would a fly from a lapel— technological progress has provided what would have been thought inconceivable as recently as a generation ago: 1) A big seaworthy sailboat with plenty of room to move about in; 2) stowage for almost everything you need or want, including an electric organ and a Jacuzzi, if that's what you want, 3) huge engines and electrical motors almost soundless—yet, 4) needing only five people to run it, to run a boat longer by 34 feet than the *Mayflower* (which, as we are all given to understand, brought over from England, in 1620, the forefather of approximately every other American everybody knows).

The next morning was Sunday, and as we had done on Sundays ten years earlier on the B.O., Christopher, Danny, and I retreated to my cabin to recite the Mass.

> **Christopher.** After breakfast (Johnston banana-walnut bread, orange slices, coffee), Pup, Dan and I retired to the aft cabin for religious services. WFB said, "Latin or English?" "Latin," I said.

I've gotten spoiled lately by the *Novus ordo* at St. Matthew's. Pup read the priest's part, Dan and I *"et cum spiritu tuo*-ed" along, sitting amid what Van calls the "swill" of WFB's cabin: two months' worth of unanswered correspondence, ammo clips, battery rechargers, insect repellent, manuscripts, peanut brittle—and, most odd of all, a wooden crock of potpourri [from ship's stores, a kind of locker deodorant]: which by day's end was strewn throughout the passageway. Safe to say ours was the only Latin Mass in mid-Pacific? Hard to say. When I was on the *Nimitz*'s bridge watching F-16s and Intruders launch, I became aware of the smell of incense. It's unmistakable to any former altar boy, but there it was wholly incongruous. Turned out it was the Russian Orthodox service.

Later that afternoon Dick made casual mention of our religious exercise and asked Danny whether he was a practicing Catholic, and Danny said yes he was, but that he was reborn, that he had slipped away from the Church for a few years after college. Dick clutched into his Meet-the-Press mode and asked why? I intervened to say that Danny and the Church had different points of view on certain questions involving Danny's first marriage, and we got into the whole business of marriages and divorces and annulments. Experience has forced me to be much less dogmatic than I was many years ago on the question of divorce, though divorce for trivial incompatibilities continues to offend. Only Christopher Little, Christo, and I, in our company, were still wed to our original spouses. Dick's attitude toward religion is very relaxed. He has not the least interest in it for himself, but is very tolerant of it. It is widely ignored by most intellectuals that religion is, among other things, a prodigious intellectual discipline. People who would faint if they could not instantly put their finger on Basutoland on the map would faint if asked to discuss the meaning of the immaculate conception. But we had asked the Lord's blessings, felt better for having done so, and not at all inconceivably, so did the Lord.

Danny, who for three days was suffering from peripatetic ailments (back, throat, neck rashes), was becoming, every day, unaccountably sicker, and Danny-depressed meant the greatest conceivable boat-

wide depressant, since his congenital exuberance is a transfusion of
spirit, aboard as on shore.

> **Christopher.** Should have known something was wrong with
> Danny. For two days he's been drinking Pepsi instead of his usual
> Lite Beer, and barely eating two GooGoo bars a day (as opposed
> to his customary five). Yesterday afternoon the spots on his back
> had multiplied exponentially—looking like a bad case of acne. Reg
> loaded him with two cortisone pills and antihistamines, which have
> knocked him absolutely flat on his ass. Danny is never sick, so on
> those rare occasions when he's laid flat he's an impatient patient.
> But Lord, the poor guy sounds awful: a flu-ish cough, fever, chills,
> dizziness, disorientation, and those nasty bumps all over his back.
> He's been in his bunk now more or less twenty hours, WFB taking
> his watches.
>
> At one point WFB started a mild panic by wondering "if he
> might have chicken pox." People practically started jumping over-
> board. (WFB was not aware that chicken pox in mature males
> frequently causes sterility.) Ears tuned in when he asked Danny if
> he'd had it as a child; a great *suspiro* of relief was heard when he
> replied, "Hell, yes."

Danny would not recover fully until a day or two after we reached
Majuro, where he was given something heady by the local doctor.

Christopher wasn't sick, but wrote of a creeping acedia, which
I had detected, but didn't know he himself had been aware of until
I saw his journal.

> **Christopher.** I have reached a new height (or depth) of listless-
> ness, and am indulging my ennui by eating more or less everything
> put in front of me and a good deal of what isn't put in front of me.
> It's just past 3 in the P.M. So far my intake consists of:
> 2 bowls of Cocoa Krispies
> 1 bowl of Sugar Pops
> 1 Lite Beer (at 11 A.M.)
> 3 helpings of Liz's (fantastic) hot sesame noodles
> 5 buttered crackers
> 1 GooGoo Cluster
> 3 of Liz's (incredible) chocolate chip cookies

By the time I get home I'll look like Jabba the Hutt.

What's truly revolting about this display of piggery is doing it while reading the life of Edmund Campion. You really want to feel degenerate, try doing that. (Something like cramming your face with bonbons and watching news reports of starving Ethiopians.) Here was a man who, condemned to be butchered at Tyburn by Elizabeth's Privy Council, *fasted* in his airless dungeon and remained, praying, on his knees for two days. I began to see why the lives of the saints and martyrs have a hold on us far greater than doctrinal abstractions.

"Oh God," said Augustine, "let me be good—but not yet."

I think I am getting closer to Yet.

Christopher Little had been worried, from the beginning, about his picture-taking. He is very original, but he had used up a lot of that originality on our Atlantic trip, and here he is: substantially the same people, the same ship, on an ocean that does not reveal to a photographer that it lies in the Eastern Hemisphere. But CL never complains, and enjoys even the routine, subject to the usual frustrations, and homesickness.

> **Christopher Little.**   I am sitting in the main saloon. It is the middle of a lazy afternoon. We've just reopened the hatches after a brief tropical shower—refreshing, more than it was unpleasant. The balmy trades continue, thankfully, unabated. We are making good speed with the main (now repaired) and the mizzen on a starboard tack and the Yankee whisker-poled wing-on-wing. Dick Clurman is sitting opposite me at the end of the dining table trying to get a weather forecast without success. He's unable to receive any short-wave, and Van, sitting on the starboard banquette, is telling him that his radio is broken. Christo is lying on my right, dressed in a towel, absorbed by the manuscript of his father's new novel. Bill is, as usual, at the chart table working his fixes. Danny's asleep, and Reg is at the helm. I'll now return to my Dick Francis. Sayonara.

You get accustomed, at sea, to very beautiful sights, but sometimes something comes along that just breaks all the rules. We ran tonight into the most extraordinary sunset, stretches of brilliant reds, each hue disinctive. It gave the impression of an artist returning to a huge canvas time after time, with great swaths of paint,

The photographer's special watch

... provides pictures like this

. . . *and this*

. . . *and this.*

trying out different colors, comparing them. Everyone was silent staring at it, and it seemed almost permanently there: it lasted a full ten minutes in its transfiguring glory. Christopher Little tried to capture it. I haven't seen the print, but I doubt that any lens could succeed in doing so. Liz was enticed from her galley to look. She is always neat, always delicately framed, however grueling her undertaking. She paused in rapt admiration, as did Maureen and Noddy. Allan needs to be prodded to express pleasure or satisfaction, so Dick wrenched it out of him: He had never seen the skies behave quite like that, Allan said.

How one cherishes these contrasts.

> **Christopher.**   I had the first good sleep since leaving Hawaii a week earlier. Woke up only four or five times, once in time to see Dick's Kaypro [computer] swan-dive from the upper berth to the deck.
>
> If Van and WFB's cabin is full of swill, Dick's, Danny's, and mine has become a sty, a veritable *porquería* of muck and detritus. Why three people have been shoehorned into the smallest cabin is of a logic only Himself could ratiocinate. (Yes, yes, I *know* the

"Muck and detritus" . . . and Danny.

verb-form probably doesn't exist.) WFB will tell you—as he told ol' Dick, ho ho—that Dan and I would sleep *al fresco*, in the gorgeous, open, spacious, cozy and select après cockpit. A week's attempts at same, however, yield the empirical conclusion that only a squid, octopus, or other suction-cup-equipped ichthyopod could comfortably slumber there in these seas.

Dick was thus taken to uttering frequent *cris de coeur* about the living arrangements he was promised, as opposed to the living arrangements he got. Yesterday after breakfast I returned to the cabin to a most peculiar (and somewhat ridiculous) spectacle, that of Dick kneeling on a dung heap of duffel and dirty laundry bags, attempting to brush his teeth, his chin level with the edge of the sink, toothpaste foam *partout*: on the sink, on the brush, on the duffel, on the movie bag. The sloth in our cabin, in other words, is rapidly approaching critical mass. In the early hours, groping for the eyeshade, I nearly wrapped some of Danny's underwear over my eyes. Maybe it *is* time to do some storage rethinking.

And Dick's complaints were no less eloquent, and he had to complain, also, of Christo's contumacious behavior . . .

Dick Clurman. The hatch could rarely be opened without taking on cascades of rain or sea water. But that could be refreshing, inasmuch as often I am occupying the hot, sweaty berth that Christo had just evacuated to go on watch. It was so bad that, after some reflection, I decided I didn't mind it. I have always hated mediocre experiences. But incontrovertibly bad ones are memorable. The sailors in *Das Boot* were no more confined. If submariners could take it, so could I. We won the war, after all.

Christo, replacing me on watch at 0500, comes bleary-eyed and unshaven on deck. In the mock jousting that we engage in all the time he says imperiously: "Now I wish to point out a thing or two, Clurman. Number one, there will be no more stepping on me while I'm asleep. Number two, that blue ditty bag of yours has got to go. Number three, give up smoking."

In retrospect, the days went quickly. On the other hand, in retrospect wars pass quickly. There is always a distraction. The

Dick Clurman, provider.

exciting catch of a 40-pound dorado, with the hilarious confusion. Dick, the professional fisherman, bounded up on hearing the swish of his line, shouting instructions to Christopher to bring in the line at the other end of the transom, so that the two lines should not be confused. Dick manfully struggles with his pole, while Christo dutifully brings in the redundant line—only to discover after three or four minutes that *he* is bringing in the fish, while Dick is laboring histrionically with a line that has a stray twig or

Allan illustrates, using gin instead of vodka,
the merciful end to a barracuda instead of a dolphin .

whatever at the end of it. The huge dorado is gaffed into the
after cockpit and the inevitable bloody business of the kill faces
us as the fish flaps ferociously and heavily about. Allan asks Danny
to fetch up some vodka. Bottle in hand, Allan reaches over and
pours a jigger of it into the fish's gill: the result is miraculous. The
fish is instantly dead. Van said he must remember never to take
any vodka into his gill.

The (first) rain came.

Christopher Little. Christo and I reveled in the drenching rains, a heavenly relief from the heat. We washed our hair with fresh-water shampoo—a real treat—and photographed one another with the two underwater cameras. Soon, of course, it became chilly, and we looked forward to the sunshine which returned in due course.

We were moving. Indeed, in due course that day we entered the Eastern Hemisphere. Majuro would come soon. Tomorrow, before

*Keeping cool and clean, using ship's hose and salt water
. . . or using the elements.*

the midnight watch was completed, I prophesied sagely, coming up from my books.

> **Christopher.** Dick and I had the International Date Line watch. Thought the occasion called for . . . something. We discussed going around every foc's'le, banging on the door and yelling, "Just crossed the International Date Line!" but on reflection we decided this approach would in all likelihood not meet with favor. Flares? We liked the idea, but it too was abandoned when we determined we'd probably set fire to the sails in the process.
>
> I then remembered: my tape of "Victory at Sea."
>
> My heavens, what perfect International Date Line music. We stood up straight, looked off into the horizon with commodorial mien. Great stuff, that overture. When I went to take a pee over the side and looked off into the moonlight I saw a line of battleships. We planned a surprise for Reg and Chris, the relieving watch. Waited until they arrived in the cockpit, groggily, then hit the Play button and on it came, full blast. It was a very funny effect—until Reg allowed as how he'd been listening to it for the last twenty minutes.
>
> "Oh," I said, "you mean you could hear it in your cabin?"
>
> "Yes," he said.
>
> Dick was funny about it. He asked me who wrote it. I said Aaron Copland. He answered that he was related to Aaron Copland and talked at some length about how you could discern Copland's "tonalities" in the piece we were listening to, though, he allowed, it seemed quite a departure for Copland. I, not knowing about these areas of sophistication, merely nodded. At this point the recording came to its dramatic finis and the announcer's voice was heard.
>
> "We've been listening to 'Victory at Sea' by Richard Rodgers."

A few hours later, while we were watching the movie *My Man Godfrey*, Allan hailed us from the wheel. He had spotted a light. Majuro.

I bounded up onto the cockpit, pleased that it was coming out when I said it should. But although we approached what turned out to be an aero beacon, the question of how to find the narrow entrance to the harbor, in the dark, with ambiguous radar sightings, was unsettled: the bearing on the light didn't correspond with the land outlines we were looking for. Moreover, the bearing to the beacon kept changing: 225 degrees, 215 degrees, 180 degrees, 160 degrees, until at 120 degrees it became clear that we had come upon a current that had set us westward. I knew now that in order to find the channel, we would need to go north for over an hour, then east into the current for over two hours, then duck south and southeast, the latter inadvisable at night.

So I said in bad bureaucratese, "Let's call it an emergency layover."

I decided against heaving to. Instead, we lowered the headsail and killed time with a reefed mainsail, coming about every hour. I gave out two-hour watches, rose at six, put on the engine, and, now that light permitted it, followed the coastline. In three hours we spotted the channel entrance. We had traveled 2300 statute miles.

16

MAJURO

Having tried and rejected the "Old Port" as a docking area (too full of junk and deserted or semideserted tankers), we put in at the "New Port," a mile and one-half down, the "District Center" of the Marshall Islands. Standing there in the sunshine was a genial young foreign service officer to greet us, Michael Senko, U.S. consul in Majuro. He was dressed in neat shorts and what looked like a strawish hat, had been expecting us following Allan's call by radio the evening before, and drove Van, Dick, and me off in his jeep while the others went through off-loading exertions and waited for Customs to clear us.

He took us to his office, a few cubicles in a building of cubicles that includes government offices. We were pretty bleary, but wanted to telephone. I recorded in my desiccated journal, for reasons I cannot now imagine, that I had asked Mike for the key to the men's room, was shown it a hundred yards down the hall, entered and found there was no toilet paper, returned to Michael's office and said could I have some toilet paper, causing him to go to a closet and fish out another key, after which I re-trekked to the men's room, and reappeared a few minutes later to inform Michael that the toilet did not flush, causing him to say that life in Majuro was a little bit that way.

My, but he was obliging. After our telephone calls he took us back to the vessel, where we ran into a little official consternation. "The Port Authority man," Christopher noted, "is all bent out of shape because half the people are ashore without having been cleared first and oh—then the Copra Man arrives and fixes things. Smiles, waves—and we're off." The "Copra Man" is one of those generic presences one comes upon in little satrapies, whose materialization brings on instant mollification. The sun was very bright overhead, we were very hot and hungry and thirsty and dirty, and we were surrounded by an appalling accumulation of bulging plastic laundry bags, twenty of them. Two weeks, eleven people, plus ship's laundry; no wonder. We went then to a huge modern shopping center—never mind that it was Sunday and that the Marshallians are very religious (and very licentious)—to pick up whatever it was we felt was indispensable that we pick up—oh, of course: newspapers! The *Marshall Islands News!* And *Newsweek* only two weeks old. Plus, of course, flashlights. No cruising man ever passes a store that sells flashlights without buying flashlights, given that no one has yet thought to engineer a flashlight that lasts more than a few days aboard an oceangoing sailing boat.

At the diner, a large, affable, bored Micronesian lady, weighing perhaps two hundred pounds, stood while the two Christophers and I, at one booth, pondered the menu. After about fifteen seconds, she sat down on the vacant part of Christopher Little's bench, as if to say, Take your time, but don't expect me to stand up through it all.

We had hamburgers, I think, and Christopher Little passed about some wine bottles we had brought from the boat. I attempted to brief the Christophers on what Mike had told me about these atolls, most of which we had read in books we had aboard. The following morning would be devoted to official business—we would meet with the president and his cabinet, and discuss "The Compact." Mike would leave us alone this afternoon, after checking us into the Marshall Sun Hotel where, in anticipation, he had reserved some rooms, and that evening would take us to a pig roast if we chose, and we could in the meantime of course walk, swim, ride about (Dick had found, and hired, a car in a matter of minutes after we arrived). Our first non-Liz meal in a fortnight, and oh, what a difference, and how we mourned those who need to eat other than at Liz's cuisine.

We drove off to the motel. As I was signing in, Christopher pointed to the sign above the air conditioner:

ATTENTION!

PLEASE DON'T TOUCH THE MACHINE.

IS COMING FREEZE!

Christopher.   Ranks with the sign in my hotel room in Puerto Barrios, Guatemala:

MANAGEMENT IS NOT RESPONSIBLE

FOR VALUES LEFT IN ROOM

The Marshall Sun Hotel looks a bit like something the U.S. military might have built for the Los Alamos boys who set off "Bravo" and the other H-bombs north of here: strictly cinderblock, plywood corridors—you kind of bounce as you walk—neoprene pillows and beaverboard air conditioners with Japanese buttons, requiring some experimentation before providing the promised "freeze." It was all painted in a yellow designed to stir feelings of sun and cheer in the guests, but which, bathed in hot fluorescence, created the atmosphere of a veterinary hospital. The Japs must have had a moment of aesthetic remorse at the last minute; each room had a wood beam, painted chocolate, spanning the ceiling. Nice touch, guys! It was spartan, but it was clean; it was dry and it didn't move. It was beautiful.

We slept that afternoon, oh my how we slept. Each in his own little room. The joys of privacy.

At the pig roast, at about 7 P.M., where we came upon Allan and Noddy and Liz, there were perhaps a hundred Americans, some of them serious Marshallians, most of them semitransients, here to work on a construction project or whatever, gone tomorrow or the day after. They all spoke to us about the island, about the natives' excitement over their forthcoming manumission (The

Compact would set them free), but also about their acknowledged dependence on American capital and welfare. The Marshall Islands are in fact a welfare project of the United States. One construction engineer who had been around for a while said he had no confidence that anyone would ever get around to changing the oil in the generator he had just finished installing (or unstick the toilet, I thought?). An airline pilot said the great pity of this cluster of Pacific islands is that people tend to come to Majuro because this is the administrative capital, but the island is surrounded by beautiful atolls, for instance, Aur. In fact, just across the lagoon, three miles west along the northern shore, he said, it becomes utterly beautiful—beach, palms, white sand, everything one goes to the Pacific for. But here, he said, life revolved, for a good while after the war, around the 10,000-foot World War II runway, and though there's a lot of commercial activity, there isn't yet any real sense of community.

We didn't eat much pig, because we would eat supper at the hotel, to which we returned in due course. The South Pacific Handbook had this under the section "Amenities of Majuro": "There are three cinemas showing American and Kung Fu movies . . . Single females on Majuro have a reputation for permissiveness, some starting as young as twelve years old. Juvenile-fixated men unfortunately still take advantage of this; a sad situation in D-U-D." That stands for Dalap-Uliga-Darrit, which is the greater metropolitan area of Majuro. Christopher's comment on this aside in the Handbook:

> There was no hanky-panky on the part of the crew of *Sealestial.* It turned out we docked right next to the local bordello, a chicken-wire and shanty affair off the rutted road. The ladies cooed and clucked at us as we drove by. We whistled back but slowed only so we could get a glimpse of the cockfight being held there.
>
> This was a long way from our Horta landfall of ten years ago, when Danny frantically told Carlos our cab driver to find us—counting us in the back seat—"one, two, three, four, *five* women, Carlos. We need five women." We're all married now, and the

blood lies a little tamer in the veins (thank *God*) as the Age of Aquarius became the age of Herpes. So we wish you well, ladies of the Majuro nights, but we'll pass all the same. Our landfall thus was not the same as Melville's on his first arrival in Pacific parts:

"Our ship was now wholly given up to every species of riot and debauchery. Not the feeblest barrier was interposed between the unholy passions of the crew and their unlimited gratification. The grossest licentiousness and the most shameful inebriety prevailed, with occasional and but short-lived interruptions, through the whole period of her stay. Alas for the poor savages when exposed to the influence of these polluting examples! Unsophisticated and confiding, they are easily led into every vice, and humanity weeps over the ruin thus remorselessly inflicted upon them by their European civilizers. Thrice happy are they who, inhabiting some yet undiscovered island in the midst of the ocean, have never been brought into contaminating contact with the white man."

Sucker could *write*.

The dinner menu was the same, but literally the same, as that at the diner. And the conversation focused very nearly exclusively on the question whether we should now head for Kosrae, easternmost of the Caroline Islands, or to Ponape, at the center of the Carolines. The difference is a couple of hundred miles, but then if we head toward Kosrae, a day or two out we'll run into the big easterly countercurrent, a sausage 300 miles wide and three thousand miles long squatting just south of us and extending all the way to Indonesia. We'll have to traverse that sausage to get to New Guinea, but if we head due west we could stay in favorable currents until ready to dip down into Ponape. I yield to Christopher's recounting . . .

Over dinner at the Sun (a not bad cabbage tempura and gristly teriyaki) Pup said *We gotta make a decision here* about whether to proceed on to Ponape or duck down to Kosrae. Old Van sort of took the floor, as he now does sort of *all* the time (being ambassador seems to have suited Van) and starts in on this pitch for Kosrae. Sounded like a one-man Chamber of Commerce. All about how it's got great volcanic formations and it's only half the distance, blah

blah. As he went on, a procession of gringos stopped by our table to chat. To each one we put the question: Ponape or Kosrae? Like a Greek chorus they all kissed their fingertips, rolled their eyes, and sang a song of Ponape; of waterfalls, mysterious ruins, night life, lagoons, the Village Hotel . . . Van meanwhile hunkered down and kept talking about Kosrae. At one point he really covered himself with snake oil, saying that well, hell, *everyone's* heard of Ponape, and we ought to be adventurous enough to go to someplace no-body's ever heard of.

"Van," says I, "you're not suggesting anyone back home has *heard* of Ponape, now, are you?"

"Look," he says, pointing at the Continental-Air Micronesia map, "it's on a major air route."

Uh-huh.

Van kept up this palaver for two hours, but WFB finally came down *firmly* on the Ponape side. Next day it occurred to me Van was just up to his trick of trying to rush-rush to Kavieng [in New Ireland] so's he can get to his farewell party in Paree.

"You really had me going there," I said to him over pancakes. "You actually sounded sincere about wanting to go to Kosrae."

He twinkled. "Well," he says, "I can sound sincere about a *lot* of things."

I decided to begin the morning by jogging with Van, which come to think of it is the first time I had ever jogged, preferring for my aerobics an indoor bicycle opposite a television set. Van's deli-cate paternalism is touching. I thought I was keeping up with his normal gait, but after about a mile, when I said I thought that was about right for half my ration, instead of turning back with me and jogging alongside until we reached the hotel, and then going on at his own clip to make his own distance, he said he would keep going and return by himself. That way he would not embarrass me by moving ahead of me while we were headed in the same direction, nor inhibit his own, greater speed.

Back at the hotel, having breakfast, Christopher, Danny, and Reg professed to be astonished at the sight of me thus engaged, which elicited from me a few homilies having to do with *mens sana in corpore sano*, and perhaps I even remembered to add that the navigator and skipper on this voyage could not afford to be self-indulgent and get sick and fat and weak from indolence and over-indulgence. I cannot recall whether that was all that I said.

Plans: Christopher Little, Reg, and Christo would go scuba diving, after formally greeting the president, even though this meant they would have to put on long pants for the brief audience. Danny would go to the hospital and be treated for his leprosy. Van, Dick, and I would stick it out with the government, and hear about The Compact, and after that perhaps tour a little with Mike Semko.

The president and his prime minister and two or three members of his cabinet were a nice combination of *gravitas* and good humor. They were dressed in slacks and open shirts. We met in an office that might have served as a middle-class living room, and introductions were made with some formality, Van always addressed as "Mr. Ambassador," our hosts addressed, by us, with their appropriate titles. The Compact is an instrument on which fifteen years of negotiation have been spent, and the special concern of the president was that individual senators and congressmen should not now pick it apart. Mike had reminded us that there were only two "free associations" surviving of the character of ours with Micronesia, the others being that of New Zealand and the Cook Islands. Something like the current Compact, yielding independence to Micronesia, had come close to fruition a few years back, but Senator Scoop Jackson didn't like a feature in it which would have permitted Majuro's government to extend equal commercial rights to Communist countries, for instance fishing rights and landing rights on our huge World War II airstrip. The president had assured everyone engaged in the negotiations that the Marshallians (one thinks, using that half-word, inevitably of the turn-of-the-century economic school) were totally pro-American, and that what mattered, after all—or ought to, on the question of strategic alignments —was that The Compact remits to the United States all rights in respect of defense policy.

The real sticker, one official freshly back from Washington candidly explained, was the business of taxation. Absolutely necessary, he said; the Marshalls *had* to have the means to attract American capital—that, or they wouldn't be able to make a go of it economically. And the way to attract American capital was seductive tax laws. Accordingly, The Compact grants to Americans who spend 183 days in the Marshalls every year immunity from U.S. taxation on any income already taxed by the Marshalls. With such hedges, Majuro couldn't become a convenient place for America's Barbara Huttons to build palazzi in for the purpose of shielding the whole of their income. Only income actually generated locally and locally taxed (highest rate: 12 percent) would be shielded. Add to this protection against abuse the high probability that the Barbara Huttons of this world would never consent to spend 183 days in the Marshalls. The president suddenly broke into a smile and asked me whether I would write a column in support of The Compact? and I said I would, provided the president would promise to erect a bronze statue of me in the center of the city park. He and I shook hands on that one and, after an hour, we left.

Mike took us on a tour of Majuro, embarrassingly easy to do: there is nothing there, to speak of, except a tiny museum and lots of shopping centers. I had a problem discharging my *petite commission*, which was to buy 300 pounds of block ice. After three false stops, I came finally on what looked like a neglected Confederate mini-plantation house in the middle of the city. I assumed I had yet again a wrong address, but after I knocked on the door a large black woman emerged, heard me out, said nothing but vaguely beckoned as she shuffled down the staircase from the porch to the ground floor, pulled a key out of her billowing floral dress, inserted it in a wooden door, and opened what turned out to be a huge freezer.

Back at the Sun Hotel, we lunched, expecting at any minute the return of the three divers, and were reunited with Danny, who was full of body-balm, pills, and his uplifting good humor. Mike told us he had had a cable from Ambassador Paul Gardner in Port Moresby. He wished to have a dinner for us on the night we would spend there before leaving for Australia to fly back to the States, and did we want only American personnel, or did we want New Guinea-Papuan officials? I opted for the former, sensing our probable fatigue by the time we got to Port Moresby, and Dick intervened and asked Mike to request that the dinner costume be tieless, which request I vetoed, promising Dick I would give him plenty of time to reintroduce him to the rigors of wearing a tie at an ambassador's dinner; Van chuckled, but was aloof from the discussion —he'd have left us before we got to Port Moresby.

After lunch, we checked everyone out of the Marshall Sun Hotel, to expedite things in general, and called for the laundry. The load must have kept the staff up all night, but out it came, what seemed like truckfuls of the stuff. Dick approached us in astonishment as he pieced his wallet back together: the entire load was done for twenty dollars. The cost, almost anywhere else we can think of, would have been twenty times that.

We got to the boat—still no divers. I became anxious. Mike called the weather station to inquire whether there had been any emergencies. Negative. When, at 3 P.M.—two hours after expected —they finally showed up, I came as close as I ever did to being censorious; but they were all glowing with such happiness over the beautiful reef they had explored, I satisfied myself with a private word to Christo.

Indeed it had apparently been extraordinary. Christopher Little described it:

> The outer motus of the atoll are unspoiled. We outboarded the length of the lagoon, out to the pass which we had traversed one and a half days earlier, and donned our scuba gear. Reg is an experienced diver; it was Christo's third dive; and I suppose I fall somewhere in between, with twelve hours underwater. Over the side we went onto one of the most spectacular reefs I've ever seen (which is saying something, since I've dived in such places as the Seychelles and Malindi, Kenya, in the Indian Ocean; St. Lucia in the Caribbean; Bermuda in the Atlantic; and Tahiti in the Pacific). We saw incredible table coral. They look like immense toadstools, the umbrellas of which are three feet in diameter and overlap one another in a great subterranean forest. A four-foot white-tipped shark passed us by, sadly (or, perhaps, happily) out of camera range. We saw a giant sea turtle making his way out to sea and a rather gruff-

looking barracuda. Poor Reg had inadequate weights on and had a
terrible problem descending. From time to time I would look up
forty feet to the surface and see Reg looking like a wounded whale
trying to squash the last cc. of air out of his buoyancy control vest
and his lungs. Christo was a natural, and we all resolved to dive
again next chance we get. Which would be?

Ponape, I had decreed.

But the next swim was only an hour or so off. The *Sealestial*
headed out, after we thanked Mike effusively for his kindness, to
the spot across the lagoon the airline pilot had told us about the
night before (never neglect, or fail to inquire after, local knowledge). It was as he said, ideal. Quiet, indeed isolated. We swam
lazily about in the clear water, using face masks. We read, and listened again to David Niven as the sun went down.

We swam lazily . . . or not at all.

Tonight it was an account of David's fast friendship with Errol Flynn. "You always knew exactly where you stood with Flynn because he always let you down, and always let himself down." He "enjoyed turmoil." Niven went through the early marriages of Flynn, including Lili, whom he married and quickly tired of, finally proposing to David that they share a house, which they proceeded to do, renting it from Rosalind Russell. There they lived the gay life of bachelors, and there was the night David thought he heard someone outside, which turned out to be Walter Wanger, given to expressing his jealousy by very direct action. He was looking for Joan Bennett and suspected she was upstairs in the bedroom with Clark Gable. David was able to swear that this was not so, concealing that Flynn was *downstairs* sharing a *couch* with Joan Bennett. "Women loved him passionately . . . not a kind man, but fun to be with. We were the best of friends." David, the impression to the contrary notwithstanding, did not like *everybody*. E.g., I know that he loathed Victor McLaglen. And he respected big Hollywood figures who, however warm in the end in friendship, were cautious in entering into them. He spoke of the legendary home of Ronald Colman, in which Robert Louis Stevenson and Galsworthy had written books and stories, where John F. Kennedy spent much of his honeymoon. Colman lived there with his wife, who loved cupcakes more even than Ronnie and lived to make a million dollars and eat all the cupcakes she wished. Colman hated only one man, Sam Goldwyn, against whom he would "fulminate, a large scotch in his hand. Apart from Goldwyn, I never heard Ronnie say an unkind word about anyone." A fine sentiment for the evening.

And then we were reintroduced to Liz's wonderful cooking. But no movie tonight. It was time to go.

Dick Clurman. Bill, as always, is eager to get moving. So we set out again, reluctant and panting. What does it sound like on deck? What is all this scintillating conversation people on land assume we constantly have? First things come first and it is often pure business —the business of sailing. So here's how it sounded that typical evening, with the strains of Bach playing in the background:

BILL: "Okay, we're going to be heading out of here with the main-sail—I think maybe we won't bother putting up the Yankee until we get up through the channel and set our regular course. We'll use a little power if necessary to augment, then when we get out we'll sail two-six-zero which is due west. If the wind is as I expect, slightly north of east—Maureen, who'd like some Sanka?—we'll be able to carry it. If it happens to be due east, then we'll face the stick [spin-naker pole] problem. That will be sort of at the changing of the shift point. There will be no—I think—point in putting up the Yankee for this six-mile stretch given that, uh—as a matter of fact, what is that, forty-five degrees? Yeah. I think we can put it up, sure we can, 'cause it's a northwest course. Sure, we can put 'em both up. Because when we head up, there isn't anything we can't do with a northeast or east wind that would overtax the Yankee. So when we set out of here we'll put up first the main, and then the Yankee. We'll be on a starboard tack."

VAN: "With or without the pole?"

BILL: "Without the pole. We may not use the pole at all, Christo, tell them to stick on the compass light."

REG: "It's [the wind] about forty degrees."

BILL: "Well, that's super. It couldn't be more northeast if it tried. That's absolutely super, forty degrees [magnetic] being of course fifty degrees [true], so we'll go out on both sails.

REG: Bring the light down a little more; we need nail polish on it [to avoid the light's glare]. We sure as hell need that."

VAN: "We could tape the flashlight on this rail."

BILL: "Take Reggie's advice. He's always right on these things. It should be down farther. Let's get it installed right now."

CHRISTO: "Is there a little bit of red wine behind you?"

BILL: You don't seriously think I wouldn't let you have some red wine?"

DICK: "You'll find duct tape in my fishing box."

BILL: "Who's on duty with me? Skipper, could we confer for a moment? We've got wind coming in at forty degrees, which is nice. We've got [a course] straight west, which is two-six-zero, to that flasher where that channel begins, then it's northwest and we should be able to see two lights at that point plus the channel, but there's no problem if we drift a little bit, i.e., in terms of depth. When we get out of the channel a course of due west is the thing to take, on a starboard tack with the Yankee up, and the mainsail up but no pole, and then tomorrow we'll do a GPS to make sure we're not in the countercurrent. If we are in the countercurrent we'll head up fifteen degrees and get out of it. So from here due west takes us right to the little flasher. What we want to do when you're ready— what we'll do—is pull up the anchor, head down a half mile, put up the mainsail and then put up the Yankee."

VAN: "Does that light show?"

BILL: "The flasher? No."

DICK: "They may have stolen the battery."

Often that was exactly what happened, the scuba guide had told Reggie and Christopher. It is one reason why night landings are less frequent than they might be. But we didn't absolutely need that flasher, not going out. Pulling out was easily done, marred only by a different reading on the radar in which I emphatically disagreed with my son, who, after a minute or two, I recognized was correct. I apologized.

On our way. We had done half the distance.

17

TO KOSRAE

I note my entry in the log, at one in the morning: "We are headed for A-I-L-I-N-G-L-A-P-A-L-A-P Atoll, for no other purpose than to avoid running into it. Its southern shore is 140 miles from NW point of Majuro. At 258 M [magnetic]. But we can only sail well at 270 deg.

"Continue at 270 deg. if wind stays as is. Then, tomorrow, we'll make necessary sail changes: probably Yankee to windward. Plenty of time. EP [estimated position] is on plotting sheet.

"Winds 20 knots ENE. Barometer at 1002. (Please return navigational tools to navigational tray.)"

A couple of reflections here. The unpronounceable atoll becomes entirely negotiable if you simply think mnemonically. Begin by breaking down those Polynesian names, which tend to run on a bit, into one- or two-syllable components. We would soon have that trouble with Kapingamarangi, until it conquered us, so much so that whatever its name, it was tattooed in the memory. The atoll we needed to watch out for now, eighteen hours' sail down the line, is easily referred to as, simply, "*Ailing.*" Watch out for "Ailing"! *If you hit Ailing, you will be ailing.* Better, in order not to hit it, *to take a lap around it*, well offshore. A *lap?* you say. We should *lap a lap* around *ailing?* I'll just contract that: Ailinglapalap.

Double-checking navigational calculations with Reg.

Nothing to it.

Another thought. The wind was crowding us on our starboard wing-and-wing course, but not enough to justify jibing to a port tack. It made sense to proceed twenty or thirty miles before doing this. We had got awfully spoiled about being able to sail dead on course.

And yes, the little housekeeping note. Dick is right that I am bad about putting things away, but absolutely indispensable things freeze me into an entirely different gear. Indispensable things, for the navigator, are his dividers, his pencil, his protractor, his parallel rules, his plotting sheet, his watch, his sextant, and his calculator. I really *didn't like it* when I had to scratch around to locate any of these. Danny is himself rather informal about where he last put something, but I find he too likes to have navigational gear at hand, though last summer, I suddenly remember, it took him a half hour to find the Tide Table. Which reminds me that I read somewhere that they now have got the tides for the principal ports on the U.S. Atlantic coast on a computer. I shall have to speak to Hugh Kenner about onloading that program to my Epson, after we get around to tuning up WhatStar.

And oh, yes, I have yet another weakness not, astonishingly, yet remarked by my colleagues or my son in their Manichaean *tours d'horizon* of my delinquencies. I *hate* to write by hand. This is in part because I am congenitally indecipherable. This has never been an affectation, rather an affliction, probably related to the same affliction that causes me to make numerous typing errors, and errors also on the piano and harpsichord. (If I practiced for ten years, I probably could not succeed in playing the Minuet in G without making at least one mistake.) Accordingly, when I need to write by hand I reach out for all available abbreviations. Thus, in the logbook, the note I entered about the navigational tools reads, exactly reproduced:

> *Please return*
> *navigational tools to*
> "   *tray*

I had thus spared myself the need to rewrite a five-syllable word. You laugh. Professor Willmoore Kendall, when I was an undergraduate, dined with me at a local eatery. I ordered a steak, he ordered hamburger steak. I asked him why, and he said that it was 25 cents cheaper, and at the end of a year the accumulation of economies practiced on that scale made the difference between balancing his budget and not. I feel a little that way when I read while shaving, watch telly while biking, and contrive to use a ditto mark when the alternative would have required me to write out, n-a-v-i-g-a-t-i-o-n-a-l. *Bon soir.*

The following morning I made an error in judgment. The winds were fractious, there were radio reports of a great doldrum in the

Ponape area, the fair current hadn't given us the 15-mile lift it was supposed to have done, so I decided to skip Ponape and head southwest for Kosrae. I gave the new heading, and prayed silently that the countercurrent would come to us leniently.

It did not. It slowed the vessel to 140 miles per day, a huge penalty. The following day Reggie, in his gentle way, drew me a vectored diagram of forces, on the basis of which I acknowledged that we'd have done better sticking to the westerly course, and dipping down to Ponape at the last minute.

But it's also true that I was feeling, at this point, a kind of hour-by-hour anxiety about the bloody schedule. Van would forgive me without second thought if he missed George Bush, the Fourth of July, his wedding anniversary, and Thanksgiving: but it is precisely because he *is* that way with his friends that I was most anxious not to make him miss his deadline, let alone the deadline forty-eight hours later on which so many others of us depended.

The distances left to go at that point: 370 miles to Kosrae, 650 to Kapingamarangi, 350 to Kavieng, 170 to Rabaul. A tight schedule.

I was experiencing a fresh frustration with navigation in the Eastern Hemisphere. I'd done, in 1978, some celestial work sailing in and around Fiji, and twice before in the Bay of Biscay, both securely situated in the Eastern Hemisphere. But my HP-41C was not giving me reliable readings when I fed it an Eastern Hemisphere assumed position. The instructions (by Hugh Kenner) clearly indicated that, in the Eastern Hemisphere, longitude entries should be preceded by a minus sign, thus (it appears on the calculator screen: "Long? E—") I dutifully entered the minus sign before putting down the longitude; but the answers were wrong, I sensed, and confirmed this by working them out mechanically. The facile solution to the problem was to postulate my position at the closest point in the Western Hemisphere, and accept a long Intercept (as they call it in navigation) even though this would look progressively ungainly on the plotting sheet as we got farther and farther away from the International Date Line, which is where west becomes east. I would think about this, and see if I could figure out what was wrong.

At lunch Dick Clurman, who likes to speculate, commented on the loneliness we had experienced during the entire time of our sail. Not one ship sighted, sail or power; not one airplane spotted.

This has never surprised me at sea, perhaps because the first ocean passage I sailed was on the 1956 Newport-Bermuda race when, beginning five hours after our departure and lasting until five hours before our arrival, we saw not a single other vessel, even though over one hundred boats were racing with us on the same course. Ocean sailing is not a gregarious exercise. Still, on the transatlantic passages we had become accustomed to spotting a commercial vessel two or three times a week, more often as we neared Gibraltar. Dick now raised his hypothetical question for that day: "Suppose POTUS wanted Van for some imperatively urgent reason?"

"Who is POTUS?" I asked.

Dick explained. Those are the initials regularly used in the relevant channels for the President of the United States. There was speculation on how long it would take a) for a satellite to spot us, our general route being known; b) then for a seaplane to be dispatched and c) to reach us from . . . Guam? Dick would settle for eighteen hours to remove Van from the *Sealestial*, nothing less. Van volunteered that he would gladly cooperate any time a President needed his advice, which should be "constantly."

> **Dick Clurman.**   I am often asked by innocents how I can get along with Bill, the real leader of the conservative movement in America. No problem. Van, however, at times makes Bill seem like a dangerous left-winger. No problem either. I delight in Van's company, even his confident, if usually off-the-wall solutions to all the world's problems. But occasionally he stretches not just *me* but even Christo. At lunch we were talking about Cristo's forthcoming *Esquire* piece on the Vietnam Memorial. Van begins to tell how "we could have won the war if we'd done the right thing." I tune out, mostly, after one or two forays that don't make a dent. Finally Christo says, "Van, you don't know what the hell you're talking about." "Okay," says Van with his usual conviviality. "Hey, look at that full moon up there."

From left, Alger, Cain, Caligula, Iago, Rasputin, Teddy.

From left, Christo, Danny, WFB, Dick, Christopher, Van, Reggie.

It lasted a full ten minutes in its transfiguring glory.

"The sea's distemper..."

Reg, after the blow.

The sailing was steady, wing-and-wing, the sky dull but placid, and those of us off watch went to attend to our off-sailing duties, I below to continue with the unanswered mail.

I reached for a letter from Walter Cronkite, a devoted fellow amateur sailor: the kind of letter that brings serenity and pleasure for hours after reading it.

He writes:

Dear Bill:

Often I have thought how lucky I have been to be a journalist, even of sorts, in perhaps the most exciting and portentous half-century of the world's history.

Occasionally something spoils that happy illusion. Such an event has just transpired. I have just read the full text of your speech at the dedication of *U.S.-44*.

I had heard many favorable comments on the talk at King's Point (it should be Kings Point, Bill Safire please note) but I had not realized until reading it how eloquent and appropriate it was.

I'm sorry I missed you at the Grove. We must stop not meeting each other like this.

All the best,
Walter

Cronkite was being copiously generous, but to the extent he meant to say that I had obviously enjoyed myself, he was right, as I had framed remarks appropriate to the rodomontade of athletic rah-rah pep talk, using the kind of hyperbole half expected in such situations, and always welcome to the ear ("You-are-the-greatest sailors-since-Ulysses" kind of thing).

I thanked him for his kindness, reflecting as I often do on the great sustaining weight the little gentilities carry, the unbought graces . . . I had in my briefcase a copy of the speech I had given a fortnight earlier, reread it after I finished the hour set aside for correspondence, and passed it around, knowing that Reggie especially would be interested, as a member of a competing syndicate.

It had been in April that Walter Cronkite had called and asked, on behalf of the "America I" syndicate, if I would do the baptismal remarks on the launching of *U.S.-44*, the sister ship of *U.S.-42*, whose launching Cronkite had consecrated a few months earlier. I am not an expert on twelve-meter racing, and never pretended to be, but I had agreed, as a longtime member of the New York Yacht Club, to serve as a member of the syndicate and said sure, though only after questioning Cronkite on what exactly was expected. "You can say any old thing," said old pro, yachtsman Cronkite. Nothing in particular occurred to me as of intrinsic importance to say, except that I made a note to touch on the tender subject of the money and time being spent on the creation of the challenger.

It was a lovely, windy, bright day in May, at Kings Point. There was a luncheon, presided over by the superintendent of the Merchant Marine Academy and the commodore of the New York Yacht Club, the principal sponsor in this venture in irredentism. There was a gallery of a few hundred people, a lot of flags flying, and the crew of the *U.S.-44*, under superskipper John Kolius, all of them standing proudly aboard their vessel during the ceremonies.

On being introduced, I launched straightaway into the hyperbolic mode:

> About fifteen years ago I attended with my wife a state dinner at the White House, in fact, for us, the first. I was not intimidated by the presence there of our host, the President of the United States, whom I had met here and there when he was engaged in climbing the grimier rungs that lead to that high office. But the prospect of being presented to him by the Chief of Protocol was positively unnerving.

That alone would stir the attention of one of my principal targets—

> Getting dressed a half hour earlier, across the street at the Hay-Adams, I said to my wife, "You do realize that the Chief of Protocol is Bus Mosbacher, who won the America's Cup?" [There—the most important thing in life is the America's Cup.] To which she replied,

"You evidently don't realize that you have told me that five times in the last five days." [The amiable sports fanatic is introduced.]

It was with great awe that I took the hand of Bus Mosbacher, staring at him as I suppose I'd have stared at Christopher Columbus or Galileo. You see, in those days I used to do ocean racing quite regularly, and hard though we tried, we never managed, somehow, to come in with the winners. [A discreet self-detachment, entirely justified, from the company of those accustomed to occupying the winners' circles.] I remember disconsolately, after my first Bermuda race, being asked by a reporter what was my ambition during those races, and replying, "My ambition is to beat at least one boat."

I went on to repeat an amusing episode involving my arriving at Halifax just ahead of F. Lee Bailey on one race, triggering at three in the morning a wail from him, on seeing who it was had come in ahead of him, "My God. Even Buckley beat us!" But there was a nice nexus that lay ahead:

> I managed, in the receiving line, to shake the awesome hand that guided the tiller that, in 1962, had defeated the Australian challenger; and then to greet the President; and then to greet the guest of honor who, by ironic masterstroke, was the Prime Minister of Australia, Mr. John Gorton.

And on to the (only) serious point I wanted to make:

> . . . It was, I think, thirty years ago that I became a member of the New York Yacht Club and my sponsor, pointing to the cup at Forty-fourth Street, said to me, "Do you know, more money has been spent attempting to win that cup than was spent on the Spanish Armada?" Well, no, I hadn't known this, nor did I know what was the anticipated reply to such an observation.
>
> But I remember groaning, at Cape Canaveral in July of 1969, when one of those awful people who write editorials said that for the cost of *Apollo 11*, which was going up the following day to land on the moon, we could build four thousand and eighty-two lower-middle-income dwelling units. But one cannot parse life's enterprises in any common coin. If Vladimir Horowitz had exercised his

fingers on a sewing machine instead of on a keyboard, stroke for stroke, he might has stitched a blanket that would keep eighty-two thousand Eskimos plus Mary McGrory warm on a cold winter's night. The sailing sport is an appanage of a class of enthusiasts who are aristocratically concerned with excellence at sea. For them—for you—no sacrifice is implausible, whether measured in savings invested in the architecture and engineering of a vessel, or hours spent in cultivating the intellectual and physical skills necessary to overcome marginally the resistance to speed at sea, the margin in question distinguishing you from the boat that, in 1987, you will have left behind.

And more of the same, sincerely congratulating and encouraging the skipper, and the designer, and the sponsors. And then of course the culminating pep talk, a requirement . . .

. . . It happened that, seated next to me at the White House banquet, was a young Australian diplomat on the staff of the Prime Minister who served as his speechwriter. This he confided to me after quite a few glasses of wine. And so, as Prime Minister Gorton

May 1985: Baptizing America's Cup contender US–44.

waxed into a heady and affectionate speech about U.S.-Australian relations, his speechwriter's face was caught in contortions of bliss as he heard pronounced, one after another, the words he had written. And toward the end of the toast he dug his elbow quietly into my side and whispered, "Listen! Listen! Listen—now!" . . . whereupon the Prime Minister, reaching for his glass to conclude his toast, declaimed to his distinguished audience, "Continue as you are, my American friends, friends of liberty and friends of progress, and we"—my Australian speechwriter closed his eyes in transport, in anticipation of the rhetorical coda he was so proud to have composed—"we will go waltzing, Matilda, with you."

In high bellicose gear I explained that, alas, dancing together was not in prospect, not for the few months that remained before the repatriation of "our" cup . . . "We are, after all, here engaged in nothing less, and nothing more, than a venture in repatriation. Here's to U.S.-11. May she bring us back what we have come to regard as an American birthright, so that my wife and I can waltz again, under the Milky Way, when all is right again at Forty-fourth Street in Manhattan."* The reassuring reaction to the short talk has caused me to reflect on the rhetorical amplitude of jock rhetoric; maybe I shall try sportswriting.

I did not complete the hour—Danny called to say there was a break in the clouds, and I could probably catch the sun before it fell. I did, and confirmed that the current was working most oppressively against us.

But it was Niven hour, and there would be no stars to be seen.

Liz served us some splendid chicken, oriental style, which catapulted Van into the game of what-is-the-question that would elicit a specified response, the challenger giving the response, the challenged having the job of thinking up the appropriate question. Van began with: "Doctor Livingstone I presume." The ear, of course, is accustomed to hearing those words uttered as a question, ad-

---

* The *America II* syndicate had an ignoble career, failing to qualify for the semifinals, won by the triumphant *Stars & Stripes*.

"Why, Dr. Livingstone I. Presume."
Enjoying the punch line.

dressed by Henry Stanley to the renowned explorer in Darkest
Africa. I caught the smile on Reggie's face. He had heard it. He
knew the question, but would not tip us off, leaving us to struggle.
We gave up. "What is it, Reg?" The correct answer, he said, in
fact the only question—Van agreed—that would get that response
is, "What is your full name, Dr. Presume?"

Reg volunteered: "Chicken Teriyaki." To which the appropriate
question was, "What was the name of the only Japanese kamikaze
survivor?" Others improvised answer/questions, but when Van
came up with: "C. S. Forester," and rejected all questions that
would elicit that answer, save his own, to wit, "What is that cock-
sucker Forester calling himself these days?" I pronounced the game
over. Christopher Little shot a picture of the merriment.

That night we saw *One Flew Over the Cuckoo's Nest,* which I found boring, greatly to the disgust of my son who pronounced it one of the six best movies he had ever seen (Dick said he did think it had an "anti-establishmentarian bias," I said I just didn't much enjoy movies about cuckoo people). Christopher and Dick Clurman had the post-midnight watch. I had checked the course, left instructions on the log and, stepping on the sill of Van's bunk, raised myself up for the ten minutes' reading which was all I ever managed in the evening before dropping off to sleep. It must have been a very sound sleep. Not so for the watch captain.

Christopher.   But I will tell you about last night. Now last night was something. It was my Dick watch, the 1 to 5 one he and I share once a cycle. The last one was—what?—a week ago, the night we crossed the International Date Line to the accompaniment of "Victory at Sea."

You know, Dick has a bunch of frustrating habits, like resting his hand on the binnacle [the container for the ship's compass, without a clear view of which it is impossible to tell in what direction the ship is headed]—the binnacle!—every five minutes, and blowing smoke in your food, but I have become *fond* of the son-of-a-bitch these last —eighteen?—days. He's a great watch partner, full of a thousand stories about all sorts of movers and shakers. I mean, he's been there —everywhere. Last night he told of Harry Luce's funeral in Mepkin, South Carolina, at H.L.'s former plantation, the one he had given to the Trappists; about arriving there with Fr. John Courtney Murray, all the monks so excited and kidlike at his visit, as if Di-Maggio had dropped in on a summer camp. He told about Harry Luce's fallings-out with the three people who really loved him: John Hersey, Teddy White, and Emmet Hughes—all three for ideological reasons. In two and a half hours we yak-yakked away, about De-Lorean, Ted Sorensen, Andrew Kopkind, Clay Felker, Harold Hayes, Billy Graham, the Kennedys, Fulton Sheen, Larry Flynt, the Prince of Liechtenstein, David Halberstam—it was awful good gab, anyway, and I was perfectly happy to keep the wheel and sip beer and listen.

About 3:15 I looked back and saw the horizon had turned black. *Very* black (as David Halberstam would say). I remembered Pup

Dick Clurman bears up, and lends the obliging hand.

telling me when I was little, one day coming back from Treasure Island in a squall, "When you look out and see a low, dark line stretching around the entire horizon, *that's* when you start to worry."

I was thinking that if this were *Patito* I'd be reefing the main and dropping the genny. But *Sealestial* is so much bigger, a sail-shortening operation, at three in the morning, with just two on watch, is not a good idea. So I thought, well, let's just see what happens, but I did wonder if we shouldn't wake up Pup or Allan. Dick and I decided to let them sleep. Dick said, "I bet Allan will be up here any second, anyway." Damned if fifteen seconds later Allan didn't materialize up through the companionway, a reassuring presence, and seconds later the rain hit.

Heavy, right away. Squall-like: torrential, warm, sweet. You have to decide right away what level of dryness you want. Since my shorts and Harvard T-shirt were basically damp anyway, I didn't bother zipping up the top of my foul weather jacket. Within two minutes I was soaked through, but it felt good and refreshing.

It was coming down so hard I thought it would pour itself out, but it continued hard until the decks were a blur and it crackled against the foul-weather jackets. You couldn't look up into it.

The wind was now up to 35–40 knots, gusting to 50, and it was a bit tricky keeping her downwind as the gusts were covering an arc of about 100 degrees. It would change from 210 degrees to 320 degrees in less than ten seconds. The only thing to do was hold on to the wheel with both hands, lean back and keep my eyes on the wind vane atop the mast. It looked eerie with the wind screaming past the shrouds, the rain driving before us at an angle of 45 or more degrees; most spooky of all was the light on the masthead, sliced and refracted by the wind shear, a kind of cubist St. Elmo's fire. (Before I die I would like to see that phenomenon.)

After some minutes of this I heard a squeaking. Usually a squeak in these conditions means no good thing: an unfair lead, loose snatch block, a line somewhere about to pop and cause havoc. But then I saw them: batlike apparitions hovering near the masthead: birds caught in the storm. I don't know if birds feel terror. These seemed to be seeking some reassurance by keeping close. The queer thing was that to stay with us they had to fly—with all their might, I would think—directly in an opposite direction to ours, the wind keeping them from passing us; so that the ship and the birds, each racing at maximum speeds in opposite directions, achieved a perfect and somewhat ironical stasis.

Now we were fizzing through the water, often at 11 knots. The rains had flattened the seas so that our progress was unimpeded by waves. The ship's lights cast a circular aura on the water around us. All was white and hissing.

The rain cut into the eyes, but it was necessary to keep the wind vane in sight at all times. The lightning, which had begun just before the rain hit us, was now directly overhead, and regular. At one

Two ways to dress for a squall.

point I looked up at the masthead from the compass just as a
gorgeous crack of lightning stitched across the sky. For two seconds
I could not see. It's a curious Old Testament feeling, being blinded
by lightning: a sense of retribution, awful judgment, awful punishment. Well, it wasn't all *that* dramatic, but it kept lighting up the
tableau around us, throwing everything into stark, hot, instantaneous
relief: a sailboat plowing through a wild-ocean storm as fast as she
could go.

   I kept the helm last night for four hours, almost two of them
spent in the storm. After the first hour I knew that we were in the
worst of it and that was a good feeling: a surge of *okay, now we
can have some fun.* And it was fun. The rain slapping into the eye-
balls, the birds screeching, the fizz of our wake, the screaming of the
wind, hands white, clutched on the helm, a slight ache in the upper
arms from the strain, just enough fear to make it interesting. After
an hour and a half of it, Allan, crouching nearby, taciturn, profes-

sional, reassuring, said, "You're doing a good job with the helm, Christo." And to Dick he explained, "That is the hardest sort of course to hold, downwind, at night, in a storm." It is awful immodest of me to write down this advertisement for myself, but that made me feel good.

Stars coming down all over. One just roared by, leaving a grainy orange flameout half the sky-width long. In four degrees latitude.

Reg reflecting yesterday: WFB's original idea was to sail to New Zealand, where it is now the seasonal equivalent of December 3, i.e., two days after the height of winter.

Next morning four inches of rain had accumulated in the fishing box.

All the next day was wet, and Christopher Little mentioned the effect of it in his journal. "The rain is almost constant now and is very debilitating to morale and skin. The cabins get so unbearably hot with the hatches dogged down that it is hard to sleep. Reg, my cabin-mate, radiates a stunning amount of body heat. It's like sleeping next to a wood stove on a humid night in August. All the foul weather gear is soaked through. When you go on watch you start off drenched and get no drier. The cabin floors are covered with soggy shorts and underwear, and the whole boat has a nasty, musty odor. So this is Paradise?"

> **Dick Clurman.** It is entirely different from day sailing. We are most definitely blue-water sailing. We are going night and day in whatever seas and weather engulf us. There's no choice. We're out there and there is no place to pull in and stop, even if we wanted to. It is a continuous, wet isometric exercise, grabbing handrails to stay upright, barking our shins as routinely as breathing, not even blinking at the flying, crashing supplies banging around below. At night, if I am not on watch, leeboards strap me into the small, hot berth to keep me from rolling out.

That was the same day that Christopher let loose on Dick, in High Elizabethan; memorable. I cannot wait for Dick's reaction when in due course my companions will see at least those excerpts from their journals that especially caught my eye—the more so, in this case, given the longtime mutual affection between Dick and The Mauler:

I relate this dreary anecdote only to acquaint the reader with the type of person Mr. C——— is, and not, I assure, to prejudice said reader against him. (Indeed, the author is himself agreeable to the "dry-cleaning" process, and upon the ship's arrival in Kavieng, plans to have himself "dry-cleaned," such is the accumulated moisture of his person and habiliments.) But it must be said that Mr. C——— can make of himself a most vexing presence, and it is in this particular that the author is compelled to manifest his grievances against him in the interest of compatibilitie and harmonie, for it is said of company aboard seagoing vessels that " 'Tis agreeable to hot-bunk with thy mate, but not to lay thy dirty underwear upon his face."

He finds pleasant that most noxious habit of tobacco, and doth contrive to pollute the air wheresoever he sits. This very afternoon I was sitting pleasantly at table, composing some descriptions of the inhabitants of Majuro Atoll, when Mr. C——— appeared and without so much as a by-your-leave plunked his person down beside me. It was the work of moments to convert my quiet writing-area into a ghetto-dwelling of computer, computer manuals, ashtray and the myriad noisome accoutrements which he doth produce from a blue purse he carries with him at all times; for it is in this purse that he keeps his Benson & Hedges cigarettes, lest he find himself with less than an entire carton.

"You have come," I said to him, "to trouble my quietude. Why doth you not repair to some other corner of the vessel whereth you may contrive an animal-sty or whicheversoever environment you pleaseth?"

He made no answer to my entreaty, but began his tapping upon the computer, shortly followed by great braying and imprecating against the maker of it. So self-absorbed does he become in his conundra with his writing machine that he payeth no mind to where his cigarette ash flieth, to wit, into various of my tender membranes, such as the eyes and mouth. When one asks if he might trouble to cause this detritus to be placed elsewhere, he makes no sign of comprehending, and continueth with his tapping.

It was not long before I found that Mr. C——— possesseth a

genius for causing a bruit without acquainting himself with its results. One day, whilst sitting across from me with his wretched
writing machine, he reached across to procure an object relating to
his tobacco; in doing so, he brushed against the volume control on
my Walkman, turning it up to such a level as to make my inner
ear ring mightily. I gnashed my teeth and made a great keening to
make manifest my pain. Yet he remarked not one iota on my consternation, and merely continued with his tapping. Not five minutes
later another disaster befell me thanks to his agency. I had procured
a cup of iced tea with a fat slice of orange to ward off the scurvy.
This I had placed beside me, buttressed against the sea motion by
means of an ingenious use of surgical tubing. It wanted no small
amount of ingenuity to consternate my iced tea, but hark, here
comes Mr. C———, and mark, soon my painstakingly prepared
beverage was a chaos of ice and brown puddles which coursed from
one end of the table like the river Lethe, a torrent of tannic acid
that staineth and corrodeth everything in its path.

Every man hath his limits, and after a fortnight of enduring these
and other affronts which shall go unmentioned, I resolved that to
keep murder out of my heart I would mount counter-vexations.
Thereupon I seized the opportunity to fill his blue purse with a
congeries of loose objects, such as Snickers' bars, clothespins, snap
hooks, and other loose objects as one doth find lying about the deck.
Last evening after the reading (our text was *Bring on the Empty
Horses*), whilst Mr. C——— was engaged in earnest conversation—
for he *only* engageth in earnest conversation—I detached his flashlight from the snap hook which dangleth from the length of line
attached to his belt loop. He noticed not the thievery—I begin to
suppose him oblivious to the greater part of that which taketh place
around him—indeed, he went on with his conversation. Thus I attached the snap hook to the accursed blue purse; the dark thought
looming not distantly in my cerebellum that he might falleth overboard and be dragged down by the Darbies by his blue purse, serving him in the office as an anchor; or like the millstone which those
aboriginals of the Old Testament used to sink their undesirables.

Perhaps I rageth out of proportion to the crime. Certainly I do
not desire that Mr. C——— be weighted down with snap hooks and
drowned. He is in many respects an excellent fellow, and he knoweth
a great quantity of celebrities with whom he treats on terms of

equality. He has written some pages of a book, which some aboard have read and found pleasing, and it promiseth to make a great noise when published. But if he continueth in his ways, making serpentine progress while at the helm, causing the sails to jibe and folk to be pitched from their bunks like cordwood, and making his copious nuisances upon our company, then I am resolved to put a dead flying fish in his blue purse, leaving him to wonder at the mysterious stink which emanateth from within. I pray, meanwhile, I will not be provoked to such an extremity of retaliation.

While this kind of thing was going on, Dick was writing in his journal:

So I find myself, aboard the *Sealestial*, the foil for much good-humored derision. Do I mind? Not at all. I would if I were entering the competition, but knowing that I've lost before I start, I go along with the unusual role for me of being the novice among the experts. In a way that makes me an outsider in Bill's sailing entourage. But the cement that binds us is personal rather than professional. So I don't mind being at the bottom of the blue-water sailing class. In recreational games I am non-competitive. But if I can't play them with grace in the company of those who can, then I watch, and lend an obliging hand.

But how very quickly moods change. Suddenly, at about six, the sun came out. Almost immediately, almost on cue, everyone began to stir. Wet clothes were brought up from below and put on clothes hangers along the lifeline. The main saloon was, lightly at first, then with Stakhanovite thoroughness, cleaned and reordered. In a spurt of energy I wrote on my Kaypro-2000 a piece on white wines commissioned by *Goodlife* magazine. Several of us were scribbling away on journals, and Van was making changes in his manuscript. I had finished reading it and was greatly encouraged as I got through it: although it needed thorough editorial revision, it is original, robust, humorous, serious, and informative.

The spirits soared with the barometer. I am amused that only one day after his lugubrious entry about the life-on-board, Christopher Little was asking that the trip be prolonged. He recorded in his journal, "We are passing Ailinglapalap Atoll on the starboard beam. I am terribly frustrated by the time constraints which restrict our shore time and prevent us from even stopping here for a swim. We are trying to do too much—I think everyone agrees—by sailing over four thousand miles in thirty days. *Racing Through Paradise*, Reggie suggested Bill entitle the book that will grow out of this trip. Already we've had to cut out two stops, Ponape and Nukuoro, to reach Rabaul, New Guinea, in time. It's too bad, but there is nothing to be done about it."

Exactly; exactly. Dick expressed himself similarly:

> **Dick Clurman.** Liz and Maureen serve incomparable food and drink, which just as often land on our laps. Bill found at Majuro, and bought yards and yards of, surgical tubing. Stretched over our plates and glasses it holds them firm, and you can't even taste the rubber. (A new Buckley invention. He is delighted with himself.) We long for the sight and stability of land. At first I thought my longing came from my relative inexperience. But it turns out that all of us and, in fact, all ocean sailors have it. Listen to Melville: "Tossed on the billows of the wide rolling Pacific—the sky above, the sea around, and nothing else! Oh for a refreshing glimpse of one blade of grass—for a sniff of the fragrance of a handful of loamy earth—that peculiar prolongation of sound that a sailor loves— 'Land ho!' "

We picked up Kosrae. Twelve miles away: gratifyingly, on the course I had specified, at about the time I predicted. It was about midnight when we caught a fleeting view of a flashing red. The chart showed that if we could simultaneously spot a Flashing Red 4 Sec, and a Quick Flashing Red, why we were on the right heading: Keep them in range, and proceed safely into the narrow neck of the harbor. If we had had Loran, or if GPS had at that hour been functioning, it would have been as easy as to travel due west at Latitude 5° 19.5′ into the harbor. Come to think of it, I guess I'd have insisted on GPS accuracy for that one: at its narrowest, the channel is only about 400 feet wide. At both ends there are submerged coral reefs.

Oh how we struggled to find access. We never did see both lights, and attempts to line ourselves up in the direction of the single light we occasionally saw, toward which the indicated bearing was 277 degrees, frustrated us time after time as we would come on course—and then lose the light. After two hours I decided to surrender. It was after three in the morning, and I told the watch to stand out, keeping the island in sight. We brought down the Yankee, and sailed with only the main. The log entry reads, "Christo and Van on duty till 0500. Sunrise at 7:54, Zone 12 Daylight Time. WFB to be awakened before channel entrance is undertaken. Merci." But I'll let Christo tell it:

> Here we went again.
>
> Fetched up the lights of Kosrae around 2300, just as the movie *The Bishop's Wife* was ending. An incongruous juxtaposition, that: Cary Grant, David Niven, Loretta Young and a South Pacific landfall. Pup and Danny said it would be two hours before we were "off the channel entrance." There was some, uh, speculation that this was going to be another jolly hove-to soiree, pitching in the swell off a reef; but after eighteen days on the road we were earnestly desirous of getting in with these by-now customary landfall protocols.
>
> I crawled off to try to get some rest in the steambox, Chris Little's bunk in this case. I burrowed in, corkscrewed my legs through his computer, camera gear, dirty laundry, hooked my arm into his storage shelves to keep me locked in and tried to sleep. No good. I'd guess the temperature was 90 degrees, humidity 100 percent and utterly airless—even the fan, in that thick stew of an atmosphere, isn't much comfort. A sleepless, sticky hour or so later I turned to.
>
> Usual array of undecipherable lights. Exultation when a red one was fleetingly spotted; desolation when it was decided, an hour later, that it had probably been a car's taillight. Where *were* those fucking range lights? We could see the harbor contours—what looked like the harbor contours. But we also saw and heard the reef.
>
> Van kept wanting to go one lump of dark landmass farther on, certain that Lelu was just around the corner. Back and forth, all eyes on the shore looking for two red lights which weren't there.
>
> We dropped the genny, and while pawing it down I burned the tips of my fingers.
>
> A squall loomed on the radar like a tumor. The eastern sky was

black. Caught between weather and an impenetrable shore, WFB decided to heave to, ride it out until the sunrise.

My new foul-weather gear is, it seems, quite popular, since it is always being worn by someone other than me. I was handed a wind-breaker the thickness of cellophane.

The squall hit—storm, really; it would last until morning—and I had a strange sense of déjà vu: *I've seen this movie, you know*: driving hard rain, gusts up to 40, strong swell. I kept the engine on to give us headway, was glad for that engine, and understood what terror it must have been for the old sailing ships, hove to off a reefy lee shore, gale blowing them back back back into the rocks. I kept the helm as long as I could, about an hour and a half, and turned it over to Van.

I went down below to get warm and within minutes was nauseated. The saloon was in its usual state of hove-to swill: wet foul-weather gear strewn about the floor, wet heaps of clothing (okay, okay: mostly mine) on the settee. Worked my way forward. As I passed the galley I inhaled a hot waft of the most unpleasant aroma: overripe papaya and evaporated milk. Ooooh . . . Slamming against the port and starboard bulwarks I passed Reg and Chris's cabin. Now here was a physical phenomenon: a human thermal layer; heat *radiating* out; body temperature plus. I'd have stayed and marveled except this, combining with the papaya and evaporated milk, had produced a foreboding in my gullet that sent me packing in the direction of the cockpit: better to be wet and shivering than barfing, I say. It was a slow watch, slowest of the trip. Every five minutes I checked my watch—and found that only two minutes had passed. This was the lowest point of the trip. I wanted my wife, I wanted to be dry, I wanted to be home. Five o'clock finally came. I told WFB and Reg we were four miles offshore and collapsed on the settee next to Liz, who had left the oven of her cabin for the saloon. The wind shifted so that every twenty seconds the sail banged; even so I was asleep in minutes.

A half hour after dawn we were tied up alongside a rusty old interchannel supply boat. Already it was hot, in the event you wonder what the weather is like on June 20, one hundred and sixty-three degrees east of Greenwich, five degrees above the equator, in the easternmost of the Caroline Islands.

18

KOSRAE

The twelve hours in Kosrae, later in the same day Christopher designated his watch as the low point of his Pacific passage, were in terms of creature-comfort criteria *my* low point. During those twelve hours, Christopher was enthralled.

Throughout our stay in Lelu Harbor we would, from necessity, be tied up alongside a rusty, oily freighter occupying the single dock space, as to a Siamese twin. In the course of the day I must have walked across it—heel-to-toe over the slim wooden plank straddling the hold of that dilapidated workhorse, over its lifeline, onto the dock—oh, fifty times?

The first business at hand, as usual, was to telephone home, and four of us got into a taxi and drove through the wet, sleepy little town up through muggy semi-forests, rising to a clearing on the hills on which lay the administrative complex of the island. We were directed to the "Communications Center," an abandoned trailer wired into a satellite dish which would reach out to any telephone system in the world, the plump brown operator told us in the crowded little room, blissfully air-conditioned. Everything was serene in the Western Hemisphere, we presently discovered, and on leaving the trailer we were accosted by a young, trimly dressed American who introduced himself as the attorney general of

The Communications Center, Kosrae.

Calling home.

Kosrae. We chatted and he told us that his wife was a qualified archaeologist who would be happy to take us through the "ruins," which lay within walking distance of *Sealestial*, so we made a date for after lunch.

At that point, in another taxi, Reggie arrived to say that Kosrae Customs was most unhappy about the *Sealestial*. To begin with there was our booze: they were disposed to seal it until our departure. Second was the problem of our arsenal—the rifle, and the skeet shotgun. They wished to seal and remove these until our departure. The attorney general said it would be tactful to call on the lieutenant governor, the governor being away from the island at the time.

Van is awfully good at that kind of thing. John Kenneth Galbraith, in his memoirs as ambassador to India, somewhere says that he does not believe in using pull unless it is convenient. Lieutenant Governor Moses Mackwelung was ever so attentive, showed an interest in our journey, and so we passed a few pleasant minutes. Along the way, Ambassador Evan Galbraith mentioned that although he would be giving up his post in government the following month, he had been asked informally whether he would agree to serve as a governor of the Overseas Private Investment Corporation. That's the outfit that surveys foreign countries, evaluating their economic climate and pronouncing Yes or No, hospitable to investment: after which, if armed with an affirmative certification, American entrepreneurs can proceed to invest with some assurance. In the event of subsequent confiscation by the foreign government, OPIC guarantees a return of capital investment. I think it is fair to say that any prospective governor of OPIC will be treated well by any country desiring the favorable attention of American capital, and it was a matter of minutes before Customs lost all interest in inhibiting our access to our wine, or in walking off with our firearms.

The lieutenant governor met later in the afternoon alone with Van for a protracted talk about this & that, including the beloved Compact about which we had been informed in Majuro. He presented Van with a canoe paddle, a wooden sword, a straw attaché case, and a cooking mortar. "I was further loaded with gifts," Van

Gifts from the lieutenant governor.

records, "when his assistant showed up at the boat, shortly after I returned, with four huge stalks of green bananas. The next day, when the lieutenant governor's assistant brought us the weather report at Port Lottin, he also delivered three woven baskets full of lettuce and fresh vegetables. We hung the bananas from the mizzen's yardarm and ate them for the rest of the trip, as they turned, gradually, from green to yellow."

Dick asked the lieutenant governor if he could recommend a restaurant in Kosrae, and he recommended two, Sterlings and Billy's, and added that Sterlings was even air-conditioned. Since it lay between the administration center and the dock, we stopped there to vet it before assembling everyone for lunch. It was a strange and lugubrious sight: so dark, as we entered, as to be difficult to see.

But soon we could see: thirty or forty men and women, totally silent, eating off wooden tables, seated on only one side of the tables because they were all watching black-and-white television, an old movie. Television had come to Kosrae only one month before. We decided to make do with sandwiches on *Sealestial*.

We wolfed them down and Debbie, the archaeologist, came with an assistant, and we walked across the way into a jungle full of rocks and blocks and decrepit structures of ancient stone. We learned that these were the remains of the Polynesian capital in the fifteenth century. It was difficult to maintain one's balance, walking over the mossy, slippery rocks, and besides it was drizzling, as off and on it did every hour or two, so that we made less than an ideal audience as we trudged about in the wet heat. Van said later that what he saw reminded him of the movie *Greystoke*: in such as this, Tarzans grow up. And I was reminded of the ineluctability of the jungle:

Christo survives a shower. His onshore smile.

Debbie kept pointing to stalks and weeds obscuring this and that, overgrowth that wasn't there as recently as three months ago. "They just don't have the money to keep it up," she complained.

Back on board I was accosted by an energetic man of quick wit and inquiring mind. It developed that he had read some of my books, seen some of my television programs, and most emphatically disagreed with me about many things, though his wife did not, he regretted to say, and what did I wish to know about the island? He had been there for a few months, supervising a large construction project having to do with water storage. He was most frustrated because, he said, the Kosraens do not have any sense of self-restraint in the matter of water consumption. The project in which he was engaged was based on American standards. In the States, I learned, we consume an average of 350 gallons per person per day. Given the laxity of Carolinian water consumption habits, David Schatzki and his partners had allowed in their planning for 500 gallons per person per day. But they had learned that the natives use over 1000 gallons per day. And that figure was only an estimate, because David could not succeed in wresting from the administration authority to interrupt the water supply only for just long enough to measure consumption.

Ah, I said, how glad I was that he had brought up the subject of water, because water was the object of my principal concern, given that *Sealestial* critically needed a mere four hundred gallons of water. Allan had been told he could not have water that day because "the pipes were closed." That would mean we would need to stay right where we were all night until the next day, a horrible prospect, unless water could be got by some other means . . .

Of course! David Schatzki said, leave it to me. He and his assistant Sean would deliver four hundred gallons.

What seemed like hours—hot, hot, airless hours—later, David reappeared. He said he had got permission of the chief of police to use the Kosrae fire truck to bring us water, subject to confirmation by his superior; then had got permission of that superior—subject to confirmation by *his* superior, our dear friend the lieutenant governor —who, unaccountably, had said: No. Especially strange in Kosrae,

The U.S. Army's reluctant water wagon.

I thought, since the only conceivable use of a fire truck must be to
put out volcanoes, given the wetness of the climate. We would not
have the use of the fire truck; and this, David said, meant we would
need to use an old army truck, which would soon arrive with a
buffalo-hide container bearing the water, never fear.

At about four the truck arrived, driven by a picture-poster model
American soldier, tall, blond, handsome, brawny, a native of Milwaukee who with an assistant stretched a hose from the buffalo
hide, squatting on top of the army truck, across the bulky beam of
the rusty freighter, to the water intake valve on *Sealestial*'s deck.

"Ready?" the soldier called out to me from the truck.

"Ready," I said, expecting a torrent to flow into our hungry tank.
What came was the most dismaying trickle. The steam was some-

thing like a leaky faucet. Dismayed, I looked up at my friend David and he said, alas, there was no pump suitable for our purpose, lacking as we were the facilities of the fire truck; not to worry, in due course our tanks would fill by the exertion of gravity. "In due course" turned out to be two excruciating hours later, during the whole of which the affable American soldier and his assistant tended the hose, so obligingly made available to us; uncomplaining, as I fed them Cokes, and anything else they inclined to, but I did find myself wondering whether, the kindness of my new friends notwithstanding, I'd have preferred at least one more moderate storm at sea to what I thought the most boring, uncomfortable day of the passage, that day in Kosrae, Caroline Islands.

> **Christopher.** [*Life on the other side of the tracks*] Reg and I went ashore. Jagged, high peaks covered with jungle, mists, dark green lagoon water. We walked through the town. It was clear we were in a remote part of the world. Only one sign in town: the Nissan dealership. Breadfruit hung over main street. We passed frangipani, hibiscus, banyan, crumbly buildings, car wrecks covered in creeping vegetation, the laundromat, a chicken-wire-enclosed area with a sign saying, DO NOT PUT PAMPERS IN MACHINES. This was the first indication of the American influence. There was a *lot* more to come. Sure enough, some moments later we came on a bright blue sign announcing a water treatment development, a gift to the people of Kosrae "from their friends in the United States." There was R.R.'s name, there was the figure $401,000. Over the day we saw about a half-dozen of these signs: $183,000 here, $55,000 there. The mother lode turned out to be the airport: $5.1 big ones. After a while we ran into a spacey-looking lad of gringo features wearing a T-shirt with a hibiscus and the legend, "A Nuclear Free Pacific." He turned out to be one of the local Peace Corps guys. We took him back to the boat and fed him the first Americano breakfast he had had in a year: French toast and eggs. He'd been eating a lot of rice and sashimi for breakfast, and he ate hungrily as we pumped him for details.
>
> *Vignettes of Our 30-Hour Stay in the Lovely Island of Kosrae:*
> • Walking the trail around Lelu Island, watching the surf rip

Boys will be boys.

over the channel reef. Asked Peace Corps about the local fauna. "No snakes. Some wild pigs, Kimono lizards, and fruit bats."

• Dating habits. It's not done to talk to a girl in public. It's assumed you're arranging an assignation. Be seen with a girl twice and her father will inform you you're getting married in two months. One young lad found himself in this position and demurred, said no, he wasn't getting married. Her family persisted. You're getting married in six weeks, they said. Four weeks. Two weeks. The lad kept denying this was the case. Peace Corps ran into him two weeks later. "Well," said the lad, "I'm getting married tomorrow."

• Wanton women . . . are rare here (unlike Majuro), but those who are are called "wanteds." Even so, said Peace Corps, "It ain't lovemaking. It's into the bushes, slackalack (meaning Hurry!) and finish!"

• Stopping at the Sandy Beach Hotel, in thatched cabanas on a beautiful beach. Young American working on the hotel sign strikes up a conversation. Invites us in for a beer. He's the Peace Corps guy for tourism, and he is sitting on top of the heap. He's gone from a job at the Waldorf-Astoria to here. He's got a cabana on a beach where he can see the sun rise and set, a refridge full of Bud. He's been here eleven months, he's got thirteen to go, and he's in *no* hurry to get back home. "Yeah," he said, "I think it'd be hard to adjust after this."

• Local geological feature is the "sleeping woman": four mountains making up a lady lying on her back, negligéed with mist, breasts protruding (1,500 feet and 1,100 feet—she's stacked), hands folded over her lap. An apt topographical curiosity on an island half of whose 5,500 inhabitants are under fifteen.

• Little kids down at the dock fishing. A two-year-old chewing on the baitfish the others were tearing bits off of.

• The Peace Corps girl from "outside Minneapolis . . ." We ducked into her family's hut during one of the sixteen rains that day. A bitch was suckling her puppies by the front door. The girl is in charge of the seaweed-farming operation. They're growing the stuff, but there's only one pharmaceutical company in the U.S. that has any use for it, and even so they don't seem to be that hot for it.

• Arrive back from drive to airport to find an army truck disgorging fresh water into our tanks. WFB in a martyrdom of waiting for the trickle to fill our tanks. Two Spec-fours from Milwaukee perch in the cockpit. One said, "What an honor it is to meet the ambassador."

• Dan and I resolve to persuade WFB we have *got* to plan to make our next landfall during daylight. He agreeable. But Dan and I, despite his protestations that tomorrow will be a "day of rest," bet ourselves we will leave Kosrae by noon.

Finally it was done. I don't remember when last I was more anxious to leave a dirty heat-trap, and I stepped eagerly behind the wheel. The head of the tourist agency volunteered to accompany us on our ten-mile trip to Port Lottin, the other harbor—uncluttered, uncommercial, and highly unnavigable; where I had decided to go to get away from Lelu.

A good thing he came along because the channel is extravagantly narrow, and by the time we got there it was not only dark, but breakers were obscuring what we'd have relied on to snake in. Unhappily, the poor tourist director had got quite seasick along the way, but he did not lose his aplomb, and, cutting the power down to less than 1000 rpm, we eased in between the breakers and put down the hook in 30 feet of water.

A little outboard came over to pick up our pilot and to bring us some more bananas. He promised to return the next morning with weather reports.

We all swam in the dark before dinner, a little breeze reached us, and I felt an emancipating touch of cool. The dinner was, as ever, inspired, including a coconut custard, fried bananas, slices of pickled pork, and wild rice. The VCR broke down, but Reggie, Danny, and Christopher managed to fix it, so we showed *Risky Business*, followed by another swim and a restful sleep, the saloon used as a dormitory since we had no watch duty to keep merely one or two anchor checks.

By ship standards, we slept late. The little outboard was back at midmorning while some were out snorkeling among the reefs. The official told us that Ponape, which had been expecting our arrival, was wild with apprehension because, far from experiencing the anticipated doldrums, it had had "hurricane force winds." As for the weather we might expect en route to New Guinea, the winds would be south southeast, going to southeast, at 18 knots.

Not so good that, our course being south.

It was almost noon.

And it was raining.

> **Christopher.**   Fuck if Pup doesn't say, at 10 A.M., might as well set off since it's raining. Dan and I look at each other, and for a few seconds I am tempted to weigh in with a "That sucks!" But I've

resolved not to complain—weather isn't really Pup's fault, though I have a feeling he'd be itching to leave *anyway*. So, in silent protest, I've resolved not to shave for the duration of the voyage. Ho, ho, ho. Last night after lovely dinner and before heated argument with Van over Vietnam, I say to Pup, "You know, this is lovely. Not moving, I mean." And he says, quote, I have a very strong feeling about this. You have to experience the lows before you can experience the highs. End quote.

19

REMEMBERING PHIL WELD

In the mail I read on leaving Kosrae I saw a letter from a single-handed racer offering me (quite extraordinary) his own boat no less, but only on the understanding that I would sail alone in it from San Francisco to Honolulu, preferably in the solo Trans-Pacific race, which the author had himself taken part in two years earlier. "The Pacific Ocean compared with the Atlantic is preferable weatherwise, the trade winds are favorable towards Hawaii and there is much less traffic. Except for minor adjustments I spent less than one percent of the time at the wheel, using either the monitor vane or the autopilot. I'll be happy to make my boat available to you; and this time there will be no question who is the captain!" Dr. Peter Strykers of Berkeley had read one of my books, knew that I was addicted to Baroque music, deplored my failure to experience solo sailing, and thought such a journey as he proposed the ideal next step for me.

Some months after my return, he sent me the manuscript of a book he had written on his solo passage. Several passages struck me, among them the difficulty he had had with his harpsichord (yes, he sailed with a harpsichord, in addition to his library of music tapes). "Two harpsichord keys are a little sticky because of the humidity, so I may leave the harpsichord in the sun for a little while. There is a saying among the Transpac sailors [the biannual race from California to Honolulu is called the Transpac], 'When you hear harpsichord music on the ocean you are not hallucinating, but you are certainly one of the last!' " The jocular reference here is to Dr. Strykers's having come in last in his solo race, though only by an hour. My eye then rested on a striking thought he enunciated. "It has occurred to me that no one can help me on this trip, but I have suddenly realized I am also unable to help them. Not my family, friends, patients. Maybe this is the most fascinating aspect of my voyage—the sense of being uninvolved. Will I be a better person for this experience?" He hopes so, and is confident he will be. A fascinating inversion of the usual temptation to self-pity. Perhaps experienced most often by doctors, whose minds go to their patients, bereft, while the doctor is at sea, of proper attention.

Finally, given the hectic concern aboard the *Sealestial* for our landfalls, my eyes lingered over Dr. Strykers's rumination during his passage. "Luckily there will be moonlight when I make my landfall at night. They told me that Hanalei Bay [his destination] is not that easy to find from the ocean. When sailing to Hawaii for the first time with a crew we were anxious for the landfall days ahead of time. I do not feel that way at all this time. Of course, I am looking forward to putting my feet on shore again. On the other hand, I dread the thought of ending this ecstasy. Maybe I am more of a loner than I thought."

I thought of Phil Weld—alas, of the late Phil Weld—and of his predilection for solo sailing.

Five years ago he wrote to ask whether I would compose an introduction to his forthcoming book, *Moxie*. (I borrow here and there from what I proceeded to write.)

I tend to resist sailing books about solo passages. Joshua Slocum is everybody's exception, and justly so. But Slocum was obstinately healthy. Most such stories, one suspects early on, are written (though this too is a problem, since the prose is more often a reproduction of long entries written in the log under traction) by dead souls, driven by misanthropic winds. The desire, never adequately excogitated, is to get "away." Anyone whose life is hectic

can understand such an impulse, but then anyone who knows anything at all about life aboard a small boat knows also that there are
times at sea when one envies the serenity of the traffic cop at Times
Square.

Even our own little voyage, by the time we had arrived at Kosrae,
was proof that Life at Sea can be demanding, and that probably is
why its measured joys are so distinctive. But these pleasures—the
obliging winds, the beneficent sky, the sweetly composed set of sail,
the fleeted motion—are building blocks for the supreme pleasure
of camaraderie. What would I have done without my companions?
Without Christo and Danny, Dick and Reg, Christopher Little and
Van? I have always thought it impossible, and if possible abomina-
ble, to harbor it all to oneself. It is as if, coming on the lone copy of
an unknown sonnet by Shakespeare, one were to read and then toss
it away; internalizing the pleasure, but only for the finite length of
time the lines stay vivid in the memory. There is no witness. You
cannot prove it existed. There is, then, none of the enduring satisfaction of the shared pleasure.

I confess I was jarred by reading *Moxie* and, as a matter of fact,
jarred also after reading the account of my correspondent Dr.
Strykers. The stereotype of the neurotic loner, on reading Phil
Weld's book, is, quite simply, shattered. I'm not yet disposed to
change my own predilection for gregariousness at sea, but I am
moved to acknowledge the pleasures it appears to hold out for
utterly adjusted people. At the time Phil asked me for the intro, I
had set eyes on him exactly one time, and we had in common only
a devotion we shared to a common friend, the book critic and
author Herb Kenny.

So that most of what I came to know about Weld I learned not
from knowing him, but from reading his book. And I wrote that
much of the book's success lay in the revelation of a wholesomely
remarkable man. Here was no fugitive from anything at all. His life
at home reminded me (I can't devise a higher compliment) of that
of my parents. In his profession (as newspaper publisher) he was
successful. His boyhood was privileged. As a soldier during the
Second World War (and he lets us learn this with singular, becom-

Kapinga's main drag.

Christo and his epigone.

Dan and Christo, exiting Kapinga.

Back at sea.

ing grace) he evidently exhibited those virtues we dare still to call manly, and when they would locate his ragged column of soldiers on those desultory missions in Burma and air-drop relief to them, the mail drops brought him from his wife one letter for every day since the last he had received.

He had sailed, as yacht club-oriented boys and girls on the eastern seaboard almost necessarily sail; but it was sometime well after he had returned from the war and raised a family that something happened that arrested his imagination. And from the imagination of a Yankee engaged comes something very like a monogamous union. A Yankee of the best kind is what Philip Weld plainly was. The reassuring reproach to Ortega's mass-man, who drifts parasitically through life without any sense of a reciprocal obligation to his patrimony. When Phil Weld got caught up in sailing, and more particularly in multi-hulled sailing, and when he discovered his hunger for solo sailing, he realized intuitively that he could only justify his self-indulgence by enhancing the sport (though what he enhanced was more than merely that). Accordingly he spent thousands of hours, and uncounted thousands of dollars, striving to develop new skills, new contrivances, fresh knowledge; and then to advertise these, so that all who cared to sail would benefit from his own thought and adventures.

And these they surely were. He combined in *Moxie* as well as anyone whose writings necessarily describe his own exploits a quality of self-deprecation with a lucidity of detail, and the result is the emergence of a truly endurable, endearing, ace. Lindbergh captured all of Gaul when, after landing and being asked why he had twice circled the field where half of Paris had assembled, agitated, to wait for him, he replied that he suddenly remembered that he had forgotten to bring his passport. There are such lines in *Moxie*, none of them synthetic. Some, in fact, are just over there on the side of otherworldliness, as when, to guard instinctively against lionization, Weld writes that such a solo passage as he undertook (in which he broke a world record) was anything but an ordeal. "A long voyage refreshes, rather than tires me." Then, "Every healthy person ought to try it to see how it tones the skin and sharpens the senses." Right.

And everyone should fly to the moon. The view from there is incomparable.

Students of technique should study not only what Phil Weld tells us about such subjects as how to behave when capsized at sea, how to prevent this from happening, what is useful to take along on an ocean passage. All those useful things are in the book, but there is also much there for students of narrative prose. It is an unusual tribute to *Moxie* that there isn't a line of it an editor would want to cut, nor (I can think of only one or two exceptions) passages one feels should have been extended. It is a perfect mix, the flashbacks, the autobiographical details, the technical descriptions, the flashes of sheer excitement, the narrative tension. And yet one has the feeling that he wrote it all not by the kind of laborious planning he invested in the devising of his beloved (and mortal) trimarans, but that he wrote it exactly in the way we read it: started with the first sentence and ended with the last, and then sent off the whole to whomever he had agreed to send it off to. When he wrote (high tribute) it was because he needed to tell us what he had to tell us; and when he stopped (high tribute) it was because, for the nonce, he had nothing to add.

I wrote "for the nonce" because I hoped that Philip Weld would not deny us, when ready, a second book; and, as someone who hasn't won a sailboat race since age fifteen, I wished him to know that it mattered not at all to me whether the next time out he won or lost; the book's success would not hang on his competitive supremacy. But having said as much I fervently hoped he would win that other struggle which, in the closing passages of his book, he merely adumbrates, rather than expostulates on, fearful as he always was— so doggedly courteous—of being pedantic, or evangelistic. He was strategically concerned not so much to win races as to harness the wind, and he saw a nexus in what he did with *Moxie*, and what others might do without *Moxie*. I turn to the text because I can't paraphrase consistently the kind of charged simplicity with which this self-effacing man communicated what he felt so deeply . . .

On *Moxie*'s 18-day spring to victory I savored my investments in windpower and windship. I seemed to be getting one good break

after another. I convinced myself that by making these commitments I had gained special favor with Aeolus. I also reflected that
here I was, at 65, making a record west-bound passage with no great
demand for physical effort. Modern gear such as my roll-into-the-
mast Stoway mainsail and my autopilot powered by batteries charged
by photovoltaic displays provided a metaphor for modern seafaring
that should be inspirational, or so I thought.

"Or so I thought." Philip Weld didn't want to be carried away,
or make you think him importunate. It was by such graces that he
achieved in *Moxie* so much more than the tribute due him as the
fastest sailor in the history of the world.

Dr. Strykers described his arrival at the end of his solo passage. "I
had put on my yachting outfit and looked like a gentleman in my
pressed trousers which had been hanging in my closet and were
saved for this occasion. The committee boat was there to welcome
me. They boarded my boat and took over the wheel! I tried to offer
them a whiskey, but they had cold beer [for me]! I had to blink
away a tear and was wondering why. Maybe it was because for the
first time in almost three weeks somebody else was doing something
for *me*. For twenty days I had done everything myself."

Aboard *Sealestial* we could hardly claim to be doing everything
for ourselves, but the boat was at our direction, and in a very palpa-
ble sense we felt that we were—jointly—alone; even as, I suppose,
the half-dozen men who form an expedition, whether in search of
buried treasure, or of the surface of the moon, feel at some moments
entirely alone. That happened on *Sealestial*, even when a live body
lay only inches away.

JOHN BLANDING BOSTON GLOBE

20

TO KAPINGAMARANGI

Christopher. The sea is calm, the stars are out, the moon's abed, the winds are light. *This* is sailing: Not-sailing!

Ah well, Pup, not to fear: we like being uncomfortable. Oh yes we do. Not as much as you . . . All this good weather. These skies! Those stars! *Boring!*

And our first night like it since Hawaii, believe it or not.

Danny has gone to sleep in the furled Yankee on the foredeck.

WFB, in one of his restless, postprandial dispositions, is eyeing groggily the wind instruments and speaking of raising sail.

"But Pup, there's only 3 knots of wind, and it's on the nose."

This followed by talk of "falling off," intimations of freshening winds.

So it was I said to Dan, Don't be surprised if you wake up being hoisted up the mast.

I have been charged with making sure Pup does *not* raise the Yankee tonight.

Christopher is a bird of paradise, and can't therefore really believe some of the numinous baloney he comes up with. He seemed to be saying—*Did you hear him?—Just now?*—that in effect powerboating is to be preferred over sailing: "*This* is sailing. Not-sailing." What he meant to say, if only he could write precisely, is that there are moments when the exercises required to hoist and maintain sail seem not to be worth it, and in such moments the sound of an engine is transmuted from an intrusive roar to a soothing purr.

On the other hand, come to think of it, I remember the shock I felt a few years ago on reading an article by Carleton Mitchell in *Motor Boating and Sailing*. He was correctly introduced in the article's headline as "America's premier yachtsman," Mitchell having among other things won the Bermuda race three times running, three races that included the slowest and the fastest races on record. "America's premier yachtsman," the headline went on, "tells why he switched to power from sail—and loves it."

Mitchell made a number of points of obvious plausibility, others unusually sophisticated. "Ever since I made my own escape from what I only half facetiously call 'the tyranny of sail,' " he wrote, "I have received [many] queries. For me, cruising and living aboard a displacement vessel driven by docile slaves under hatches has been very much like cruising the sailing craft I have owned, except there is more room, less dependence on others, and a new-found leisure making it possible to enjoy more of what I think of as the fringe benefits of cruising: scuba diving, poking into gunkholes, ham radio, reading, listening to music, lolling in the sun, whomping up meals in a spacious galley, or simply taking it easy, even under way, while the autopilot does the work and the soporific hum of the engines brings into focus thoughts which never seem to take form ashore. Thus, as I have tried to say reassuringly to others, the transition can be considered a way of life, instead of only a time of life."

Mitchell spoke of his gradually crystallized "yearning for space." And, finally, he came to the Great Watershed: "I found I could charter a 36-foot Grand Banks [motor yacht] based on St. Thomas, and two weeks of lazy meandering through the British Virgins had me hooked. *The simple fact of being afloat seemed more important than the kind of vessel I was aboard.*" (My italics.)

That is the raw, the numbing question. Christopher knows the sensations uniquely attaching to a boat-under-sail. No one who was ever airborne in a glider would compare that sensation to traveling in an airplane, though travel by air is of course the great polarizer. One does not, really, "travel" by glider; one merely experiences gliding, though I suppose that the day after tomorrow, Malcolm Forbes will travel in a glider from Tierra del Fuego to Point Baker, Alaska, nonstop. A cruising sailboat will take you—as we were at this very moment in the process of reestablishing—across the Pacific; indeed around the world, as is routinely done nowadays; well, perhaps not quite routinely. What Christopher was saying, really, was that the ordeal associated with sailing, the work required to raise sails, to fine-tune them, and to maintain them in proper position, is at the margin not worth it, the margin being when the price is exhaustion, or interrupted lassitude. I think he is wrong, and though I doubt that I would ever buy a powerboat (unless, for whatever reason, I could no longer handle a sailboat), I feel about this less strenuously than I once did. Certain kinds of experiences at sea would seem to me entirely eliminated by powerboats, for instance my little Friday night cruises on *Patito*. Others wouldn't be, one supposes: quite the opposite—more frequent visits to St. John River, weekend cruises to Nantucket.

Mitchell makes three emphatic points. He explains: "Confusing to the uninitiated is the lack of a proper generic term to identify the true offshore motorboat, combining seaworthiness—in the real meaning of the word—with characteristics enabling the crew to live comfortably for extended periods in remote areas. 'Trawler yacht' has been so misused as to have become almost meaningless, although nothing else seems to fit so well the concept of a pleasure version of working vessels combining carrying capacity, spaciousness, low fuel consumption, long range, and the ability to cope with rough seas.

"Perhaps the term 'displacement speed yacht' comes closer to the mark, although it lacks glamor. For 'displacement' translates as 'weight,' and from weight stem most of the virtues we are seeking: meaty construction to withstand the inevitable buffeting; ample fuel and water to provide range and independence; heavy ground tackle, including a powerful windlass capable of handling a spread of anchors, at least one on 30 to 50 fathoms of chain, insuring sound sleep when port is achieved; the space and reserve buoyance to accommodate a seemingly endless accumulation of equipment, spares, personal gear and ship's gear and, finally, consumable stores for weeks or months away from supermarkets. To say nothing of a useful dinghy, inflatable rubber raft and other survival equipment, medicines and first aid supplies, fishing tackle and/or scuba gear, books to use and amuse, and whatever else your way of life requires." A piano, for instance?

Carleton Mitchell instantly relieves us of any notion that he is playing for speed *qua* speed: "Perhaps the simplest rule of thumb to find how closely a vessel approaches the ideal is to consider her speed. It is generally conceded that a true displacement hull [i.e., a hull designed among other things not to rise in the water as it gains speed] has a maximum efficient speed of 1.34 times the square root of the waterline. Above, greatly increased horsepower—and fuel consumption—will result, producing only larger waves astern as the stern squats, unless weight is reduced or underbody form allows lifting to a 'planc' over the surface, at which point the vessel ceases to displace water commensurate with the physical dimensions of the hull. Thus a true displacement 'trawler' of 36 feet on the water would be limited to a top speed of 8.04 knots ($\sqrt{36} = 6$); $6 \times 1.34 = 8.04$." That is a good speed for the 71-foot *Sealestial*, though we can make ten knots when the wind and direction are both exactly right. (The square root of 56, *Sealestial's* waterline, is 7.5. Times 1.34 gives you 10 knots.) If you think in terms of 40 feet, waterline 35 feet—a common size in sailboats—you get a speed of 7.9. Say, eight knots ($\sqrt{35} = 5.9 \times 1.34 = 7.9$).

I think it very important to get used to the slower speeds for two reasons, the first being that the slower speed is in harmony with the winds and the natural movements of the sea. The second, that it is only with moderate speeds that one can hope in a small boat to control and even eliminate artificial sound (the indispensable requirement, in my judgment, of tolerable powerboating), and of course to minimize fuel consumption, which adds up to effective range. Carleton Mitchell's third point is that a powerboat's generator oughtn't to need to run more than a couple of hours a day, so that when at anchor, a powerboat can give the same protracted stillness as a sailboat.

Suppose, then, that by the wave of a wand I might have transformed *Sealestial* into a 71-foot powerboat during the post-midnight watch? It would be interesting to read Christo's journal over the ensuing eight days. There would be something missing in it. He would here comment, no doubt, that what would be missing in it would be the tortures of the experience. With respect to heat and ventilation, I'd concede this. Some of the intense discomforts would be missing from the experience, but so would the highest pleasures, the absence of noise, the absence of roll, the sense of motion, and the symbiosis of sail and surge. Accordingly I appeal, as the old English expression has it, from Philip drunk to Philip sober: If Christo accosted these points, I'd win that argument. Either that or simply disinherit him.

One needs quickly to concede these obvious points, which are that you get more room in a motorboat than ever you can have on a sailboat, unless you marry Marjorie Merriweather Post, or Rafael Trujillo, or whoever it is who now owns the *Sea Cloud*. I have mentioned also the factor of noise, and right away one needs to eliminate any thought of owning one of those powerboats that are so noisy as to make conversation almost anywhere aboard all but impossible. I have never quite understood how it is possible to relax when you need to shout in order to get somebody to pass you the peanut butter. Loud, throbbing engines do not conduce to the diffuser graces of rhetoric, as Charles Lamb once put it, referring to leisurely and imaginative and spontaneous conversation.

I should admit that there was a powerboat in my own history. Though I began life (age thirteen) with my own 16-foot sailing sloop, seven or eight years later my father decided to get a boat for his own use.

The *North Star* had been built during the thirties for Bernard Baruch, who desired a boat he could cruise about on the Chesapeake. This meant that its draft must be shallow because, as we all know, much of the Chesapeake is inhospitable to deep-draft boats.

On the other hand, Barney Baruch was a very tall man (six five, my memory tells me), so that what the ship gained going up it lost, so to speak, going down.

The overall length of the *North Star* was 100 feet exactly, half again as long as the *Sealestial*, and the whisper of a wind or sea would cause it to roll quite uncomfortably. I remember one time making the adventurous passage from Darien to Oyster Bay, a distance of approximately ten miles, and being grateful that I gave up seasickness, along with poison ivy, at age twelve, because I'd otherwise have been as sick as most of my guests were, just ambling about on the *North Star*. The wind was screeching at all of twelve miles per hour. I asked Captain Jones whether the *North Star* always behaved this way in williwaws, and he replied, What was I to expect of a boat designed to reach into the shallow corners of the Chesapeake? Except that I was afraid my father would overhear me, I'd have replied that what I would expect was that no one other than the original, mad owner-designer would buy such a boat.

But we had some jolly times aboard the *North Star*, even though it was what one would call a formal boat. As I remember, my father and mother frequently dressed for dinner, by which term it is useful to specify that, in those days, dressing for dinner meant putting on a black tie, as distinguished from putting on clothing. The crew of eight took excellent care of you and the vessel. There were on board five comfortable double cabins, and the boat went down to Florida via the Intracoastal for the winters; but, since I cannot tell a lie, when my father sold the *North Star* I did not grieve. My eyes were on a different kind of boat, and the interval between the death of the *North Star* and the advent of the *Panic*, my 42-foot cutter, was only about a year or two.

It was ten years before I had what one might think of as an entirely orthodox experience with a powerboat. We had been sailing to Maine and were invited for a day's outing on a 40-foot Hatteras. Its owner, a gentleman of near infinite resources, tended to be rather blasé about the amenities of life, having got used to them when he was born. But when he spoke of his powerboat his eyes shone.

Did I realize that this boat would travel at 19 knots?

Did I realize that he had made it to Mount Desert Island from Greenwich in just two days?

"How long did it take *you*, Bill, to get up here? Two weeks?"

I had put my polemical glands to sleep on this trip, and so I said nothing; and in due course we set out for a picnic on an island owned by his wife, way around at the other end of Mount Desert. He got behind the wheel of his speedy boat, high up on the bridge (a second wheel was below in the cockpit), and he invited me to feel, alongside him, the joys of true speed over the water.

It was a singular experience, riding 20 feet above the sea at 20 knots, seeing the sands and hills of Mount Desert Island gliding past at a speed reminiscent more of what you see out of the windows of small airplanes than small boats. Mostly I was struck by the sheer joy the voyage brought to the owner and captain. The distance of 40 miles was covered in just two hours, but before we got there I had retreated to the main cockpit section to read. Conversation, in that noise, was quite simply excluded. The Walk-man had not then been invented. It it had, I'd have been more comfortable.

On my return, deliberating the experience, the sheer usefulness of a powerboat was engraved on my mind, raising provocative questions that have to do with speed. In some vehicles one is never quite satisfied with their speed: we are comfortable only with pre-accepted ranges of speed. I have seen grown men weep when they cannot flog their sailboats to go one eighth of a knot faster; they are racers, generally. The same men, the next day, are calm piloting airplanes at 600 miles per hour, or driving automobiles at 55 mph, philosophically resigned to prestipulated speeds.

Using power instead of wind totally relieves you of anxieties concerning speed, unless you suspect that the barnacles on your powerboat are slowing you down, or that a cylinder is misfiring. It tends to be as simple as that when you hit the desired rpm, you will have hit your cruising speed. And if that speed is on the zippy side of the powerboat range, you will sport such a smile as was engraved on my friend's face that bright afternoon in Maine.

But I was not seriously introduced to speed on a powerboat until the day in Cat Cay in the Bahamas when a tall and fatherly gentleman asked if I would like to cruise with him to Bimini the next morning to fetch the morning paper.

"To fetch the morning paper?"—I looked at him quizzically, thinking him rather nonchalant about a 24-mile round trip for the purpose of getting the *Miami Herald*. I had better ways to spend two hours.

"Should take fifteen minutes, maybe sixteen, seventeen." John Wayne could not have sounded more casual about the length of time it would take him to dispatch Billy the Kid.

Yes, he owned a Cigarette. And I knew that there would probably be quite a few other passengers on the trip to Bimini, because that afternoon I had casually invited him and his wife over to my schooner, *Cyrano*, for a drink.

Might he bring his children? he asked.

Of course, I said. And that afternoon *eleven* blond children accompanied him and his wife to my boat. I was delighted to entertain them, but since all of them, father and mother included, were teetotalers, I quickly exhausted the ship's supply of Coca-Cola. *Cyrano* could without strain have handled a hundred alcoholics.

The Cigarette zoomed off, north, to leeward of the little coral islands, and in a minute was traveling at 60 mph. I have not had such an experience since taking the hydrofoil from Capri to Naples. I chatted with the mother of the brood and she told me that it was wonderfully comforting to be able to bring the family from Miami to Cat Cay in a matter of fifty minutes (the day before, it had taken me eight hours to go the same distance). But weren't there any bumpy experiences, I asked, in her life on a Cigarette?

Well yes, true: There were, as a matter of fact. She remembered when, the December before—"Really, I said to Charlie, why don't we just *postpone* the trip until tomorrow? But, well, Charlie just doesn't believe in postponing things."

To get to Cat Cay, they had had to cross the Gulf Stream, of course, which comes in from the south. But there was a hard northerly that day and as the meteorologists like to put it, the seas were "confused." So confused that Charlie had had to reduce the speed of the Cigarette to a humiliating 20 knots. This was unnerving for several reasons.

For one thing the boat could not plane at that speed. For another, it consumed fuel at about 90 percent of full speed rate, so that after an hour the question arose whether they would have enough fuel to complete the crossing of the Straits of Florida.

And since the Cigarette is of course an open boat, the children had ducked below to protect themselves from the drenching waves. This presents problems when there are eleven children competing for scant space. This was before we came to know about the Boat People, but it was that kind of feeling, I gathered, as Charlie's wife relived Four Hours Aboard a Cigarette in a Very Confused Sea. When they finally made it to Cat Cay they were haggard, and the following morning there were no volunteers to go with Dad to Bimini to get the morning paper.

I think of the Cigarette as an instrumental boat, absolutely perfect when you need to go from here to there, thirty miles away, when there is water in between. The alternative is a helicopter, to be sure. But on a helicopter, you can't really think of yourself as having been out boating. And that is very important.

I terribly regret that I accepted the invitation for Pat and me to cruise in Greece with friends aboard their boat, which I shall call *Elixir*. No, that isn't true, because we had a splendid time. But my wife has not, since that time, been easily satisfied with life aboard my little junks.

The *Elixir*'s staterooms are limited: there are only five. To be sure, each one is splendidly furnished, and of course air-conditioned. The boat has stabilizers, and it is hard to know when we are in motion and when we are anchored. One rises to the main deck level, where the dining room is and the public quarters, and the outdoor section with the beach chairs. There is a bar, open day and night, where you help yourself.

That bar is not to be confused with the main bar, which is one level up, under the awnings on the top deck, which is all open. There are four tenders there, nicely situated in their cradles. The

largest tender will carry ten people comfortably, and since no one
has ever been uncomfortable on the *Elixir*, I must assume eleven
people have never been on that tender at the same time.

Did I say the boat was 245 feet? Yes, and it has a crew of nineteen. There are many lovely, distinctive touches about life on that
motor vessel, but I think I remember most the little cassette
players, four of them on coffee tables here and there. You are
sitting, reading, when suddenly you feel a curiosity about world
affairs. So you lean over and depress the button that has PLAY
written on it. This you need do *all by yourself*, mind. Having done
that, you will hear, for fifteen minutes, the latest news broadcast
as delivered by the BBC. But doesn't the news get stale? Not
aboard the *Elixir*. Because every two hours a quiet steward appears
from the Radio Room with four cassettes. He goes to each of the
players, removes the stale cassette, and replaces it with the fresh
one. You wouldn't want to hear two-hour-old news, would you?

That was a lovely way to go about those islands—from Piraeus
to Andros, to Khios, overnight to Sérifos, down to Milos, around to
Kimolos, and back: a serene 16 knots, usually anchored at night,
with a tender ride into town to do a little walking, visit a tavern,
buy a souvenir, stare at the ruins, and return for dinner, served at
10:30—mustn't keep the staff up too late.

I suppose there aren't a dozen ships of that size floating about as
private caravanserais. It is a way of life. I have a friend who was
invited by Mr. Onassis aboard his yacht in connection with a
romantic anniversary, and the ultimate hospitality was shown. The
host told his guest that, whenever he felt like it, but sometime
before dinner, he should inform the captain where, during the
ten-day cruise, he desired the vessel to go—not to bother to tell
the host; he couldn't care less. He had a lot of reading to do. So
the guest elected to go from Casablanca to Marbella, to Naples, to
Haifa, to Rhodes, and then to Piraeus. A trip like that would have
taken Ulysses twenty years. It's nice to know that kind of thing
still happens.

And, finally, there was that routine weekend. Routine for our
hosts, who lived in Caracas, but who like to spend their weekends

at sea. At least, that is what they call life aboard their 48-foot powerboat, with its three air-conditioned guest cabins, captain, cook, and steward.

You begin by going to the little airport, just outside the city, where a private jet lifts you up and out to Los Roques, a matter of thirty minutes. A car is waiting, and you are taken to the little wharf on the beach. There the tender is, and in ten minutes you are at your destination, the little powerboat bobbing up and down off the Venezuelan coast as though it were in the Bahamas or in Aegean waters, so blue is it, and so white the nearby sand.

It does not occur to our Venezuelan hosts themselves to take the 100-mile sea passage. They want a houseboat. One thinks of a treehouse with the comforts of home, which is the only treehouse I would myself consent to live in. And on such a powerboat you do have potential mobility, and that means something—even if you never get around to moving.

And when you do move in a powerboat you can move decisively, and it does not matter where the wind is blowing in from, and the hull does not need to shrink to such miserable dimensions as sailors put up with. All you need is a little power, and now that OPEC is under control, we have that, do we not?

People live happily in boats used as houseboats. At the slip next to the *Panic*, and subsequently next to *Suzy Wong*, my 40-foot yawl, lay a powerboat of hefty dimensions. We were neighbors for about twenty years, and two or three times every week the owners came at about six, had cocktails and watched a little television and often had supper, leaving the boat at nine. I never saw their boat leave the dock, not once, though the captain was charged to take the boat down the waterway to Miami every year, which he reached, one assumes, in time for cocktails. It would be quite foolish, I always conceded, to own a sailboat as a houseboat, quite utterly foolish. I would need to remember to tell Christopher that when he gets up for the next watch. Or perhaps I'd just put it in the log?

Speaking of which—I roused myself from my power vs. sail

reverie—it was time to do some housekeeping duties. I went below to the chart table and pulled out my calculator:

Kosrae 5–16 N, 162–58 East. Kapinga 1–15N, 154–45 E. Distance, 548 miles. Direction 244° True, 236° Magnetic.

For two or three days we were without substantial winds, though we were able to sail beginning on Day Two. The pilot chart shows prevailing easterlies and northeasterlies, but less emphatically so than when more securely in the trades. I was experiencing difficulties with navigation which absorbed and frustrated me. Kapingamarangi is a very small, low-lying atoll and it would not do, would not do at all, to glide by it. I would not know the principal source of my problems until a post-dinner conversation the following January in Baltimore with Hugh Kenner, during which he asked whether I had correctly triggered the minus sign in the Hewlett-Packard. I had not (one doesn't use the minus sign, but the CHS key; not before the lat/lon numbers, but after them) and so had been driven to calisthenics with almanacs and tables which, while they refreshed my rudimentary skills, dampened my spirits. I pursued the WhatStar on the computer, but then put it to one side, working out the star sights on the calculator, with irregular success.

Having abandoned any hope of using the H-P calculator to give me accurate distances within the Eastern Hemisphere, I had resorted, as mentioned, to simply continuing the Western Hemisphere arbitrarily (much as, by the way, H.O. 249 Sight Reduction Tables do). The following entry in the logbook for June 24 tells about all there is to tell about my episodic ignominies as a navigator. I wrote:

>1100   The bad news is:
>
>1) No sun
>
>2) No wind
>
>3) The Great Circle program on computer is *not* working when operated conventionally. It *does* work if you add longitudes sequentially past 180° [e.g., 170° East Longitude would become 190 West Longitude]. This means that the distance to Kapinga is not

269 miles (at 246° M), but 326 miles (at 242° M). This means we will arrive on Wednesday

at	1700	if we do 6 knots
at	1500 " " "	6.2 "
at	1400 " " "	6.4 "
at	1330 " " "	6.6 "
at	1100 " " "	6.8 "
at	1030 " " "	7 "

The good news is that we are having pizza for lunch.

[one hour later]

The very good news is that the above is buncombe. Based on a mathematical error. *However*, Great Circle calculations should indeed be executed by longitudinal westward additions. [To Kapinga] 269 miles at 246° M.

So it was that time and again I was reacquainted with the preternatural failing I have for silly errors, on the order of subtracting seven from nine and getting three, I mean grossness of that order, which I suppose would have got me keelhauled under Captain Bligh, reminding me of the convenience of being Bligh, rather than serving under him.

Though the weather did not inspirit, the mood was good—in fact, it was always good, the Weltschmerz confined, in general, to the journals. And added to the disagreeable weather there was the temperature in the saloon. On top of the regular heat factor in the saloon we had a new problem. The fan in the galley, necessary to make it possible to breathe in there, broke. There was no alternative: I took the fan from the saloon and handed it to Liz. This left us, when crowded in the saloon for dinner or for the movie, without ventilation of any sort. It was quite creepy-crawly awful, and Reg promised to devote himself the very next day to attempting to fix it. Allan, taking a cursory look inside the motor, said it surely needed a new electrical spring, and Reg said, well, if necessary he would attempt to fashion a new electrical spring.

And, with Dick as always cheerfully leading the way, everything that happened reminded someone of something interesting. That evening we saw *Apocalypse Now* with Martin Sheen, which prompted Christo to say that surely the landing scene featuring the marine colonel was a near-unique cinematic triumph. And the movie reminded Christopher Little of some of the tribulations of a professional photographer. The day the three-part program on JFK began on NBC on the twentieth anniversary of his assassination, ABC went on at the same hour with "The Day After," which swamped the competition, getting an audience of fifty million or so, leaving the JFK drama, starring Martin Sheen, in the rating basement. So what? So a few weeks earlier *People* magazine had sent Christopher Little out to photograph Martin Sheen, advising him that the editors were considering cover treatment for Sheen in connection with the upcoming JFK business. So Christopher Little takes pictures of Martin Sheen, telling him it might be a cover story. But when the *People* people weigh the low ratings for JFK, they come up with a completely different cover, and Sheen calls Christopher Little raising hell, saying he *was promised a cover,* and the editor of *People* calls Christopher Little and says, Christopher Little, did you really promise a cover to Martin Sheen? and he says hell no, I know better than ever to do that . . . It was funny, hearing that story, after seeing three hours of Martin Sheen sweating his way through Vietnam, in situations that certainly warranted cover treatment for self-abnegation.

Dick let out a howl before dinner. He had inadvertently closed the lid on his Kaypro 2000 without committing a long passage he had written to the computer's memory. There is nothing quite like the sense of utter irretrievability one experiences on losing out in the running *mano a mano*, adversary relationship with a computer. I tell him with some condescension that the Epson PX-80, which Christopher Little is using (until the disk drive stopped working), automatically saves if you go ten minutes without using the machine, the point being thus to husband battery power.

The nightly movies, I note, have a greater holding power on us when the day's workload is lighter: more people stay and more of those who do stay, stay awake. My original idea of running the movie a second time for the crew was a splendid example of a *fausse*

No way. The computer is adamant.

idée claire: Wouldn't it be a fine idea, I thought while making up the watch roster in my study in Stamford, Connecticut, to screen the movie again, later, for Liz, Maureen, Noddy, and Allan? That way Liz and Maureen could finish cleaning up after dinner, and Allan and Noddy would be through with their one watch. But by 10:30 Noddy and Allan were ready to turn in, and Liz and Maureen had finished quickly with the dishes and that part of the movie they hadn't seen directly during cleanup they could easily hear in the galley, so that for two thirds of the movie they were in the saloon watching. Abstract planning, welfare-state-style, crashes one more time.

Christopher, in his journals as recorded, reverts from time to time to the Elizabethan mode when writing about the delinquencies of his roommate, Richard Clurman, whom he now refers to only as "Mr. C———." As in, "Concerning certain recent incidents involving Mr. C———: At lunch today he drippeth tahini [sesame paste] on my plate, and following the dinner hour, his cigarette was observed lying lit beside him on the floor. He possesseth the remarkable ability of stepping on you on the *top* bunk. He doth make a powerful nuisance of himself. Crew wroth; preparing hot pitch and feathers."

Dick has his own complaints, which lead to great feats of fortitude:

> My friend Bill is oblivious to physical disorder. His clothes and his stuff (lots of stuff) lie in disarray around him, wherever he happens to drop them. His shipmates unconsciously follow his lead. So I pretty much give up and except for rare moments when it's too much for everybody, we live in the clutter that belies the notion "on a boat, everything has its place." With Bill, nothing has its place—only essential emergency and sailing equipment. All the rest is where he last dropped it. He has other virtues. And everybody knows that "neatness doesn't count," even though its converse drives me crazy, unless I ignore it. So I do.

"My friend Bill is oblivious to physical disorder . . ."

And, I now note, Dick had one or two bouts of melancholy, which were never visible to any of us, so reliable was his good humor. But he would write:

> I'm feeling a little sea-weary so I ask myself, without the challenge and game of navigation, which is played all day and half the night, what's really the point of round-the-clock sailing on one course for days and days, eating extraordinarily, watching movies, reading, being banged around and never seeing anything off the boat but the same sea all the time? Silly question. My momentary downer is broken by Maureen coming on deck and announcing lunch below. Bill, even more ebullient than usual because his gadgets are working, says, "But it's only 1:01. I asked for lunch at 1:05."

Christopher, as Entertainment Officer, had unused reserves:

> 9 A.M.
> Went on watch just in time for a four-hour rainstorm. I'd seen this movie before—most of my recent watches have been wet ones —so it was with a jaded eye that I took my position in the cockpit.

The Entertainment Officer posts notices for the Children's Hour.

Pup was at the helm and in a chatty mood. He, Chris, and I devised a new ending for his novel which is very good and will go far toward prolonging the comeuppance of Bertram Oliver Heath [the Bad Man in *High Jinx*]. This done, I went below to fetch the model of the *Titanic*.

Christopher Little and I set to work on the *Titanic*. Christopher was very good company on this endeavor since Walter Lord is a kind of uncle. (His father and Lord were in OSS together during the war.) So he knows all sorts of things about the *Titanic*. He and Reg did a little *mano a mano*:

—Do you know how many compartments got flooded?

—Six.

—Did you know that one of the funnels was fake?

—Yes.

—Do you know the name of the woman sleeping in the forward section who woke up on the iceberg?

To this Christopher unhesitatingly answered, "Sophie Schwartz." Reg said, "Boy, you *do* know your *Titanic*!" Later Christopher allowed as how he'd just made the name up. That's one of the nice things about Reg: he'll believe you.

Now it's not that easy putting together a model during a driving rainstorm. Our hull started to take on water the moment we glued it together, and for a while it looked like we were going to have to put a man down to run the pumps.

After about an hour we had things under way; our hands were about to grow webs. The instructions were stuck together, causing a near disaster when I turned from Step 3 to Step 8, not noticing Steps 4, 5, 6, and 7 because they were stuck together. Christopher averted the near disaster when he noticed me trying to glue the boat deck on before the promenade deck. By this time the rain had half filled the box the model came in, so it was necessary to fish for winches, cargo booms, Dorades and the like. The little pieces proved most vexing.

Reg reemerged with some cotton swabs and a good sharp knife.

"I think it was neat the way they handled the people in steerage," he said, sarcastically.

"What did they do with them?"

"They didn't let them on deck until all the lifeboats had been filled."

Raising the Titanic.

"Oh yeah. How many of them were there?"

"About fifteen hundred."

"Funny, that's about how many went down . . ."

. . . Sinking protocol . . . Van mentioned that when the *Andrea Doria* was going down, the Italian waiters elbowed their way into the lifeboats; and I seemed to remember [incorrectly, I am told] a few years back when an American liner caught fire off Alaska with a passenger manifest full of old people. The crew distinguished itself by throwing the poor senior citizens out of the lifeboats so as to make room for themselves. Women and children first—except in emergencies.

I was having great difficulty with the Dorades on the promenade deck. My hands at this point had that waterlogged, mummified look, and the Dorades were the size of two ants, but the old *Titanic* was definitely starting to take shape.

I was thinking about the title of Walter Lord's book. I don't know why it hadn't ever occurred before, but on reflection *A Night to Remember* seems a little, well, understated, doesn't it? The first time you got laid, the time you got dysentery in Tangier, the night Aunt Matilda fell down the stairs—these are nights to remember. History's greatest ocean disaster would seem to warrant something more.

Reg and I were putting finishing touches on the *Titanic* when the fishing line started to pay out at a thousand licks per minute. While attempting to bound out of the cockpit I caught my kneecap on the rim of the winch. I had to lie in the scuppers grinding my teeth for a few moments before I could move. David Niven continued to talk on about Humphrey Bogart, and I listened to a small commotion aft about another swallowed fishing lure. Overhead, the skies were the color of lead.

As I was musing on this, the storm intensified. Our visibility was now about 100 yards in the rain. I stood, angled over the table, gluing on the observation tower and the false funnel, thinking what a piquant irony it'd be to get run over in mid-Pacific while putting together a model of the *Titanic*.

Read another three pages of *Typee*. Melville and Toby, having jumped ship, are now in the care of the Typees, who are being very hospitable, giving them tons of food, etc. Toby is convinced they're just fattening them up as they would swine, but Melville is taking the Rousseauean view—for the time being. It's going to take me 3–4 years to finish the book at this rate, but I can't seem to stay awake for more than three pages of anything on board. With a week to go I think it is safe to say *The Brothers Karamazov* will *not* get read this trip.

COCKTAIL HOUR: Oh yes, David Niven spoke about Humphrey Bogart, his odd lisp, his early unhappy marriages, ending in a fine mature union with nineteen-year-old Lauren Bacall, his soaring career beginning with *The Petrified Forest* and reaching its apogee in *Casablanca*, and then of the cough, the visit with the doctor, the slow attrition of his body, not unlike, Pup said, what happened to David Niven twenty-five years later. We heard of the delirious happiness Clark Gable finally found in his union with Carole Lombard, who had "booked a sleeper to Los Angeles but at the last second, anxious to be home, caught a milk-run plane instead. Gable was delighted and made plans for the early return. He was just getting into his car when a call came in from the studio police department."

Clark Gable refused to delegate responsibility for the funeral, at-
tending himself to everything, including the selection of the hymns.
Then he went fishing and "for three weeks drank himself to stupor."
Back in Hollywood, he kidded with old friends, memorized his lines
well and uncomplainingly, "the complete professional."

The storms are hours off, the light failing, seas calm. A bird lands
on the Bimini, exhausted, with that traumatized look such creatures have after finding something to perch on in mid-ocean with
only a few hours of energy left to them. This one is a long-beaked
green one the size of a pigeon.

On June 24, after sight-time, I wrote in my journal, "Should
arrive tomorrow between ten and eleven."

June 26, from ship's log:

    0500   DR plotted.   30 miles to go.
    Sunrise at 6-34
    Stars at 5-45
    0600   Stars plotted (Altair
                    Achernar
                    Venus
                    Jupiter) $1°$-18
                                 $155°$-17
    Changed course to 236°
    Distance = 34m
    0800   EP distance 22m
    0920   Sighted K on radar
    1015   "   " visually
    1230   Entered channel, with aid of pilot

0500	DR plotted: 30 miles to go.
	Sunrise at 6-34
	Stars at 6-45
0600	Stars plotted (Altair 1° - 18
	Archenar 155 - 17
	Venus
	Jupiter)
	Changed course to 236°
	Distance = 34m
0800	E P distance 22 m
0920	Dighton [K] on Radar
1015	" " visually
1230	entered Channel, with aid of pilot

21

KAPINGA

As we neared the atoll we could see a dinghy. It seemed to be circling. It was circling, waiting for us. Allan had radioed for a pilot boat, and it was here. Four men, two of whom boarded *Sealestial*—Harry and Salter. Salter sat behind me, dictating stiff, British-style instructions.

"Left five degrees."

"Steady as she goes."

"Right ten degrees."

"Steady as she goes."

It took a lot of these, at reduced rpm, to wiggle our way through the channel. There'd have been no way to do it without Salter, though with the sun overhead, a dinghy forward, one man driving, the second looking out, we might have got through by following the darker waters this way and that. A hairy business, though, because there are currents, and currents tend to prevent the behemoth behind from following an absolutely straight course pursuing the dinghy doing fugleman's duty at a cautious two or three knots. But it's what I'd have done if I had been Magellan. I wonder if Christo ever gave thought to how these things were done? He had written in his journal (presumably an exchange he had had with Danny):

"No *way* we could have come in here without the pilot. No fuck-ing way."

"Just be thankful Himself didn't try."

"Oh I am, I am."

The pilot and his friend Harry were not too busy both to give me instructions and to suggest that any food and drink we might have for them would be welcome. Accordingly we gave them beer and oranges, just to begin with. This brought on an imperishable exercise of Dick's maladroitness, celebrated by the entire company as Clurman's *ne plus ultra*. The islanders' 12-foot dinghy, propelled by its 24hp outboard motor, was all along following us abeam, eight or ten yards out, one native at the helm, the other standing, holding on to the dinghy's painter for balance. They were making gestures I finally interpreted as their desire to share in the refreshments, so we got word to Liz, who handed up four oranges to Dick. His cigarette in his mouth, he placed all four oranges in his cupped hands, approached the lifeline, and threw them at the natives' boat. All four oranges landed in the water. It was beautiful.

We were coming in now to the three principal little islands of the atoll, connected by tiny walkways. The atoll is about five miles by five miles, and all the islands that sit up above the water are on the arc between one o'clock and five o'clock, measured as on the face of a watch. The circle is completed by submerged reefs, save for the windy entrance at six o'clock. There are reefs, submerged and visible, freckled about the lagoon, so that piloting had to be done with caution. But we were led right up to an anchorage we selected, a few hundred feet from the principal island where, we were told, the chief was waiting to meet the ambassador—Ponape had done its hospitable work of advising the island of our probable call.

So we disembarked, leaving the others to bask in the startling beauty of our surroundings. (Christo: "We drop our usual four hernias' worth of anchor chain in 20 feet of water off the village. Murmurs of appreciation on deck. Rampant coconut palm, thatched huts, a hundred children giggling at the end of the dock, nestled in the green, a tiny white church steeple, tourmaline water, not so

much as a telephone pole to locate the century we were living in—
just the Evinrude outboard.") Van, Christopher Little, and I went
off in Salter's dinghy.

Van. This was, without doubt, the first time that an American
Ambassador had called at Kapinga, and they held an exaggerated
belief as to my importance. My physical appearance, on stepping
ashore out of our small Zodiac, did not live up to their ambassadorial
expectations—bare feet, short pants, Lacoste tennis shirt, and a
white Greek fisherman's cap. I should have given the sartorial matter more thought and donned my double-breasted blue blazer, white
trousers and, above all, my Topsiders, because the 25 yards across
ground coral to the village meeting hall were painful, and my stride
lacked dignity.

Notwithstanding, the people were all smiles, happy to see Bill
and me as we made our way (me with the aid of a strong Polynesian
arm) to be received by the chief. He greeted us at the door of his
low concrete-block building with a tin roof and showed us to a long
table at which we sat opposite the chief and about eight councillors.
Immediately someone lopped the heads off two milk coconuts with
a long machete, and we were urged to drink. I did so with pleasure,
but I noticed out of the corner of my eye that Bill's enthusiasm was
perfunctory.

The chief expressed an interest in our coming (Kapinga had not
seen a sailboat in three years, it turned out, and could count only on
the monthly supply ship from Ponape). He invited us to a scheduled island banquet two days later but we explained we would need
to leave the following day. He then asked whether we had television
on board and we learned—about this there was confirmation from
all sides—that, at Kapingamarangi, the biggest treat of all for the
350 islanders is when a little steamer comes in with movies on tapes.
Then the steamer hands over the television set for the night, and a
VHS auxiliary and four or five video tapes. The entire village con-
venes about the chief's dwelling, the generator is turned on, and
through the night the movies are shown, sometimes over and over
again, until the provider recalls his set and pulls out. I told the chief,
Sure we had a television and movies, and I'd see to it that they got
them as soon as we returned to the vessel.

This proved impossible. Danny and Christopher and Reggie pooled their energy and resources, but finally opined that the wire disconnections needed in order to disengage the telly could never thereafter be made right again, that the set would never again work in the *Sealestial* and most probably would not work for the chief; so we had to carry back the doleful news with consolation fare, presenting the chief with an assortment of articles, including my book *Atlantic High* which he had requested on learning that we had on board a book that included pictures of a voyage in *Sealestial* across the Atlantic.

Everyone made plans. Van intended to investigate the little islands, and also to jog. So did Danny and Christopher plan to visit, and they also scheduled some snorkeling. Dick and Reg would rest, swim, and sight-see. I would do a little of everything, including nap. We sat down for lunch. All of Liz's repasts were memorable, but this one was extraordinary even by her standards. I wish Van or Christopher or Reggie or Dick had recorded the fare because, as with flowers, I stare at edible delicacies and don't quite know what to call them. But I did scratch down that they included meat, salad, sandwiches, Mexican salad with corn, corn bread, dates, cheeses, and a freshly baked chestnut pie.

In the afternoon we came again on an American who that morning had greeted us along with the islanders, a retiring scientist in his late thirties—Ted Murphy—who had told us that if he could help in any way, we could find him in a little thatched shelter kitty-corner from the chief's, that he was on the atoll doing research for an oceanographic institute. I asked him to join us for dinner and he gleefully accepted.

He arrived at about six, an hour or so before sundown, and was carrying, astonishingly, a copy of *Airborne*. He told us he was at Kapinga for a fortnight to conduct some researches, and that he had brought the book with him and had finished reading it only the day before, and was, well, surprised when the following morning he came upon its author. You can't get smaller-world stuff than that, I tell you, at Kapingamarangi, if you please, one degree above the equator, 26 degrees west of the International Date Line.

Kapinga is in touch once a day with Ponape, using the single side band radio and relaying weather and ocean current information. These data are carefully tabulated by the University of Hawaii, and Ted is on the island intending to set up an automatic system for measuring currents. The northeast trades, which had blown us here all the way from Hawaii, create an easterly current. Water, Ted reminded us, inasmuch as it seeks its own level, causes the strong easterly current—the huge countercurrent I've referred to—just north of the equator, which bumps into the Humbolt Current off South America (the El Niño condition, we are always being told, causes climatic difficulties of one sort or another in California and other western states). This collision is bad for the anchovy crop, hurting in turn the fish meal production and the economy of Peru. In turn this means a shortage of protein, creating a demand for more U.S. soybeans to make up the deficiency. We never quite got it from Ted what an exact knowledge of the currents would do to prevent the unhappy union between the countercurrent and the Humboldt, but we were greatly impressed by the weight he attached to his researches, reflecting the gravity of his mission.

It was, really, a splendid evening. *Sealestial* looked quite beautiful, her huge, all-encompassing yellow awning up for the first time since Hawaii, shielding us from sun all the way aft, covering the two cockpits and, like visors on a car's window, shielding us from the sun until its angle came down to innocent eye level. The sun's evening rays shone on the green little islands and their yellowing beaches, and the blues of the water kept changing hue.

Tonight, Christo said, would be the last of David Niven, the last of four hours. David ended his story by telling of the corrupting influences of Hollywood. He spoke of a youngish actor who had got on wonderfully well with a small agent called Gersh, who had looked after the interests of the young actor and befriended him over the years. Along came a big-timer called Allenberg. Hollywood was at his feet. He could get his clients choice roles, triple their salary. The young actor fell under his influence and in due course resolved he would let his contact with Gersh expire the following month and sign up with Allenberg. Telling this to Gersh had not been easy, Gersh's reaction being that he would never again deal with actors, that from now on he would confine himself to authors, who knew what friendship and loyalty were like. The actor was upset, and relayed his misgivings to Allenberg who had said, Forget it, Gersh will get over it, just give him a little time. The following day the actor called Allenberg, his new agent, on a professional matter. The receptionist gave the news that Allenberg had died the night before.

"The name of that young actor? David Niven."

David had told me the story ten years earlier, and I suppose he told it often, his form of expiation. Look, he was saying, all of you who admire me so, look at the kind of thing I am capable of doing . . .

Admirable.

We would miss David on board *Sealestial*, as we always will, away from the *Sealestial*.

We went below for dinner and I proposed a modest toast to M.I.T. because Reggie had fixed the delinquent fan. The temperature was 91 degrees, but the fan made life bearable again. Allan, trying the radio, was surprised to get a clear connection with Oakland, California, so I called Frances Bronson of my office, with much compunction since it was 4 A.M. in New York, but I didn't know when next the radio might chance to work. She had no news in particular, save to say that the package I had air-mailed to her of tapes and correspondence had arrived only the day before. Fifteen days from Johnston Atoll to New York! "It figures," Van commented, and there was general unanimity. "They probably played your tapes to check for security."

And in due course we were watching *Lolita*, utterly relaxed in the knowledge that there were no sails to be maneuvered, no navigational work to be done. We swam again, and sat about in the cockpit talking and drinking a cold beer. At that moment we got a squall. Allan and I conferred. It made sense, to guard against the possibility of dragging, to move the ship one hundred yards farther away from shore. Ah, but this meant pulling up that anchor chain by hand, because our windlass had stopped working in Majuro. So

"The anchor was truly stuck."

—out we trundled, I at the wheel, six men pulling together on the chain, in rhythm. But the anchor was truly stuck. Van recorded, "The anchor was firmly wedged into a large chunk of coral, it turned out. Danny went down with an air tank and a flashlight and unscrewed the anchor chain, and replaced it with the line. He loosed the anchor as much as he could. We all then pulled in on the chain, Bill powered up over the anchor, and we broke it loose and hauled it in. During this operation, Dick kept dropping the chain on my feet, much to the amusement of Danny." After *that* we slept.

Christopher.   Next day Dan, C.L. and I are in the Zodiac scouring the shallows for the U.S. plane shot down by the Japanese. I drag Danny, with the snorkel, behind. The Zodiac has a hole in it the

Kapingamarangi's World War II memorial.

size of a golf ball, so I bail as I troll. We hail an outrigger canoe and ask directions. Ten minutes later we're diving on the plane.

It's in about 30 feet of water, in four big, shiny pieces. The propeller is bent from the impact of the crash, its red paint thickened and gooey from forty years underwater. Just below the engine cowling I spot the holes made by the anti-aircraft guns: size of a quarter. Little blue fish dart in and out of the twisted wreckage: a sword, beaten into a reef. We offer a watery prayer for the crew and ascend toward the light.

Three hundred yards north is a sunken Japanese ship in 50 feet of water. We let ourselves sink down into her. She's on her side, and because her hull was perfectly intact we supposed she'd been sunk by a hit on her other side—or scuttled. One curious detail was the 10-inch projectile I found—lying on top of her side, near the water-

line. How did *that* get there? I rolled it on the side and it fell with
several thumps to the floor, near where an enormous crayfish had
defiantly stared us down.

Dan found a large bottle, a jeroboam maybe, which I tried re-
peatedly to smash against the prow in a posthumous christening
ceremony, but repeated blows produced only a hollow, glassy
thwack. Then Danny found the Oerlikon (antiaircraft) guns, all
encrusted with iron oxide. We moved by the hatches to her holds
and, exchanging "after you, Gaston's," decided not to enter those
darkened spaces for fear of disturbing some creature's slumber. Our
air was now running out and we reluctantly bubbled our way back
up to the Zodiac.

I walked, with Van and Reggie. A circumnavigation of the village, including all three islands, requires only about twenty minutes. Every forty or fifty yards, to seaward, there was a walkway—
narrow elevated docks they looked like—held up on wooden pylons,
leading out to a tiny thatched enclosure above the water, twenty
feet below. Inside the hut was a round hole, toilet-size. These are
Kapinga's toilets. I tried to forget that they were on the windward
side of the island. Still, the swimming is all in the lagoon, so far as
we could see.

Kapinga's well-thatched W.C.

Christopher Little, back from his dive, joined us. The morning's gifts to greater Kapinga included two 55-gallon drums we'd have no further use for. "And," Christopher Little noted, "in a particularly inspired moment Christo and Danny brought the Ping-Pong table ashore. It was immediately set up in the village square adjacent to the Men's Hut, Kapinga's version of the Century Club, and was a major hit. We left considerable loot in Kapinga. A partial list was compiled from memory:

> Two cases of beer
> Seven bottles of shampoo
> 1 Ping-Pong table (including 30 orange Ping-Pong balls)
> 1 jumping rope
> At least a dozen *Sealestial* T-shirts
> Cash "for gas"; i.e., for the pilots.
> 24 Milky Way bars
> 24 chocolate-covered Granola bars
> 30 mint sweets
> Assorted bottles of wine (red & white)
> Assorted bottles of booze (hard: brown & white)
> Matches

And, Christo added finally,

"1 carton of Dick's Benson & Hedges (sequestered without the owner's knowledge). In fact, the suggestion was made that *all* of Dick's cigarettes be given to the good people of Kapinga, but this was vetoed on the grounds it would constitute cruel and unusual punishment. It was then counter-suggested that Dick be given to the islanders. This was vetoed on the grounds that it would constitute cruel and unusual punishment."

"Everyone," Christopher Little wrote, "was uniformly friendly although in the distance I could see the women cover their breasts as we approached. In brash photographer/Ugly American fashion I smiled my way into countless homes and photographed the friendliest strangers I've ever met. From little babies in hammocks being lulled by their mothers to old men tending their okra fires. We visited the school, the dispensary, and the Kapingamarangi Co-op

The shoeless ambassador calls on the chief.

Refreshments are served.

(its nearly empty shelves bearing cans of condensed milk and soup, a few jars of instant coffee, and eleven packages of Winston cigarettes). Our young guide explained that the copra boat wasn't due in for another two weeks."

The big adventure for *Sealestial* would be an onshore lunch, a picnic on the beach, by the passage between two of the islands.

> **Christopher.** Lunch was the long-postponed "cookout." Roasted chicken wings, green bean salad, chips, the inevitable and now very dreaded Swedish crackers ("our hardtack," observed one embittered companion) [I found this animadversion on the Swedish crackers I had scoured two continents to get for my palate-dead Philistines intolerable], wine, and beer. When Dan, C.L., and I arrived on the island, the rest of our company was arrayed on the yellow tarp in the shade. Several drinking coconuts were laid on the tarp, with some of the yellowish stuff poured incongruously into our Italianate plastic wineglasses. Nearby huddled a company of Kapingamarangese, looking on.
>
> After gnawing the meat off several chicken wings and draining a few beers, we decided to go sit in the shallows. This we did, and exceedingly pleasant it was, though the water temperature, as one observer observed, was the temperature of urine.
>
> Within no time we found ourselves surrounded by the children, who seemed to find us curious specimens and a source of amusement, and didn't mind sharing the picnic. They crowded in around us, pointing out our oddities among themselves, giggling, submerging. The ship was off in the distance; the smoke from their pig roast wafted over the little channel; the sun, bright and declining, shone above a distant squall line. Dan brought over more beers, and we sat there experiencing a contentment rarely felt by mortal souls.
>
> "Tell my mother I'm staying," said Noddy when a boat was sent ashore in an attempt to induce us to return, for our departure from that uncharted isle was not far off. "Tell her I love her."

Danny had scooted off to the artisan who was completing the wooden shark we had secretly commissioned as a gift for Liz. It was huge, skillfully crafted, and lifelike, its hungry teeth open and ready to eat man or beast. Danny had thought to buy a turtle shell as a

Ping-Pong coaching, a part of our Marshall Plan.

A night swim.

gift for me from the crew, but Christopher had discouraged him, predicting that Pat would not permit it on the premises. Danny and Noddy came on the Zodiac to pick Christopher, Reg, and Christopher Little up from their beloved shallows by the beach.

> **Christopher.** Now the launch had returned, and we with heavy hearts pulled ourselves aboard. The children swarmed around our craft with a profusion of "Bye-byes!" One little girl lunged for the transom, but soon she and Kapingamarangi were astern, and our course set for the wilder shores of New Guinea. It was sad to consider that probably none of us would ever return here but alas, such is the nature of paradises.

22

TO KAVIENG

Kapinga to Kavieng was our shortest leg, a mere 312 miles (one becomes blasé, but 312 miles is 121 nautical miles farther than from New York to Washington). Two days, two nights, I projected. Of course it was not to be.

We had dead-on head winds for the first time, and the most obstinate and eccentric foul currents I've ever experienced. We were under special psychological pressure because Van's professional/personal life was coming to shreds before Arcturus's very eyes. As, by the way, did the clew of the Yankee, the first night out, turn to shreds, leaving us with our last set of headsails, a jib topsail and a staysail. At one point it became obvious that Van would not catch the connection that would permit him to entertain the Vice President. It was problematical whether he would be in Paris in time to be the guest of honor at the farewell party the following day, and we reached a point where I even wondered whether he would be there at the embassy's obligatory Fourth of July Party. I have no doubt he was finally brooding on whether he would still have a wife on July fifth.

The rest of us, who were not scheduled to fly out of New Guinea until two days later, were ourselves made a little tense by Van's quite uncharacteristic tension. At one point he came to me and asked whether we wouldn't be better off powering into our course rather than tacking. I drew a sketch demonstrating that if *Sealestial* split one hundred degrees at eight and a half knots, which was what we were doing tacking under sail, as compared to doing five knots dead into the wind under power, it would take us twenty-seven hours under power to do what we could under sail in twenty-two hours. For a very few hours it irritated . . .

> **Christopher.** Van has gotten obsessive about getting to Kavieng. Every time I lower the rpm's by one or two hundred, he sits up and demands to know what I am thinking of. Or if I fall off the wind by as much as two degrees—*two* degrees!—I am treated to ten minutes of complaining. It is . . . slightly vexing. While I understand Van's anxiety, it has introduced an unfortunate element to the end of our trip. We've been running hard, Lord knows, very little R & R. As they might say in the Foreign Service, I'm not sure Van realizes his obsessiveness is *impacting* on us.

But that was a spastic reaction: Van hadn't really changed, never would. And in the end he greeted our reversals, one after another, with jocular stoicism. Each of us appeased his own impatience in different ways. Christo slept, or tried to, more than usual. Dick, one day after lunch, rather extraordinarily asked for some chocolates (he is anti-sweet). M & M's were served up. He took a handful, paused, extracted from the lot of us the pledge *never* to reveal what he had done—"It would ruin me for life"—and ate them. Danny, Reggie, and Christopher Little occupied themselves with this and that. I turned obsessively to my own opiate: celestial navigation in the electronic age.

On the second day the wind picked up, and although we needed to continue tacking, we had fine weather—scattered clouds but almost always bright sun. We were, however briefly, sailing at over eight knots, though the log would show, when I did my next sights, that we were making good, over the ground, less than six knots.

Danny and I thought during our watch to make up a list of what *Sealestial* had suffered from during the trip, combined with what she suffered from before we even set out, twenty-nine days ago.

Memo on Sealestial and Condition
- Baggy wrinkle was needed for sail chafing.
- The genoa shredded almost immediately, was of no use through the passage.
- The Yankee's clew detached, rendering it inoperative.
- The mainsail's seams needed mending.
- The starboard upper spreader support was broken, probably causing much of the damage to the main.
- Spinnaker poles are corroding, dangerous to use.
- Genoa sheet track pulled out; the bolts were corroded.
- The sheets were frayed.
- The main halyard reel winch was broken, also the anchor windlass.
- Insufficient stitching tools on board.
- Digital Brooks & Gateshouse log milometer not working [that is the instrument that records distance traversed through the water].
- The lighting is out on all cockpit instruments [a heavy handicap at night].
- The Zodiac [dinghy] has numerous leaks.
- The cockpit table is loose.
- Port running light not working.
- SATNAV never worked.
- Galley fan not working.
- Weatherfax not working.
- Video camera not working.
- Deck showerhead missing.
- Main companionway glass panel won't stay down.
- Water maker not functioning.
- Autopilot was not working; fixed by Reggie.
- Pump for Zodiac missing.
- Auto bilge pump not working.
- Main blower fan in engine room not working.
- Spare part inventory apparently nonexistent.
- Generator cutoff switch for fan not working.

We felt better, having put together a comprehensive list. The General Accounting Office would have been pleased.

Danny and I also composed a list of recommendations to Charles Trimble, who had been so obliging in lending us the $40,000 GPS prototype. We noted that the unit had worked about four (consecutive) hours per day until we arrived at approximately 4 degrees North Latitude and 170 East Longitude, after which it worked for only about one hour per day, even though it indicated, however spasmodically, that it had the requisite three satellites in sight. We made recommendations, especially aimed at facilitating the engagement of the satellites when they came within operative range of the antenna. A problem, of course, that will not exist after the Defense Department has launched all of the twenty-one scheduled satellites that will complete the unbroken belt around the sky.

Occasionally the fish at sea would continue to tease us.

> **Christopher.** Made tea at 0600. Put out fishing line which hadn't been out 20 seconds before line started paying out like mad. The fish took the lure and most of the leader in under a minute. These waters showed talent, so I put on another lure and dropped that in and went off to make another pot of tea. Came up three minutes later. Van was at the wheel. He asked if I wanted to read his book. I said I did, he said he'd fetch it. I took the helm, and chanced to look back. The rod was bent almost double. I hollered for Van to come back up—how had he not heard the line pay out?—and scrambled back. *All* the line had gone out. I started to reel in. This fish was strong. I put the butt of the rod between my legs for leverage and quickly regretted it. I got maybe 20 yards of line in when the fish broke water 100 yards astern, a huge, fantastic white froth of ocean. I knew then I'd never get it aboard. A moment later he sounded, almost pulling the rod out of my hands. Suddenly there was that depressing telltale spring in the line, then the slack. Damn!

Christopher's preoccupation with the fish did not mean he would neglect his chronicle of Dick's disposition to fiasco.

> Dick appeared on deck, smelling of shaving cream. (This is his fragrant time of day—before his first cigarette.) I told him about my adventure with the creature of the deep, whereupon he delivered a lecture on the landing of fish.

"Let's put up the Bimini," I said. In the attempt, Dick thrust the bar so it banged sharply into my knee, also knocking off my eyeglasses.

"Don't feel bad," I said. "It's probably only a fracture."

They were, they are, the best of friends. Dick wrote, in those closing days:

> The more I know the closer I feel to this remarkable younger man, full of wit, talent, irreverent intelligence, insight, and internal storms rarely reflected in his external charm. He is a thoroughly modern young man with a spacious capacity for all kinds of other people. Tonight on the midnight watch we are talking, not fooling around. "Reg really wanted to stop at Ailinglapalap," says Christo. I say we all did. "We're really pressing on," he mentions, aware that whenever we stop, Bill wants to get on with it so we can stay on schedule. "It's sort of the way Pup lives," he says. He knows Bill as well as, or better than, anyone. After my own son Michael, I think I probably now feel attached to this lad more than to any young man I know of his generation. He may be a chip off the old Buckley block, but from that chip his own new spreading tree has grown—disciplined, but slightly wild, traditional in formal manners and religion, but effervescing with his own variations.

The star sights on the second day finally and absolutely establish that only estimated positions, not convenient assumed positions, will get any juice at all out of the WhatStar. I gave out the dismaying news: we had averaged 5.6 knots in forty hours. It was now officially out of the question that Van would catch the first of his connections. We would need to play for the second and, finally, the third, depending on how it went that evening.

Dinner was as usual superb, though there was what Christopher designated as a "Kosraen vegetable puree" which Liz was urged not to stock up on the next time she was in Kosrae. Van was asked to give a toast in the French style, as though he were in diplomatic circumstances. He would have used both hands to perform, except that he needed one to compensate for the ship's tossing. He did in

Bonne cuisine, bonhomie.

fine French a spectacular dithyrambic toast to all and sundry for a couple of minutes, punctuated by *"Tiens!"* We fell to a discussion of the unique usefulness of that French word. My colleague Bill Rusher once recalled an exchange he had heard between General Charles de Gaulle and Governor Thomas E. Dewey when the general made his first postwar trip to the United States in 1945. Their exchange, made near a live microphone, was overheard in the large banquet hall.

"I forget," General de Gaulle had said (probably he had not forgotten it at all), "just who was it who ran against President Roosevelt in the last presidential election?"

"Why," Thomas E. Dewey beamed, "that was I!" General de Gaulle looked all the way down at his 5-foot 8-inch host and said, *"Tiens!"* I told them the coincidence that a dear friend with whom I regularly correspond, a Belgian living in Atlanta, recently remarked in passing that the word *"tiens"* has no English equivalent, to which I had responded, yes it does, try: *Whaddayaknow*. That word, depending on the inflection given it, can do everything for you that *tiens* can do—I think.

The saloon lights dimmed for the movie, lighting the tobacco smoke . . .

> **Christopher.**   Our movie supply is down to those we've not shown because no one wanted to see them. Dan ate four Oreos before lunch, two with, and four following. Having mashed two into his mouth simultaneously, he then poured in a mouthful of Rosé. I expressed revulsion at this and asked if he might eat atop the mast so as to spare us the grievous spectacle. But asking people aboard to eschew their less endearing mealtime habits is a lost cause. Dick lights up his cigarette between courses, during courses: my favorite moment came when, the night Liz served curry, he reached over and ashed into the raisin dish, just as I was reaching for a handful.
>
> But here Dick is not the only offender. No matter how nauseating the action of the seas, each night after dinner out come the cigars, and soon the saloon is rendered foul with smoke. On top of this, WFB has introduced a most piquant quirk. Saying he cannot enjoy his cigar unless "I can see the smoke come out," he ordered the hatch shut, depriving us of the only source of fresh air. When I demurred, rather heavily, he replied that he could not sit "in a wind tunnel"! Perceiving this to be another lost cause, I went out to take my customary movie seat, at the top of the companionway, where a stray whiff of oxygen might reach my beleaguered lungs.

After star-tending, I stayed up and went forward to chat with Allan who was sitting (his *querencia*) by the mainmast, on the forward end of the cabin top, a can of beer in one hand, looking out at the sea. We talked again of his forthcoming engagement with *Freedom*, and of the many hours he would spend at sea. Do you know, he said, the owner doesn't think it's safe to go through the Suez Canal, figures we'd be too tempting a target for the terrorists —you know, big pleasure boat. So we're going back through the

Mediterranean, down the western shore of Africa to Capetown. After that, to Perth. Five thousand miles—there's nothing in between the tip of Africa and the tip of Australia.

I told Allan I thought that was an awfully long distance to go to avoid the Suez Canal, and he shrugged his shoulders, as he would if suddenly told I had decided to go, instead of to New Guinea, back to Hawaii. "That's for Mr. Simon to decide," he said. And then he chuckled a bit, and spoke of the long summer on the *White Eagle,* a previous command before going to Bill Simon—a boat owned, as it turned out, by a classmate of Van's and mine with a passion to dive: all summer in the Central Pacific, finding this place and the other place to dive. But—Daphne had been with Allan. And now they were married and had a child. It wasn't like Allan, so it sent a shaft of pleasurable electricity through me when he said this year had been "very good" for him. I said something about how I hoped the current trip hadn't interrupted that stretch of good fortune. He smiled, and said nothing. I told him I'd go back and see how Christo, who appeared to be alone in the cockpit, was doing.

Christo was, for an hour or so, alone—I didn't wake up his watch companion. We talked discursively and privately. "Odd," Christopher wrote in his journal, "that this should have been our first time alone; mostly due to my promotion to watch captain, he and I haven't had any watches together." We talked about the guillotine-finishes of our passages, where everyone lands and promptly disappears, risking a clinical ending to the entire operation, like actors hurrying off in different directions after the curtain goes down. He agreed, though he reminded me that after he had landed in Spain on the B.O. [we were still so referring to that passage, the "Big One"], he and Danny had gone off to Morocco, while I had flown back directly, as all of us would now do.

He wrote in his journal, "You find out on a trip like this who you can absolutely depend on. And really the answer is, Pup and I agreed, that the person who is *absolutely* dependable in every situation is Reggie." We didn't mean that anyone on board had ever broken the absolute rule of intrapersonal courtesy, merely that Reg is a critical mass of intelligence, good nature, and composure. He has never complained, about anything.

In fact, on the trip, just last night, I had broken down and told a story on (or about) Reggie I had kept a secret for seven years. Pat and I, in Hong Kong in 1978, were most hospitably treated by Reggie's nephew, a business journalist, a suave and sophisticated young writer-operator. Reggie had written to him, and to me about him, a letter in which he casually mentioned that he continued to be disappointed that on one or two trips back to America, his nephew had neglected to bring Reggie one of those yellow underwater cameras you use while scuba diving, which are available in Hong Kong at a small fraction of what they cost in New York.

I chided young Billy on his neglect of his uncle while making a gleeful private commitment. Pat had given me one of those yellow cameras for Christmas three or four years earlier. I had never used it, on the grounds that one has quite enough to do while scuba diving without worrying about taking pictures, and longed to be rid of it. On my return to Stamford, I packed the yellow camera and sent it to Reggie with a note that it had been given me in Hong Kong by his dutiful nephew Billy, to deliver to his uncle.

It happened that one month later, Billy's best Hong Kong friend returned to Newport to be married—and, having overheard my conversation with Billy, brought one of those yellow cameras to Reggie as a gift. Which prompted Reggie to send *that* yellow camera to me, with a note that he was sure I would want to have one of the cameras which he now had two of. I felt like Lady Macbeth staring at the bloodstain.

Yes, Christo and I concluded, there had been some disappointments in the passage, though most of these had been imposed on us: the tight schedule, the bad ventilation, the heat, the squalls, the rain, the crowding in the forward cabin. Christopher wrote directly to me in that particular journal entry, "It was good having the talk, Pup. Just hope I haven't been one of the disappointments." And, a little later, "As the end draws nearer, I'm weighing my hankering for my wife, a warm, unmoving bed, and a hot shower against the knowledge that we'll never do this again. Never will

Van, Reg, Dick, Chris, Pup, Dan, and I sail all together again. Sad to think so. Can't believe I'm getting sentimental about it. Must be the malaria pills."

We had one more squall to go through.

Christopher. Not long after Pup had gone down to sleep, some spray started reaching me in the cockpit. The moon was high above, throwing light down on the seas. The winds were up to 25, 30. Reg and Dick came on watch, Dick taking the helm. In these seas, an interesting proposition.

I remember concentrating on the wind indicator (with some misgiving as the gusts built up to 40), looking up and seeing Dick, helm white-knuckled in both hands, look of (understandable) terror on his face as the ship's nose reared up and then plunged into the troughs. On either side of him the Bimini had come loose and was flapping madly.

"What can we do about this?" he said with a motion toward the disarry surrounding and disconcerting him.

I said I'd get it and climbed up behind him to throw some line around the canvas. From my perch above him I had a too-good view of the sea. Just then we reached the crest of a sizable wave. I thought, "I'm up here, we're about to crash, Dick's down there at the helm . . . I don't want to watch this." So I turned back to the line and went on uncleating it. This was a pure ostrich-reaction. Sure enough, seconds later I felt the water disappear from under the bow, the surge of speed as we began the plunge, then the shudder as the next sea crashed against the bow. A great sheet of water flew up over the deck and trajectoried down on top of us. The next morning Danny, who had been asleep in the after cockpit, would say, "You wouldn't believe this fucking wave we took. Dumped 15 gallons on me." To which I was able to say, "The reason it wasn't 25 gallons is that I intercepted the difference."

Gotta say, Dick didn't do bad at all. The wind was doing a lot of screaming by now, and that can unnerve you a bit. Reg took the helm and I went below, glad to leave it all up on deck—the moon, wind, and seas—'cause I had the feeling this could be the last (real) night of our trip, even though I could be reasonably sure Pup will order the bow lines cast off in Kavieng as soon as we get the Worried Ambassador off.

And Dick was writing, reflectively,

I begin to realize that for much of the time none of us enjoys, in the conventional sense, what we are committed to doing. The surest sign is that we all long for land. I'm reminded that most tourists do not enjoy traveling in itself. They enjoy having done it rather than the experience of doing it. Not I. But this trip seems to be edging toward that kind of perverse pleasure in inducing pain to enjoy its absence. I mention this to Bill on watch one night and to my utter surprise he agrees. Of course no one enjoys the mountain climb, he says. It's getting there that matters. Too simple. Parts of the trip were ecstasy—much of it an adventuresome agony. The balance was not enough to make me change my mind that having done something is still incomparable to doing it. Including crossing the wide Pacific, with all its downers.

I am amused to discover that the very last entry in the ship's logbook ends at 0600 on the morning of June 30. That has happened before, I recall: When a trip is thought psychologically to be over, the logbook degenerates into something of a formality and, its utilitarian function over, is ignored. The final log readings, given what happened, are provocative to read. And what happened was anticipated by that last reading, in Danny's handwriting. "DTM and Van take over. Reg says we are 60 miles away. Disagree. I think we are less than 30 miles. We'll soon know." Dan would more accurately have written, "We'll eventually know."

At dawn we spotted the coast of New Ireland. Christopher wrote, "There she is—the coast of New Guinea! [I had, as already noted, been using "New Guinea" to refer to the whole Solomon Sea archipelago, including New Britain and New Ireland, which is actually 180 miles north of New Guinea.] I miss the old Land-ho-ho, but our landfalls have tended to be night ones. You sort of feel like you're sneaking up on the land when you fetch it up at night. Give me sparkling bright seas, gusts on the rigging, and two hours of peeled retina, Cabo de São Vicente finally appearing between the wave tops, a gobbled lungful, heart-quickening Laaaand ho!!"

Christo was referring to the southwestern coast of Portugal when we spotted it on the B.O., exactly (to the day) ten years ago . . .

We had been heading west since spotting Tabar on the radar, and the 30-mile estimate was reasonable. We moved in toward land slowly (the cursed current again) and now the wind failed, so that we were under power.

Christopher Little tape-recorded the heroically exasperating effort by Allan to get through to the American Embassy in Rabaul to reinstigate the air charter Van would now need if he was to be in Paris on July 4:

> "Rabaul Radio, this is Mike Charlie Bravo Zulu Three. Do you read me? Rabaul Radio, this is Mike Charlie Bravo Zulu Three. Do you read me? Rabaul Radio, this is Mike Charlie Bravo Zulu Three. Do you read me? Over." This continued for twenty minutes. Finally:
>
> "Mike Charlie Bravo Zulu Three, this is Rabaul Radio. I read you. Please stand by."
>
> Ten minutes pass.
>
> "Mike Charlie Bravo Zulu Three, come in please. Over."
>
> "Yes, Rabaul Radio, this is Mike Charlie Bravo Zulu Three. This is the Yacht *Sealestial*. That's Sierra Echo Alpha Lima Echo Sierra

Van and Allan wrestle with the radio in search of . . . Paris.

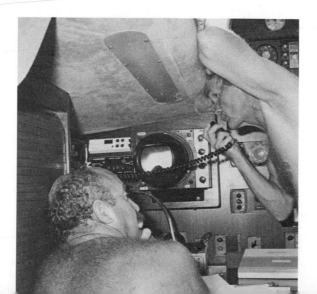

Tango India Alpha Lima. We'd like to place a telephone call to the American Embassy in Port Moresby. Over."

"I do not read you, Mike Charlie Bravo Zulu Three. Please repeat. Over."

We repeat.

"Still do not read you. Over."

Finally, Rabaul heaves in and even contributes the telephone number of the embassy.

"Ah, Mike Charlie Bravo Zulu Three, how do you wish to pay for the call? Over."

"Can we use a U.S. telephone credit card number? Over."

"Negative. Over."

"Can we give you a billing address? Over."

"Negative."

"Well, how do *you* suggest we pay for the call? Over." (Mustn't sound too exasperated at this point. We need them more than they need us.)

"*Sealestial,* you can only pay for this call by calling collect. Over." (*Well why didn't you say so in the first place!*)

"Thank you, Rabaul. This is a collect call from Ambassador Evan Galbraith to Ambassador Paul Gardner. Over."

"What?" (You can imagine how long it took to straighten that out.)

But finally Van got through, the duty officer made and confirmed the flight arrangements (it would cost Van $1900 to fly from Kavieng to Port Moresby, he would leave the following morning at dawn and arrive in time to catch the flight Manila-Zurich-Paris; and all would be well. *Sealestial* needed only to be in Kavieng by dawn tomorrow, and I expected to be there not long after noon today.

By 1230, by common agreement we had gulped down our lunch, expecting to round North Cape into Kavieng within the hour. Allan had pointed to a promontory a few miles up and said, "Gotta be just around that point."

I have gradually learned a lesson about the responsibility for navigation, punctuated as recently as last Christmas when *Sealestial*'s sister ship (not under my command) ran into coral off Anguilla. It is this: The navigator, whoever he is, should assume *sole* responsibility for navigating. *Never* share his duties. If others wish to do their own platonic navigating or piloting calculations, fine. But what tends to happen—or does so in my case—is that when a qualified companion begins to get into the act, however informally, he osmotically absorbs responsibility; which is what happened only just now. Within sight of New Ireland, I ceded psychologically to that person's navigational conclusions. When Allan said Kavieng had to be around that bend, and knowing it had been only fifty miles away at three in the morning when we passed Tabar on the port beam, twelve miles away, it did not occur to me to question Allan's judgment. By the same token, my instant acquiescence in his projection had a reciprocal effect on Allan; so it happened that what was, after all, only the loosest conjecture became ratified by its implicit confirmation in my own calculations. It is a situation in which the sum of the parts is equal to much less than the whole. If I had seriously explored Allan's guess, I'd have soon figured out just how far away we actually were—every now and again, between the squalls, the sun was briefly out.

We were sailing only a mile or two off New Ireland, which stretches northwestward. After the point to which Allan had motioned, we soon found that there was another point. Well, that had to be the one. After that there was a third; well, that one, certainly. And so for the fourth, fifth, and sixth. Christopher Little examined the chart and said plainspokenly that so long as we were able to see any land at all beyond the next point, it could not be North Cape because there is no land beyond North Cape (actually, there is a stretch of islands, but they begin twenty miles beyond North Cape). That cold rational shower, added to the warm shower from another little squall, gave us fatalistic stamina, and we stopped expecting Kavieng within the next five minutes.

As ever, Christopher was amused when, finally, I was persuaded, dammit, to try to establish exactly *where* we were—but only after the sun had permanently receded.

After several hours of this asymptotic frustration, Pup and Reggie went on deck to do some divination. They called for a hand-held compass (Pup couldn't understand why I hadn't interpreted his demand for a "protractor" as meaning that he wanted a hand-held compass) [Amusing. I had meant to ask for a pelorus], and he and Reg, masters of Global Positioning System, H.O. 249, myriad computer star-finding programs, calmly went about in the rain trying to analyze our situation by means of good old-fashioned four-point-eight-point.

[A little solecism here. A four-point-eight-point fix will tell you how far away you are from land by timing the interval between when an object bears four points—forty-five degrees—off your vessel, and when it bears eight points—ninety degrees. If you are traveling at 8 knots and it takes a half hour for the ship's bearing to traverse those forty-five degrees, why you are four miles away from land, by the simple geometrical law of the isosceles triangle, as also the speed you are traveling, and therefore the speed of the current. But we knew how far from land we were: the radar tells you that. Reg and I were attempting to match chart and land contours.]

In due course they satisfied themselves that we were making a speed of six knots. At this point the rest of us began to speculate that the land we were coasting by was not New Ireland, but Australia. (My own hypothesis was that it was the northeast coast of Mindanao in the Philippines, but WFB would brook no serious discussion on that point.)

Eventually—at about six, or five hours after we expected it—fifteen hours after nailing the island of Tabar a mere fifty-five miles away, giving us a speed over the ground of less than four knots, we ran out of the southern coast of New Ireland, rounded the Cape, and there it was, Kavieng.

I intended to let Van disembark after dinner to stay at a hotel until his charter flight time tomorrow, and be off ourselves for our final destination, 130 miles southeast at Rabaul. But the charter pilot, who had flown in from Port Moresby over Rabaul and was waiting to board Sealestial—a happy Australian overflowing with good cheer—was full of weather information.

Christo gets into the navigational act.

Arrival at Kavieng.

Christopher.   Dick came to me. "You know what his plan is?"

"No," I said warily.

Oh boy. WFB was already itching to go. He really is allergic to stationary vessels. The "plan" was to leave at seven in the morning and run straight through the night for Rabaul, getting in just in time to pack and catch the flight to Port Moresby.

Sighs. But *resigned* sighs. As one captain I know would have said as he said of all intolerable situations, "Whaddaya gonna do?"

But help was present. Van's charter pilot, a trim Aussie who accepted (several) scotches, told Pup he'd just flown over the stretch from Rabaul to Kavieng, and said there were 30-knot head-winds and "a lot of whitecaps." This sounded distinctly unlovely, and though I hated to see Pup's crestfallen look, I knew then that we had come to the end of our line, the last leg of our last big trip.

"Well," said Pup, "our trip is over."

23

ARRIVING—
THE FINAL EVENING

Dinner would be late. Van packed while Danny, Reggie, and the two Christophers sight-saw along the quay. They ran into Dick, who had already befriended and learned all the secrets of the neighboring Japanese fishing boat. He offered to introduce his shipmates to the Japanese captain, but first he ducked into *Sealestial* and came out with a bottle.

Christopher. I had put on the clean shirt I've been saving since Majuro and we ran into Dick. He told us about the Jap fishing boat, and came up with a bottle of Bordeaux, which seems an incongruous thing to give a fishing captain, but that's what he's going to do, in that ineffable way of his, Cortez among the savages.

"Uhhh," he says to the captain, "would you be good enough to take my friends aboard your lovely vessel and give them a tour?"

The skipper, a squat fellow missing most of the fingers on his right hand, speaks no English at all, except for "thanka you," but kindly obliges after trying to refuse the Château Fleuri or whatever.

We end up in the galley where he produces a tray of—to my mind—singularly unappetizing-looking raw fish. While the others are urged to plunge in, I wander off to stare at the piston heads clack-clack-clacking. At length I am induced to partake, and of all the scores of sashimi dinners I have had, none has been better. A

huge bottle of Okinawa sake was brought out. I went back to
Sealestial and brought over two bottles of Johnnie Walker Black
for the skipper, who, remarking on our appreciation of the sashimi,
promptly dispatched one of his men in a launch to the mother ship
to bring us back a skipjack tuna. This done, he proceeded, with no
small flourish, to fillet the thing himself. It was a scene of utter,
non-lingual bonhomie; ironic to reflect that had we met here forty
years ago it would have been as enemies. By now the 30-proof sake
had taken its toll, so I left him and Reg and the others to their
continued libations and went back to *Sealestial*.

Our final meal together aboard, and Liz was as ever unstinting.
Van had already packed, and after dinner we ourselves would pack
the fourteen bags he would take along in his plane to Port Moresby,
to reduce the luggage we'd be bringing with us later on the commercial flight. Dick Wellstood was playing jazz piano on the tape,
and there was general animation, though the quality of it, after a
landfall, after so long a passage, is in my experience strangely non-
hysterical in quality: It demands to incorporate some of the sobriety
that attaches to the sensation of a quite-large endeavor undertaken
and consummated by amateurs: We had sailed a boat approximately the distance from Chicago to Honolulu.

After dinner, Dick Clurman made an exuberant, tender toast.
And turned to Christopher.

> **Christopher.**   Dick said in front of all, "I think you ought to say a
> few words." I started to feel that clutch I always experience on being
> told I have to make a toast; but it passed in nanoseconds. The sake,
> beer, and rum had done noble work toward beating back the in-
> hibitions, and I was, after all, sitting down at table not with an
> audience, but with my shipmates. *Shipmates*.
>
>   "Haven't we, together and upon the immortal sea, wrung out a
> meaning from our sinful lives?" Conrad said . . . After a month on
> that sea, sleeping in each other's bunks amongst the dirty laundry,
> we had few secrets. How could I have been nervous? Yet in those
> seconds I had to think about what to say; reaching my seat by step-
> ping over Dick, behind Danny, I wanted so terribly to say something

to make Pup know the joy—there is no other word for post-landfall elation—that he had given us.

So I raised my glass and said (I remember maybe half of this), "Here's to the man who shot the sun, who shot the stars, but who, most of all, shot the moon."

To which all I could add—despite the two dozen times during the last month, blasted by seas, drenched by storms, hove-to in air-less cabins smelling decomposing eggplant, when I kept saying to myself *never again*—was, "And all I could ask is that this not be the last time we happy few sail together." With that Pup and I ex-changed a furtive squeeze and moments later, at our last meal aboard the ship that had gotten us from West to East, Dick asked Pup what, conceivably, might be the itinerary of another trip. He said, with that twinkle that drives Mum so up the wall, "Rio–St. Helena–Capetown."

I had checked into the hotel during the *Sealestial*'s invasion of Japan, leaving in the room everything I needed for the night, and so now I thought to walk there, slowly adapting to the dislocating stability of land. But Christo said no, he would drive me to the hotel in the car Dick had rented, he insisted on it. We elected to drive without headlights—they weren't really necessary, along that faintly luminous quiet road, the solemn deadwood trees on either side, the air so still and fragrant. It was a short drive, and Chris-topher saw me silently to the door, where we embraced.

Epilogue

Christopher. Aboard Air Niugini. I'm seated behind Dick, who has just spilled coffee all over himself. My legs are wedged against Liz's Kapinga hammerhead, and I seem to be wolfing down finger sandwiches of indeterminate meat. (Dan gave his to Christopher Little; I made him get them back.) Now Dick, in order to tell me about some of his more famous spills, has pushed his seat back, causing extreme pain in both knees and inhibiting the flow of blood to my lower legs. But the hangover is improved, and the landing strip at Port Moresby is looming. The problem is: What to do with the thirty bags? One of them feels like it's got a small nuclear reactor in it. Come to think of it, why *didn't* we bring a small nuclear reactor with us? We'd have found room for it in Dick's cabin.

The coffee on Dick's groin still appears to be causing him some distress, though our concern is primarily for the two-year-old child he has probably scalded with the same. He tells these stories— stories at his expense, mind—with more gusto than we'd ever have contemplated: about how he spilled a martini on Ping Ferry's groin three minutes before Ping was to stand up and address three hundred people—without a podium. How piquant that as Dick tells this story he should be dropping cigarette ashes on the head of the child he has just scalded.

Index

Airborne (Buckley, William), 135, 301
Andrea Doria, 294
Anguilla, 60
Apocalypse Now (movie), 289
Ashjaee, Javad, 153–54
Atlantic Bound, Inc., 168
Atlantic High (Buckley, William), 74, 164, 301
Auchincloss, Louis, 125
Azores, 65, 66–74

Bacall, Lauren, 295
Bailey, F. Lee, 243
Baker, Colonel Phil J., 143n
Banfield, Noddy, 4, 7, 8–10, 134, 184, 187, 216, 225, 290, 309
Baruch, Bernard, 280, 281
Bass, Dick, 3
Bass, John, 74
Bennett, Joan, 233
Bishop's Wife, The (movie), 256
Block Island, 46, 48
Block Island Race, 150n
Bogart, Humphrey, 295
Bring on the Empty Horses (Niven), 207–8
Bronson, Frances, 37, 42, 117, 188, 303
Brooke, Rupert, 86
Buckley, John, 161
Buckley, Mrs. Christopher, *see* Gregg, Lucy
Buckley, Pat, 5, 46, 48, 50, 60, 62, 65, 70, 80, 187, 191, 284, 311, 320
Buckley, Priscilla, 65, 69, 70, 80, 83

Cabalho Blanco (Azores restaurant), 72
Cadogan, David, 66, 68, 69–70, 71, 164, 165, 166, 167, 168, 169
Caine Mutiny, The (movie), 179
Caine Mutiny Court-Martial, The (play), 179
Captain Cook (MacLean), 84
Caribbean Enterprises, Inc., 17
Caroline Islands, 227, 257
Casablanca (movie), 295
Chamberlain, Neville, 184
Charterers, 64
Clancy, Tom, 125, 153
Colman, Ronald, 233
Concorde (sloop), 59, 62–63, 97
Cook, Captain, 82, 83, 116–17
Cozumel, Mexico, 22
Craven, Matt, 46, 47–48
Cronkite, Walter, 241–42
Cruising Guide to the New England Coast, A, 43
Cruising Information Center, 102
Cruising Speed (Buckley, William), 121
Cyrano, 15–18, 19, 57, 63, 67, 92, 191, 198, 205, 283

Darwin, Charles, 76, 77, 78
Davis, Peter, 124
De Gaulle, Charles, 317
Denaro, Robert P., 148
Dewey, Thomas E., 317
Disney, Roy, 129
Duncan, Roger, 43, 44

East Indies, 6
Eatons Neck, Long Island, 50

Edgartown, 46
Electronics Week, 143*n*
El Niño, 302
Endeavour, 117
Eschenbach, Ralph, 145–46, 147
Esquire, 93, 240

Felker, Clay, 93, 247
Finucane, Kathleen (Auntie Bill), 176*n*
"Firing Line," 66
Flanigan, Peter, 49, 53
Flynn, Errol, 233
Forbes, Malcolm, 278
Forrestal (U.S. aircraft carrier), 47
Freedom, 206, 207, 209–10, 318
Fundy, Bay of, 35

Gable, Clark, 295–96
Galapagos: Islands Lost in Time
   (Moore), 76
Galapagos Islands, 75–79, 84, 86, 100
Galbraith, John Kenneth, 260
Gardner, Paul, 230
Gauguin, Paul, 81
Gauguin Museum, 81
Geometric Dilution of Position
   (GDOP), 149
Global Positioning System (GPS), 118–
   19, 135–36, 141–54, 210, 255, 315
Goldwyn, Samuel, 189, 233
Goodlife, 254
GooGoo bars, 119–20
Gorton, John, 243, 244
Gregg, Lucy, 80, 111
Greystoke (movie), 262
Grunwald, Henry, 123

Hahn, Emily, 67*n*
Hallowell, Roger, 102, 103, 111
Hammer, Josh, 42–43
Hawaii, University of, 302
Helkey, Roger, 147
Hewlett-Packard (H-P), 144, 145, 146
Hinz, Earl R., 102, 112
Honolulu, 2, 3, 5, 6, 12, 75
Hopper, Hedda, 208
Horowitz, Vladimir, 243
Horta (Azores), 66, 69, 70, 71, 73, 74
Huie, William Bradford, 189
Humboldt Current, 302
Hunt for Red October, The (Clancy),
   125, 153

Integrated Operational Nuclear Detonation System (IONDS), 144–45
Isla Mujeres, 22

Johnson, Captain Irving, 103, 104–8
Johnston Atoll, 118, 182–89
Jouning, Allan, 4, 11, 97, 100, 101, 112,
   132, 134, 173, 175, 179–80, 181, 184,
   193, 197, 198, 202, 204–7, 216, 219,

225, 249, 250–51, 263, 288, 290, 291,
   301, 303, 318–19, 323, 324, 325

Kapingamarangi (Kapinga), 298–311
Kavieng, 312, 324, 325, 326
Kemp, Jack, 161
Kendall, Willmoore, 238
Kennedy, John F., 233
Kenner, Hugh, 115, 156, 238, 239, 287
Kenny, Herb, 272
Kenya, 65–66
Kilpatrick, James Jackson, 161–62
Kolius, John, 242
Kosrae, 227, 239, 255, 258–68, 272

Lamb, Charles, 280
Landes, David, 125
Landfalls of Paradise (Hinz), 102, 112
Langan, William, 208, 209
Latitude 38 (magazine), 55
Leggett, Tony, 49–50, 51, 53
Lehman, John, 182
Léontieff, Alexander, 86–87
Levinson, Daniel, 164
Life, 55
Little, Betsy, 65, 69, 70, 80, 94
Logbook for Helen (Watson), 131–32
Lolita (movie), 303
Lombard, Carole, 295
Loran, 136, 137, 255
Lord, Walter, 293, 294
Luce, Clare Boothe, 123–24
Luce, Henry, 123, 247

Mackwelung, Moses, 260
McLagen, Victor, 233
MacLean, Alistair, 84
Majuro, 221, 223–32
Man and His Island (Neal), 104
Marshall Islands, 226
Marshall Islands News, 224
Marshall Sun Hotel, 224, 225, 230, 231
Melville, Herman, 76, 85–86, 135, 295
Merritt, Gloria, 3, 4, 8, 18, 92
Micronesia, 2, 229
Mitchell, Carleton, 227, 278, 279
Moby Dick (Melville), 135
Moore, Tui De Roy, 76, 77
Morbidity and Mortality Weekly Report,
   116
Mosbacher, Bus, 242, 243
Motor Boating and Sailing, 277
Moxie (Weld), 271, 272, 273, 274–75
Murphy, Ted, 301, 302
My Man Godfrey (movie), 221

National Review, 82, 161, 204
Navstar Global Positioning System, *see*
   Global Positioning System (GPS)
Neal, Tom, 104
New Guinea, 2, 11, 322
New Ireland, 322, 325, 326

Newport-Bermuda race (1956), 240
Newsweek, 224
New York, 124
New Yorker, The, 67, 160
New York Times, The, 18, 53
New York Yacht Club, 164, 242, 243
Nicholson, Julie, 97
Niven, David, 120, 132–33, 189, 207, 232, 233, 295, 302–3
Norell, Judith, 124
Normandie, 65
North Star (power boat), 280–81
Nova Scotia, 45

Olivier, Laurence, 189
Olsson, Dexter, 150n
One Flew Over the Cuckoo's Nest (movie), 247
Ormond, Maureen, 4, 11, 193, 216, 255, 290
Overboard (Searls), 131
Overseas Private Investment Corporation (OPIC), 260

Panama Canal, 75
Panic, The, 136, 205, 281, 286
Papo, Dr. Michael, 59, 63, 75, 97, 98, 160
Papo, Judy, 59, 114
Parkinson, Brad, 144, 145, 146
Parsons, Louella, 208
Patito, 18, 19, 20, 35, 37, 42, 46, 48, 49, 50, 125, 129, 203, 248, 278
Pearl Harbor, 6
People, 42–43, 44, 289
Pete's Bar (Azores), 73
Petrified Forest, The (movie), 295
Polynesian Magazine for Tourists, The, 86
Ponape, 302
Pope, Aubrey, 41–42
Pope, Kempton, 42
Portuguese Tourist Agency, 66
Power and Motoryacht, 92, 142

Querencia, xiii, xiv

Rabaul, 326, 328
Reagan, Nancy, 5, 187
Reagan, Ronald, 123, 161
Rebozo, Bebe, 191
"Reporter at Large in the Azores, A" (Hahn), 67n
Revolt of Mamie Stover, The (Huie), 189
Revolution in Time (Landes), 125
Risky Business (movie), 268
Royal Kennebecasis Yacht Club, 35
Rusher, Bill, 82, 204, 317
Russell, Rosalind, 233

St. John, New Brunswick, 34, 36, 37, 39–44

St. John River, 20, 35, 45
St. John Telegraph-Journal, 37, 38–42
St. Martin, 59, 60
Sand, George, 68
Sandy Beach Hotel (Kosrae), 267
São Miguel (Azores), 71, 72
Scarlett O'Hara, 164
Schatzki, David, 263, 264, 265
Schiff, Andras, 124
Sea Cloud, 280
Searls, Hank, 131
Seasons of a Man's Life, The (Levinson), 164
Selected Worldwide Marine Weather Broadcast, 114
Semko, Michael, 223–24, 229, 230, 231, 232
Seven Seas Cruising Association (SSCA), 104
Sheen, Martin, 289
Simon, William, 202–4, 210, 319
Siolberberg, Miriam, 163
Slocum, Joshua, 271
Society Islands, 82, 83, 84
Sparkman & Stephens, 204, 208
Stars & Stripes, 245n
Steaming to Bamboola (Buckley, Christopher), 93
Steib, Lars, 130
Sterlings (Kosrae restaurant), 261–62
Stevenson, James, 160–61
Strykers, Dr. Peter, 270–71, 272, 275
Suzy Wong, 17, 18, 205, 286
Swedish Cracker, The, 117
Sweet Isolation, 20

Tahiti, 75, 80–88
TAU Corporation, 148
Terceira (Azores), 68, 72, 76
Thalberg, Irving, 189
Thomson, Virgil, 63
Time, 123
Time Inc., 123
Titanic, 293–94
Tortola, 62
Transit (satellite navigational system), 144
Trimble, Charles, 26, 141, 142, 145, 146, 147, 148, 152, 315
Trimble Loran-C computer, 23, 24–32, 33, 137
Trimble Navigation, 141, 147, 153
Typee (Melville), 295

U.S.-42, 242
U.S.-44, 241, 242, 244, 245
Universal Press Syndicate, 2

Wackiest Ship in the Army, The (movie), 119, 134

Walter, Mrs. Laurel, 162
Wanger, Walter, 233
Ware, John, 43
Washington Post, The, 131
Watson, Tom, Jr., 131, 160
Weld, Phil, 271, 272–75
Wellstood, Dick, 124, 330
Wendel, Tom, 20, 21, 27, 32, 36, 37, 42, 45, 51, 125
Westward Bound in the Schooner Yankee (Johnson), 105
Wheeler, Liz, xiii, 11, 112, 116, 160, 161, 216, 225, 245, 255, 257, 288, 290, 299, 301, 309, 316, 318, 330
White Eagle, 319
White House Mess, The (Buckley, Christopher), 93, 119
Wolfe, Tom, 145
Women's Wear Daily, 46
Writer's Art, The (Kilpatrick), 161
Wuthering Heights (movie), 189
Wyler, William, 189

Yale Daily News, 161